T0202872

Lecture Notes in Computer Science   13476

More information about this series at https://link.springer.com/bookseries/558

Heinrich Söbke · Pia Spangenberger ·
Philipp Müller · Stefan Göbel (Eds.)

Serious Games

Joint International Conference, JCSG 2022
Weimar, Germany, September 22–23, 2022
Proceedings

 Springer

Editors
Heinrich Söbke 🆔
Bauhaus University, Weimar
Weimar, Thüringen, Germany

Pia Spangenberger 🆔
Technical University of Berlin
Berlin, Germany

Philipp Müller 🆔
TU Darmstadt
Darmstadt, Germany

Stefan Göbel 🆔
TU Darmstadt
Darmstadt, Germany

ISSN 0302-9743   ISSN 1611-3349 (electronic)
Lecture Notes in Computer Science
ISBN 978-3-031-15324-2   ISBN 978-3-031-15325-9 (eBook)
https://doi.org/10.1007/978-3-031-15325-9

This Springer imprint is published by the registered company Springer Nature Switzerland AG
The registered company address is: Gewerbestrasse 11, 6330 Cham, Switzerland

Preface

The Joint Conference on Serious Games 2022 (JCSG 2022) was held at Bauhaus-Universität Weimar, Weimar, Germany, during September 22–23, 2022. The JCSG conference series has been established as a vivid opportunity for discourse on innovative topics in the emerging and developing field of serious games. Thus, new media, such as virtual reality and augmented reality, are included as well as emerging application domains, such as educational games and health games. The conference is a gathering place for individuals and decision makers from academic research, industry, education, and administration. With this diversity of participants, the conference has the capacity to stimulate an interdisciplinary and challenging field of research.

All submissions were carefully reviewed in a double-blind review process by at least three members of the international Program Committee. Based on the reviews, the Program Committee selected 19 of the submissions for presentation at the conference. The authors of the papers are affiliated to institutions from 12 countries, covering all habited continents acoss the world.

A full-day workshop on Instructional Design for Location-based Augmented Reality (IDLARL) was held as a conference pre-event on September 21, 2022. This workshop also helped to attract a number of distinguished experts for invited talks. We were honored to welcome Kathrin Gerling from KU Leuven, Belgium, Alexander Kulik from Consensive GmbH, Germany, Anton Nijholt from the University of Twente, The Netherlands, Samuli Laato from Tampere University, Finland, Helmut Niegemann from Saarland University, Germany, Johanna Pirker from TU Graz, Austria, and Jan L. Plass from New York University, USA, to Weimar and enjoyed their inspiring insights.

A total of six presentation sessions were held, each thematically framed by an invited talk, namely, Learning Psychology, Design Aspects, Game Design, Health Games, Games Application, and Mixed Reality.

We cordially thank the authors for submitting their interesting papers, the Program Committee members for their constructive and thoughtful reviews of the papers, and the fellow members of the steering committee. Without the long-term commitment of all the above, this conference would not have taken place and the JCSG conference series would not exist. May JCSG 2022 give rise to fruitful discussions whose innovative products will enrich one of the forthcoming JCSG editions.

September 2022

Heinrich Söbke
Pia Spangenberger
Philipp Müller
Stefan Göbel

Organization

General Chairs/Program Committee Chairs

Heinrich Söbke	Bauhaus-Universität Weimar, Germany
Pia Spangenberger	TU Berlin, Germany
Philipp Müller	Technical University of Darmstadt, Germany
Stefan Göbel	Technical University of Darmstadt, Germany

Steering Committee

Jannicke Baalsrud Hauge	University of Bremen, Germany, and KTH, Sweden
Stefan Göbel	Technical University of Darmstadt, Germany
Minhua Eunice Ma	Falmouth University, UK
Tim Marsh	Griffith University, Australia
Manuel Fradinho Oliveira	KIT-AR, UK
David White	Staffordshire University, UK

Program Committee

Mariano Alcaniz	Universidad Politécnica Valencia, Spain
Jannicke Baalsrud Hauge	University of Bremen, Germany
Per Backlund	University of Skövde, Sweden
Josep Blat	Universitat Pompeu Fabra, Spain
Polona Caserman	Technical University of Darmstadt, Germany
Michael Christel	Carnegie Mellon University, USA
Karin Coninx	Hasselt University, Belgium
Ralf Doerner	RheinMain University of Applied Sciences, Germany
Kai Erenli	UAS BFI Vienna, Austria
Baltasar Fernandez-Manjon	Universidad Complutense de Madrid, Spain
Mateus Finco	Universidade Federal da Paraíba, Brazil
Augusto Garcia-Agundez	Brown University, USA
Tom Gedeon	Australian National University, Australia
Pascual Gonzalez	University of Castilla-La Mancha, Spain
Pedro González Calero	Universidad Politécnica de Madrid, Spain
Stefan Göbel	Technical University of Darmstadt, Germany
Mads Haahr	Trinity College Dublin, Ireland

Matthias Hemmje	FernUniversität in Hagen, Germany
Helmut Hlavacs	University of Vienna, Austria
Jun Hu	Eindhoven University of Technology, The Netherlands
Petar Jerčić	Blekinge Institute of Technology, Sweden
Michael Kickmeier-Rust	St. Gallen University of Teacher Education, Switzerland
Troy Kohwalter	Universidade Federal Fluminense, Brazil
Linda Kruse	University of Applied Science Mainz, Germany
Minhua Eunice Ma	Falmouth University, UK
Tim Marsh	Griffith University, Australia
Athanasios Mazarakis	Kiel University and ZBW, Germany
Wolfgang Mueller	University of Education Weingarten, Germany
Philipp Müller	Technical University of Darmstadt, Germany
Manuel Fradinho Oliveira	KIT-AR, UK
Sobah Abbas Petersen	Norwegian University of Science and Technology, Norway
Alenka Poplin	Iowa State University, USA
Nikitas Sgouros	University of Piraeus, Greece
Pia Spangenberger	TU Berlin, Germany
Heinrich Söbke	Bauhaus-Universität Weimar, Germany
Thomas Tregel	Technical University of Darmstadt, Germany
Thrasyvoulos Tsiatsos	Aristotle University of Thessaloniki, Greece
David White	Staffordshire University, UK
Josef Wiemeyer	Technical University of Darmstadt

Contents

Health Games

Games Application

Mixed Reality

Learning Psychology

Flow and Self-efficacy in a Serious Game for STEM Education

Phoebe Perlwitz[(✉)] and Jennifer Stemmann

Pädagogische Hochschule Freiburg, Kunzenweg 21, 79117 Freiburg im Breisgau, Germany
{phoebe.perlwitz,jennifer.stemmann}@ph-freiburg.de

Abstract. Although the performance of female students in STEM subjects is as good as that of male students, their self-efficacy expectations are at a low level. Given the influence of self-efficacy expectations on academic careers and later career decisions, measures are needed in this area. Serious games could be one way of increasing the self-efficacy expectations of adolescents and girls in particular. The property of serious games to enable flow experiences is said to have a positive effect on motivation and possibly also a positive influence on self-efficacy expectations. In order to investigate this, a serious game on the topic of electricity theory was developed and the flow experience and the influence on self-efficacy expectations were examined in a pre-post design. The results indicate a positive effect, which is partly mediated by the flow.

Keywords: Self-efficacy · Flow · Serious games · STEM

1 Introduction

The construct of self-efficacy expectation describes the subjective perception of being able to cope with demands based on one's own competence in order to achieve goals [1–3]. The differences in boys and girls in STEM revealed by studies [4] can be attributed to the fact that girls get fewer opportunities to engage with technology at a young age [5]. The confrontation with stereotypical expectations that women and technology do not match also leads to lower self-efficacy expectations [6]. Regarding computer use, for example, men are more likely to report an interest and positive feelings than women, who are more anxious [7]. Although the objective level of knowledge is the same, girls rate their computer-related skills significantly lower than men and accordingly have a lower computer-related self-efficacy expectation [8].

These differences explain a general underrepresentation of women in STEM occupations, as self-efficacy expectancy predicts not only school outcomes [9] but also later career choices [10]. Therefore, measures to increase self-efficacy expectations are of particular interest in STEM. The results of studies that report a positive change in self-efficacy expectations through serious games [11, 12] inspire hope.

Bandura [2] identified four resources that can influence a person's self-efficacy expectation: 1) Experiencing success by mastering difficult tasks increases self-efficacy expectation. 2) But also, the experience of people with similar abilities help to increase

H. Söbke et al. (Eds.): JCSG 2022, LNCS 13476, pp. 3–16, 2022.
https://doi.org/10.1007/978-3-031-15325-9_1

confidence in one's own abilities. The more one identifies with the observed person, the stronger the influence. 3) In addition, verbal encouragement from teachers, parents and peers exerts an influence on the development of self-efficacy expectations. 4) The perception of one's own feelings also plays a decisive role [2].

The potential of serious games to have a positive effect on self-efficacy expectations is clear in this context. The use of serious games enables learners to solve tasks independently and without direct instruction and thus experience success. The possibility to explore causes and effects in a risk-free environment [13] and the partitioning of a game into smaller tasks of increasing difficulty that are completed continuously lead to a continuous sense of achievement [14]. Studies have reported a positive change in self-efficacy expectations through serious games, e.g. [11, 12, 15, 16]. For example, inherent in the possibility of creating an avatar is the possibility of increasing self-efficacy expectation, as the adaptation of the virtual presence to the ideal self should lead to a stronger identification with the game character and the game [17, 18]. In a study on the Proteus effect, Yee and Bailenson [19] were able to show that larger or more attractive avatars lead to more self-confidence. It can be concluded, that players adopt the goals and attitudes of the avatar and consequently their self-efficacy expectations can be increased. Verbal persuasion is also taken into account, in that positive feedback can be given through implemented chat functions but also through the serious game itself [20]. The temporal stability of the game's responsiveness allows players to continue the rewarding experience over long periods of time [21]. It was found that low self-efficacy expectations of students could be overcome by the high motivation in the game-based environment (ibid.).

Researchers see a predictor for the motivating effect of serious games in the flow theory [22, 23]. Flow describes a state of complete concentration on the here and now; the activity performed is simultaneously the reward itself. Through complete absorption in the activity, the sense of time and space disappears [22]. According to Stadler [24], it is mainly people with high self-efficacy expectations who experience flow.

Pavlas et al. [25] provided initial results on the reciprocal relationship between flow experience and self-efficacy expectations in serious games in a study in which the relationship between flow, game-related self-efficacy expectations and learning outcomes in a serious game was examined. Specifically, flow and self-efficacy expectancy predicted motivation and acquired declarative knowledge from serious games. Furthermore, Flow was able to fully explain the effects of self-efficacy expectancy of serious games on intrinsic motivation [25]. In her meta-analysis of comparative studies, Sitzmann [12] was able to identify the flow experience as the important element of the motivational effect and found an increase in self-efficacy expectation - also in the long term - as a result of playing serious games. Consequently, due to its relationship to the flow state, the self-efficacy expectation of serious games may be a key component for ensuring motivation and learning outcomes in serious games. The connection between an improvement in self-efficacy expectation through flow experience has already been suspected by studies, but has not been researched in the scientific-technical field in particular, although a potential is suspected [26].

In order to gain further insight into the interaction of flow and self-efficacy expectations, a serious game named *Lights Out* on the topic of electricity theory was designed within the scope of a research project and compared with a conventional learning setting. The results can be used to show which flow-promoting elements should be used in school lessons in order to enable an increase in self-efficacy expectations for students in addition to an increase in subject knowledge. Positive results can also help to reduce teachers' prejudices against the use of digital games in the classroom. A large proportion of teachers do not use games because they are not convinced of their effectiveness. They want more knowledge about the use of digital games in the classroom and more access to studies that research the use of such games [27]. By researching the use of *Lights Out*, there will be a serious game that can be used directly in the classroom due to its direct educational curriculum reference. The game and the results of an exploratory study are presented hereby.

2   Methods

2.1   The Serious Game *Lights Out*

The learning content of *Lights Out* covers the basic principles of electricity according to the educational plan for Baden-Württemberg, Germany [28]. This learning content is an important prerequisite for understanding later topics in electrical engineering. Since the target group, 7th and 8th grade students, predominantly favor the game *Minecraft* [29], the pixel art design was chosen for the design of *Lights Out*. The development of the game took into account previously published studies on features of serious games related to learning efficacy and motivation (e.g., immersion through narrative framing [30], personal relevance [31], appropriate cognitive load [32–34], short periods of explicit learning [35], feedback and assistance via chats [18, 36].

The game is divided into four chapters in which the learners acquire new topics in electricity theory, gradually building on each other and increasing in difficulty. Starting with electricity in our everyday life, the electric current and the voltage are elaborated. In order to avoid a cognitive load due to excessive immersion, the narrative is limited to a few sequences and texts; the focus is on learning content. The contextualization as an everyday problem (a house is to be lightened after a power failure by appropriately combining lamps and batteries) is intended to increase girls' interest in electricity in particular [37].

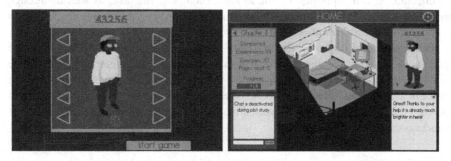

Fig. 1. Creation of an avatar (left), in the house it is possible to switch between rooms (right)

Once the avatar has been created (see Fig. 1, left), the control is explained and can be called up again at any time via the escape menu. Further help on the controls or the tasks is displayed in the course of the game as short texts or videos. In addition, the avatar provides assistance and positive feedback. After the intro scene, the learners enter a (yet) dark house, which gradually lightens up as the game progresses. Via a chat interface, students have the opportunity to discuss problems with their teacher and classmates.

Inside the house, the learners can switch between different rooms (see Fig. 1, right):

- A kitchen where the detailed learning progress can be viewed in the form of badges (see Fig. 2, top left). A badge is a common term in digital learning for badges that confirm the acquired knowledge. Through this and the feedback on the player's progress, the influence of encouragement is considered.
- A living room containing a book in which the required knowledge about electricity can be looked up (see Fig. 2, top right). The texts contained in the book are supported by appropriate animations. The players can choose whether to use the book as a guide during the game or to read it in advance.
- A children's room in which tasks on the respective topics are worked on (see Fig. 2, bottom left). The matching pages of the book are also linked here. In addition, there is the possibility to take the respective task to the attic and check it there in experiments.
- An attic where experiments have to be carried out (see Fig. 2, bottom right). Here, lamps, batteries and conductors can be combined to form various circuits. As the game progresses, measuring devices (ammeter/voltmeter) are also unlocked. At any time, it is possible to jump to the appropriate book page in the living room.

In line with van Roy and Zaman's [38] recommendations for increasing self-efficacy expectations in serious games, the order of activities in *Lights Out* is not predetermined, so as to allow the greatest possible freedom of action. Thus, learners can choose for themselves whether they first read technical texts, solve tasks or carry out experiments. However, all these activities must be completed in order to move on to the next chapter of the game. The tasks are structured in such a way that they are not too difficult as to avoid anxiety or frustration. However, they should not be too easy because this would lead to boredom. Successfully completed tasks are rewarded by badges, completed chapters are rewarded by new achievements, such as multimeters.

During the game, verbal persuasion takes place in inquiry learning, where learners are encouraged and supported by the avatar to complete the task, as well as through group activities and chat communication. During the surveys, the chat is deactivated in order to avoid possible confusion.

In a first trial of *Lights Out* with 47 8th grade students of a secondary school, the students indicated in feedback forms that they appreciated the game as an alternative to conventional lessons, but also wished for more variety in the types of tasks and the choice of avatar. In addition, the book was mentioned several times as particularly useful and the creation of an avatar was named many times as the most important feature of immersion.

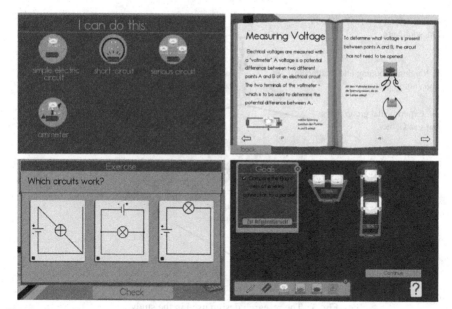

Fig. 2. The badges in the kitchen (top left); a book page (top right); a sample task in the children's room (bottom left); an experiment in the attic (bottom right)

2.2 Participants and Design

The research design is presented in Fig. 3. The assignment of learners to the experimental and control groups is randomised. First, all students filled out a paper questionnaire, which measured their self-efficacy expectations as well as their age and gender. In order to determine computer-related attitudes, behavior and emotions, the computer-related self-concept was also surveyed.

While the experimental group learned the contents of electricity theory with a serious game, the control group received work assignments and information sheets in paper form as well as the opportunity to carry out the identical experiments.

Once the learners had completed the work assignments respectively the serious game, the self-efficacy expectation was measured again in order to determine in which treatment a greater change in self-efficacy expectation was achieved and whether the experienced flow was causal for this. The survey was conducted with students from secondary schools (Gymnasien and Realschulen) in Baden-Württemberg, Germany. All students attend 8th grade and had no previous lessons on electricity topics. Allocation to the treatment groups was randomised. There were 60 participants in the experimental group and 51 in the control group ($n = 111$, 46% female).

2.3 Instruments

School-related self-efficacy expectations were measured with a scale from Jerusalem et al. [39]. The wording was adapted to the subject of physics and the items had good reliability (Cronbach's $\alpha = .86$). An example item is "I am confident in physics". The

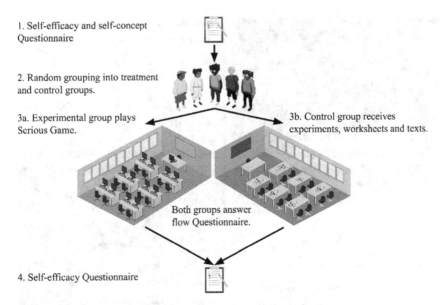

1. Self-efficacy and self-concept
Questionnaire

2. Random grouping into treatment
and control groups.

3a. Experimental group plays
Serious Game.

3b. Control group receives
experiments, worksheets and texts.

Both groups answer
flow Questionnaire.

4. Self-efficacy Questionnaire

Fig. 3. The research design used in the study.

questions were answered on a 5-point Likert scale. In both groups, flow was also assessed during the intervention on a 5-point Likert scale with linguistically adapted items from the Flow Short Scale by Rheinberg et al. [40] (Cronbach's $\alpha = .89$). Computer-related self-concept was assessed with parts of the Conative, Motivational and Cognitive subscales (Cronbach's $\alpha = .86$) from Janneck et al. [8]. All items were piloted beforehand ($n = 47$ participants).

2.4 Statistical Analysis

Mann-Whitney-U-tests were used to examine possible differences in computer-related self-concept, change in self-efficacy expectancy and experienced flow between the control and experimental groups as well as between the genders. The change in self-efficacy expectancy was determined using Wilcoxon signed-rank. Finally, regression analyses were used to examine the correlations of computer-related self-concept and experienced flow with the change in self-efficacy. The change in self-efficacy expectation was calculated from the difference self-efficacy expectation [pre] − self-efficacy expectation [post]. Bootstrapping with 5000 iterations together with heteroskedasticity-consistent standard errors [41] calculated confidence intervals and inferential statistics.

3 Results

3.1 Comparing Treatments

The Mann-Whitney-U-test revealed no differences between intervention groups in computer-related self-concept ($U = 1353.50$, $Z = -1.05$, $p = .296$) in change in self-efficacy expectancy ($U = 1467.50$, $Z = -.37$, $p = .709$) and experienced flow ($U = 1381.00$, $Z = -.88$, $p = .377$) (Tables 1 and 2).

Table 1. Change in self-efficacy expectations in the intervention groups

Intervention	n	Self-efficacy					
		M [pre]	SD [pre]	M [post]	SD [post]	M	SD
Experimental group	60	2.96	.87	3.20	.90	.22	.50
Control group	51	2.91	.93	3.11	.90	.20	.62

Note. n = sum of Students and sample sizes of each pairwise comparison; [pre] = pretest; [post] = mean posttest; M = mean; SD = standard deviation.

Table 2. Flow and self-concept in the intervention groups

Variable		Flow		Self-concept	
Intervention	n	M	SD	M	SD
Experimental group	60	3.46	.83	3.43	.78
Control group	51	3.31	.78	3.59	.85

Note. n = sum of Students and sample sizes of each pairwise comparison; M = mean; SD = standard deviation.

3.2 Changes in Self-efficacy Expectancy

A Wilcoxon signed-rank test was calculated to determine the change in self-efficacy. The distribution of differences was symmetrical according to visual inspection of the histogram. The increase before the intervention compared to after the intervention was significant in the experimental group ($z = 3.12$, $p = .002$, $r = .40$) as well as in the control group ($z = 2.22$, $p = .027$, $r = .31$).

3.3 Comparing Genders

The Mann-Whitney-U-test revealed no differences in self-efficacy expectations between the genders in the experimental group ($U = 423.00$, $Z = -.41$, $p = .685$). However, there were significant differences in computer-related self-concept ($U = 251.00$, $Z = 2.96$, $p = .003$) and experienced flow ($U = 301.00$, $Z = -2.20$, $p = .028$) in favor of the male students (Tables 3 and 4).

Table 3. Self-efficacy comparison by gender

Intervention	n	M [pre]	SD [pre]	M [post]	SD [post]	M	SD
	Self-efficacy						
Male	30	3.13	.84	3.35	.81	.23	.53
Female	30	2.79	.87	3.01	.97	.21	.58

Note. n = sum of Students and sample sizes of each pairwise comparison; [pre] = pretest; [post] = posttest; M = mean; SD = standard deviation.

Table 4. Flow and self-efficacy by gender

Variable		Flow		Self-concept	
Intervention	n	M	SD	M	SD
Male	30	3.70	.82	3.73	.84
Female	30	3.22	.78	3.14	.60

3.4 Relationship Between Self-concept, Self-efficacy and Flow

In order to gain further insight if the effect of flow on the change in self-efficacy expectancy is moderated by the computer-related self-concept and thus explain possible gender differences, a moderated regression analysis was conducted for the experimental group (Table 5).

Table 5. Results of the regression analysis

Predictors	β	p
Flow	.20	.010
Computer-related self-concept	−.18	.037
Interaction	−.11	.044

Note. β = standardized regression coefficient, $F(3,56) = 4.32, p = .008, R^2 = .13, n = 60$.

The overall model was significant ($p = .008$), predicting a variance of 13%. Computer-related self-concept weakly significant moderated the effect of flow on change in self-efficacy expectancy $\Delta R^2 = 2.14\%$, $F(1, 56) = 4.22$, $p = .045$, 95% CI[−0.24, 0.04]. The Johnson-Neyman plot in Fig. 4 indicates the conditional effect of flow on the change in self-efficacy is significant when the computer-related self-concept has lower mean scores than 3.85.

To test for a possible mediation effect of the flow state on the relationship between pre-game and post-game self-efficacy, a mediation analysis was conducted. Unstandardized path coefficients of the total, direct and indirect effect were determined using the least

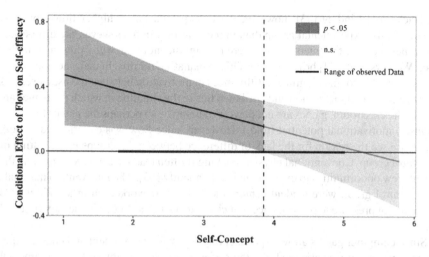

Fig. 4. Johnson-Neyman plot of the moderation effect

squares method. The relationship between the variables was linear according to visual inspection after LOESS smoothing. The path diagram is shown in Fig. 5.

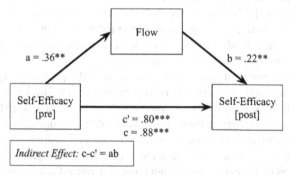

Fig. 5. Path diagram of the mediation analysis ($**p < .01$, $***p < .001$).

An effect of pre-intervention self-efficacy expectancy on post-intervention self-efficacy expectancy was found, $c = .88$, $p < .001$. After the mediator was included in the model, pre-intervention self-efficacy significantly predicted the mediator, $a = .36$, $p = .003$. The mediator in turn significantly predicted self-efficacy after the intervention, $b = .22$, $p = .009$. The change in self-efficacy experience was thus partially mediated with small effect size by the experienced flow, indirect effect $ab = .08$, 95% CI [0.01, 0.17].

4 Discussion and Next Steps

Initial findings indicate that all learners in the study were motivated; above-average values were determined for flow in both groups. Following the studies by Kiili [42] and Nacke and Lindley [43], however, it was expected that a higher flow would be observed in the experimental group than in the control group. However, the differences in flow between the treatment groups were not significant in the study presented in this paper. Wouters et al. [44] bring up a possible explanation for this. In their meta-analysis, they were unable to find significant differences in motivation between the use of serious games versus direct instruction and attributed this to the situation in which the games are used. In the classroom, games are not played voluntarily, so perhaps the games lose their (intrinsic) motivational potential (ibid.). However, since flow was experienced in both groups, we see the reason for the lack of difference between the groups in the setting of the control group. Conventional physics teaching is often teacher-centered and offers the students few opportunities to experiment independently [45]. The intervention materials of the control group were student-centered and could be worked on in a self-selected order without pressure to performance, which led to a similar flow as in the experimental group.

Since computer games allow experimenting in a safe environment and enable experiencing success, it was assumed that the self-efficacy expectation of the experimental group would change more positively. However, this could not be determined. Although the change in self-efficacy expectancy was significant in both groups, no differences were found between the experimental group and the control group with regard to the change in self-efficacy.

Again, the reason may lie in the setting of the control group. This assumption is also shared by Sitzman [12]. She determined that a majority of the studies examined in her meta-analysis did not offer an adequate substitute for the control group. This seems to be the reason why these studies find a larger increase in self-efficacy expectancy in the serious game group than in the control group.

Since the development of the serious game used in the present study already took care to address both genders as effectively as possible [16, 18, 38], it was expected that the change in self-efficacy expectations would not differ between men and women in the experimental group. This was indeed shown by the data and probably suggests that it was indeed successful, e.g., by implementing an avatar or embedding it in an everyday problem, to address women as well and to motivate them for the game context.

It was expected that subjects with a high computer-related self-concept would interact more with the serious game, which would lead to a greater experience of success and thus to a higher self-efficacy expectation. It is well known that male subjects usually have a higher computer-related self-concept. Thus, adolescents with positive perceptions of their own computer competencies also rated their experiences with computer-related activities as positive. Christoph, Goldhammer et al. [46] also uncovered significant relationships between self-concept and motivation. In our own study, these findings could largely be replicated. Significant differences in both computer-related self-concept and flow were observed in favor of the boys. To investigate the interaction effect of the computer-related self-concept and flow on the change in self-efficacy, a moderation analysis was performed. The results were significant for low computer-related self-concepts. For subjects who had a high computer-related self-concept, flow was no longer able to produce large changes in self-efficacy expectations. In particular, subjects with low computer-related self-concepts benefited in terms of changes in self-efficacy due to flow.

This result can be regarded as positive, since it can be assumed that the computer-related self-concept is not decisive and that subjects with low self-concept also have the opportunity to experience flow. The role of flow in the change of self-efficacy expectation could be confirmed by a mediation analysis, in which a partial mediator effect could be observed.

In summary, the present study was able to show that self-efficacy expectations can be improved by suitable teaching scenarios. Such teaching scenarios are characterized, among other things, by the fact that they enable flow by providing a suitable fit between requirement and ability. However, such instructional scenarios are difficult to implement in everyday life because they require a lot of planning and materials. For example, the possibilities for hands-on experiments in schools are limited, on the one hand due to time constraints, but also because experimental equipment is often not available for each individual student in a class. In addition, teachers frequently lack the opportunity to give students tasks that are precisely adapted to their abilities and thus enable flow.

The study showed that serious games can be used to facilitate flow and improve self-efficacy expectations. The advantage of serious games is that they are cost- and time-efficient, since no experiments have to be set up and differentiated exercises have to be created, copied and distributed. Each student gets exactly the help they need and direct feedback when they need it. This also makes teaching self-efficacy enhancing when the teacher does not have the opportunity or ability to reach all students equally through verbal encouragement. Another advantage of serious games for the teacher is the simplified evaluation of results and process data. The teacher can better monitor learning progress and better account for diversity to tailor individualized support.

The results of this study are important in that they provide an indication of how women can be encouraged to pursue careers in STEM fields in which their STEM-related self-efficacy expectations are increased. By experiencing being self-efficacious, women are more confident in performing more difficult tasks in the STEM field, which in turn leads to increased self-efficacy expectations.

Of course, there are also limitations to be mentioned. On the one hand, the results may have been biased by the sole implementation at German schools in Baden-Württemberg, but also by the small sample size. Specifically, the results of the moderator analysis of self-concept showed weak significance and a zero crossing in the confidence interval and should be further investigated. Also, it is still unclear whether subjects with different self-concepts interacted differently with the serious game. Here, a detailed analysis of the process data is needed.

In order to determine the mediation effect or a presumed moderator effect of flow on the change in self-efficacy expectancy, a suitable group size in the experimental group is to be achieved in the next study. In addition, an expertise test on the subject of electricity in the pre-post design should reveal whether and which effects there are between the constructs flow, learning outcome and self-efficacy expectation. Finally, it has to be considered that although the results are promising, ultimately the use of the game in the classroom is still influenced by the teacher. An unsuitable embedding of the game may even nullify the characteristics of the game.

Acknowledgments. The authors would like to thank Anouar Chaari for his constant help and support creating the game.

References

1. Beierlein, C., Kemper, C.J., Kovaleva, A., Rammstedt, B.: Short scale for measuring general self-efficacy beliefs (ASKU). Methods Data Anal. **7**, 251–278 (2013). https://doi.org/10.12758/MDA.2013.014
2. Bandura, A.: Self-efficacy: toward a unifying theory of behavioral change. Toward a unifying theory of behavioral change. Psychol. Rev. **84**, 191–215 (1977). https://doi.org/10.1037/0033-295X.84.2.191
3. Jerusalem, M., Mittag, W.: Selbstwirksamkeit, Bezugsnormen, Leistung und Wohlbefinden in der Schule. Emotion, Motivation und Leistung 223–245 (1999)
4. Stemmann, J.: Metakognition und Selbstkonzept - Motivationsbezogene Einflussgrößen auf technisches Handeln. J. Tech. Educ. **9**, 74–90 (2021). https://doi.org/10.48513/joted.v9i1.224
5. Hirsch, E.: Frauen und Computer-Bildung in der Informationsgesellschaft: Informations- und Kommunikationstechnologie als Herausforderung frauenspezifischer Bildungsarbeit. IFF, Klagenfurt (2002)
6. Wächter, C.: Technik-Bildung und Geschlecht. Profil-Verl, München (2003)
7. Chua, S.L., Chen, D.-T., Wong, A.F.L.: Computer anxiety and its correlates: a meta-analysis. Comput. Hum. Behav. **15**, 609–623 (1999)
8. Janneck, M., Vincent-Höper, S., Ehrhardt, J.: The computer-related self concept. Int. J. Soc. Organ. Dyn. IT **3**, 1–16 (2013). https://doi.org/10.4018/ijsodit.2013070101
9. Williams, T., Williams, K.: Self-efficacy and performance in mathematics: reciprocal determinism in 33 nations. J. Educ. Psychol. **102**, 453 (2010). https://doi.org/10.1037/a0017271
10. Bandura, A., et al.: Self-efficacy beliefs as shapers of children's aspirations and career trajectories. Child Dev. **72**, 187–206 (2001). https://doi.org/10.1111/1467-8624.00273
11. Ketelhut, D.J.: The impact of student self-efficacy on scientific inquiry skills. An exploratory investigation in River city, a multi-user virtual environment. J. Sci. Educ. Technol. **16**, 99–111 (2007). https://doi.org/10.1007/s10956-006-9038-y
12. Sitzmann, T.: A meta-analytic examination of the instructional effectiveness of computer-based simulation games. Pers. Psychol. **64**, 489–528 (2011). https://doi.org/10.1111/j.1744-6570.2011.01190.x
13. Cheng, M.-T., Chen, J.-H., Chu, S.-J., Chen, S.-Y.: The use of serious games in science education: a review of selected empirical research from 2002 to 2013. J. Comput. Educ. **2**(3), 353–375 (2015). https://doi.org/10.1007/s40692-015-0039-9
14. Bandura, A., Schunk, D.H.: Cultivating competence, self-efficacy, and intrinsic interest through proximal self-motivation. J. Pers. Soc. Psychol. **41**, 586–598 (1981). https://doi.org/10.1037/0022-3514.41.3.586
15. Pavlas, D.: A Model of Flow and Play in Game-Based Learning. The Impact of Game Characteristics, Player Traits and Player States. Orlando, FL (2010)
16. Spangenberger, P., Kapp, F., Kruse, L., Hartmann, M., Narciss, S.: Can a serious game attract girls to technology professions? Int. J. Gend. Sci. Technol. **10**, 253–264 (2018)
17. de Freitas, S.: Learning in immersive worlds. A review of game-based learning. Joint Information Systems Committee, Bristol
18. Alserri, S.A., Zin, N.A.M., Wook, T.S.M., Wook, T.S.M.T.: Gender-based game engagement model validation using low fidelity prototype. Int. J. Eng. Adv. Technol. **8**, 1350–1357 (2018). https://doi.org/10.35940/ijeat.D9042.049420
19. Yee, N., Bailenson, J.: The Proteus effect: the effect of transformed self-representation on behavior. Hum. Commun. Res. **33**, 271–290 (2007). https://doi.org/10.1111/j.1468-2958.2007.00299.x

20. Burgers, C., Eden, A., van Engelenburg, M.D., Buningh, S.: How feedback boosts motivation and play in a brain-training game. Comput. Hum. Behav. **48**, 94–103 (2015). https://doi.org/10.1016/j.chb.2015.01.038
21. Klimmt, C., Hartmann, T.: Effectance, self-efficacy, and the motivation to play video games. In: Vorderer, P., Bryant, J. (eds.) Playing Video Games: Motives, Responses, and Consequences. Motives, Responses, and Consequences, pp. 153–168. Lawrence Erlbaum Associates Publishers (2006)
22. Csikzentmihalyi, M.: Beyond Boredom and Anxiety. Jossey-Bass, San Francisco (1975)
23. Ravyse, W.S., Seugnet Blignaut, A., Leendertz, V., Woolner, A.: Success factors for serious games to enhance learning: a systematic review. Virtual Reality **21**(1), 31–58 (2016). https://doi.org/10.1007/s10055-016-0298-4
24. Stadler, J.: Die soziale Lerntheorie von Bandura. In: Frey, D., Irle, M. (eds.) Theorien der Sozialpsychologie, Gruppen-, Interaktions- und Lerntheorien, pp. 240–272. Huber, Bern (1985)
25. Pavlas, D., Heyne, K., Bedwell, W.L., Lazzara, E.H., Salas, E.: Game-based learning. The impact of flow state and videogame self-efficacy. In: Human Factors and Ergonomics Society (ed.) Proceedings of the Human Factors and Ergonomics Society Annual Meeting, vol. 54, pp. 2398–2402. SAGE Publications, Los Angeles (2010). https://doi.org/10.1177/154193121005402808
26. Hung, C.-Y., Sun, J.C.-Y., Yu, P.-T.: The benefits of a challenge: student motivation and flow experience in tablet-PC-game-based learning. Interact. Learn. Environ. **23**, 172–190 (2015). https://doi.org/10.1080/10494820.2014.997248
27. Wastiau, P., Kearney, C., Van den Berghe, W.: How are Digital Games Used in Schools? European Schoolnet, Brussels (2009)
28. MKJS: Ministerium für Kultus, Jugend und Sport Baden-Württemberg (2015): Bildungsplan 2016. Allgemeinbildende Schulen. Gymnasium. Physik. (2015). https://www.bildungsplaene-bw.de/site/bildungsplan/get/documents/lsbw/export-pdf/depot-pdf/ALLG/BP2016BW_ALLG_GYM_PH.pdf
29. Feierabend, S., Rathgeb, T., Kheredmand, H., Glöckler, S.: JIM-Studie 2020. Jugend, Information, Medien: Basisuntersuchung zum Medienumgang 12-bis 19-Jähriger. mpfs, Stuttgart (2020)
30. Mäyrä, F., Ermi, L.: Fundamental components of the gameplay experience. Digarec Ser. (6), 88–115 (2011)
31. Klimmt, C.: Serious games and social change: why they (should) work. In: Ritterfeld, U., Cody, M., Vorderer, P. (eds.) Serious Games. Mechanisms and Effects, pp. 270–292. Routledge, NY (2009)
32. Böhme, R., Munser-Kiefer, M., Prestridge, S.: Lernunterstützung mit digitalen Medien in der Grundschule. Zeitschrift für Grundschulforschung **13**(1), 1–14 (2020). https://doi.org/10.1007/s42278-019-00066-3
33. Ke, F., Abras, T.: Games for engaged learning of middle school children with special learning needs. Br. J. Educ. Technol. **44**, 225–242 (2013). https://doi.org/10.1111/j.1467-8535.2012.01326.x
34. Admiraal, W., Huizenga, J., Akkerman, S., Dam, G.t.: The concept of flow in collaborative game-based learning. Comput. Hum. Behav. **27**, 1185–1194 (2011). https://doi.org/10.1016/j.chb.2010.12.013
35. Quandt, T., Wimmer, J., Wolling, J.: Die Computerspieler: Studien zur Nutzung von Computergames. Springer (2008). https://doi.org/10.1007/978-3-531-90823-6
36. Arnab, S., et al.: Mapping learning and game mechanics for serious games analysis. Br. J. Educ. Technol. **46**, 391–411 (2015). https://doi.org/10.1111/bjet.12113

37. Dopatka, L., et al.: Kontexte in der Elektrizitätslehre im Rahmen des Projekts EPo-EKo. In: Maurer, C. (ed.) Naturwissenschaftliche Bildung als Grundlage für berufliche und gesellschaftliche Teilhabe. Gesellschaft für Didaktik der Chemie und Physik Jahrestagung in Kiel 2018, pp. 217–220. Regensburg (2018)

38. van Roy, R., Zaman, B.: Why gamification fails in education and how to make it successful: introducing nine gamification heuristics based on self-determination theory. In: Ma, M., Oikonomou, A. (eds.) Serious Games and Edutainment Applications, pp. 485–509. Springer, Cham (2017). https://doi.org/10.1007/978-3-319-51645-5_22

39. Jerusalem, M., Drössler, S., Kleine, D., Klein-Heßling, J., Mittag, W., Röder, B.: Skalen zur Erfassung von Lehrer-und Schülermerkmalen. Dokumentation der psychometrischen Verfahren im Rahmen der Wissenschaftlichen Begleitung des Modellversuchs Selbstwirksame Schulen (2009)

40. Rheinberg, F., Vollmeyer, R., Engeser, S., Rheinberg, F., Vollmeyer, R., Engeser, S.: FKS - Flow-Kurzskala. ZPID (Leibniz Institute for Psychology Information) – Testarchiv (2019)

41. Davidson, R., MacKinnon, J.G.: Estimation and Inference in Econometrics. Oxford, New York (1993)

42. Kiili, K.: Digital game-based learning: towards an experiential gaming model. Internet High. Educ. **8**, 13–24 (2005). https://doi.org/10.1016/j.iheduc.2004.12.001

43. Nacke, L.E., Lindley, C.A.: Affective ludology, flow and immersion in a first-person shooter: measurement of player experience. J. Can. Game Stud. Assoc. **3**, 1–21 (2009)

44. Wouters, P., van Nimwegen, C., van Oostendorp, H., van der Spek, E.D.: A meta-analysis of the cognitive and motivational effects of serious games. J. Educ. Psychol. **105**, 249–265 (2013). https://doi.org/10.1037/a0031311

45. Seidel, T., et al.: Blicke auf den Physikunterricht. Ergebnisse der IPN Videostudie. Zeitschrift für Pädagogik **52**, 799–821 (2006)

46. Christoph, G., Goldhammer, F., Zylka, J., Hartig, J.: Adolescents' computer performance: the role of self-concept and motivational aspects. Comput. Educ. **81**, 1–12 (2015)

Gaming Experience as a Nuisance or Confounding Variable in Serious Games for Research: Creating a Scale Measuring RTS Experience in a Serious Game Exploring the Sunk Cost Effect

Andrew Reilly$^{(\boxtimes)}$ ⓘ, Laura Kelly, and Kira Lough

Monash University, Melbourne, Australia
drew@www.adaptivebehaviour.com

Abstract. A scale measuring real-time strategy (RTS) game experience was created and used to determine whether RTS experience acted as a nuisance or confounding variable in a serious game examining sunk cost effects (SCE). A sample of 164 males, 324 females, 11 non-binary and 2 unclassified participants with a mean age of 43.53 completed the Real-Time Strategy Experience Scale (RTSES). A smaller sample of 63 males, 79 females, 2 non-binary and 1 unclassified participant with a mean age of 40.9 also played *Magnate*: an RTS-style serious game measuring SCE. Contrary to expectations, a single factor of general and strategy gaming experience was found, while two factors of RTS gaming experience were found: one comprised of experience playing popular titles, and another playing titles with more diverse game mechanics. However, a weak, positive relationship between RTS experience and game performance was found, as well as a weak, negative relationship between SCE and game performance. There was insufficient evidence of a relationship between RTS experience and SCE, which meant that the positive relationship between SCE and game performance remained largely unchanged after accounting for RTS experience. These results suggest that while RTS experience can act as a nuisance variable in studies using serious game performance as a dependent variable, there was no evidence of a confounding relationship with SCE as an independent variable in this instance. Validity of the RTSES could be improved with items focusing more on game mechanics rather than genre, which may make it easier to identify these relationships.

Keywords: Real-time strategy games · Serious games · Scale construction · Gaming experience · Sunk cost effects · Nuisance variable · Confounding variable

1 Introduction

1.1 The Potential Influence of Experience in Serious Games for Research

The use of serious games in research has been examined in a number of contexts including psychology [1], economics [2], and engineering [3]. These games tend to prioritise

H. Söbke et al. (Eds.): JCSG 2022, LNCS 13476, pp. 17–29, 2022.
https://doi.org/10.1007/978-3-031-15325-9_2

design around a particular problem or situation directly relevant to training or research goals [4]. In contrast, some studies have made effective use of data from commercially available games [5, 6], and it has been argued that an effective means of engaging research participants is to design games that draw on mechanisms from popular genres [7]. However, participants with previous experience in playing games of the selected genre could potentially display a performance advantage, and this may compromise the validity of the research when mechanisms essential to the genre are used to examine constructs of interest. This study aims to explore the construct of real-time-strategy (RTS) game experience by constructing a scale and then using this to evaluate experience as a potential nuisance or confounding variable in the development of a serious game designed for decision-making research.

1.2   The Construct of RTS Experience

Following the approach suggested by Apperley [8], the RTS genre was defined in terms of both narrative – the socially constructed classification of games – and ludology – the common player interactions required to play games of a given genre. Through a process of informal discussion and reviews of websites and blogs focusing on RTS games, series titles such as *Age of Empires* and *Starcraft* were identified as having strong name recognition and were frequently associated with the RTS genre. Common features attributed to RTS games were:

- a landscape in which gameplay takes place
- game objects that move around the landscape under the player's control
- collectible resources located across the landscape that allow the player to progress further in the game
- game objects that the player can use to create other game objects
- gameplay that includes an element of real-time decision-making.

Furthermore, common mechanisms, UI elements and consequences of actions that enable players to learn how to play a new RTS game faster than a player without this experience include, but are not limited to:

- the use of icons and numerals to indicate levels of resources collected, and the change in these resulting from spending or gathering further resources
- the use of a pointer in moving game objects across the landscape
- the use of build menus to create new game objects
- the need to both focus on and switch attention to multiple elements in the game in real time, such as UI elements that show resource levels, resources located across the landscape, and changes in game object behaviour
- the ability to explore a landscape and an understanding of how this can promote progress in the game.

The experience and learning acquired from repeated exposure to these features could conceivably overlap conceptually with typical elements of decision-making that may be of interest to researchers, such that individual differences in experience could be measured as differences in decision-making performance. For example, a player who hoards resources in an RTS game may do so due to an underlying insecurity regarding the expenditure of resources [9] (decision-making), or their lack of experience in playing RTS games may mean that they are unaware that these resources are accumulating (experience). Therefore, a scale measuring experience in playing RTS games should allow for this level of experience to be controlled for when examining player performance in areas such as decision-making.

However, the distinction between unique learning acquired from playing RTS games and learning acquired from other types of strategy games, or games in general, is not always clear. For example, city-building games also tend to take place on an isometric landscape, and the use of a pointer to manipulate game objects is common in many different types of games. Therefore, scale items covering general gaming experience, experience in playing strategy games, and games that incorporate many but perhaps not all features of RTS games were included as a means of conducting a full exploration of the construct. It was expected that a factor analysis of the scale would indicate the presence of three factors: one relating to general gaming experience, one relating to experience playing strategy games, and another relating specifically to experience playing RTS games.

1.3 The Sunk Cost Effect: RTS Experience as a Nuisance or Confounding Variable

The sunk cost effect (SCE) is a common example of irrational decision making that occurs when people decide on a course of action based on the reasoning that resources have already been committed to that action, despite evidence that that action results in loss or diminishing returns [10]. The SCE can be particularly damaging financially when in the form of a progress decision: an extended period of escalating commitment in which time and or money is continually poured into a project on the basis that ending the project would waste resources already spent [11]. A notable example in terms of cost is that of the Concorde, a project to build and maintain a supersonic passenger aircraft that ran at a loss over decades despite large and continual government subsidies [12]. This suggests that there is some educative value in developing a serious game that allows players to experience the pressure of sunk costs in decision-making.

Magnate is a serious RTS game currently in development that is designed for decision-making training and research. *Magnate* simulates the SCE by creating a situation where players initially commit resources to a course of action that results in limited returns but then have the option of switching to a more beneficial course of action at the expense of discounting existing commitments. Therefore, players who are vulnerable to SCE should perform worse than those who are not. When developing *Magnate*, the RTS genre was adopted due to its commercial track record in appealing to a large audience, and also because it typically includes mechanisms that involve resource allocation over time that lend themselves well simulating escalation of commitment. This is particularly valuable as previous attempts to capture the SCE have tended to examine decisions in greater isolation, which may have contributed to the small effect sizes found [13]. Furthermore, the real-time aspect of RTS gameplay was seen as advantageous in magnifying these small effects as it requires players to make quick decisions with short-term consequences, while exercising deliberation and focused attention, thus increasing cognitive load, both of which are associated with the SCE [14, 15].

This tendency towards smaller effect sizes suggests that the SCE may easily be masked or confounded with other factors, particularly those that relate to prior experience. Several skills matching this description are required in *Magnate* to avoid SCE and perform well. Players must be able to recognise cues in the landscape and in the UI that signal progression and opportunities for performance, and many of these cues may already be familiar to players with previous experience in playing RTS games. Examples include understanding how the gathering and storage of resources contributes to the stockpile of resources shown elsewhere on the screen, how these resources are depleted when buildings are constructed, and how the choice of a building's location can have long-term impacts on performance due to the distance units travel when transporting resources. These factors can be of concern to researchers as they contribute to variance in game performance as a dependent variable but are not related to the independent variable of interest, i.e., they are nuisance variables.

Another concern occurs when both the independent and dependent variables are related to another independent variable, making it difficult to determine which of the independent variables contributes to variance in the dependent variable. For example, players in *Magnate* with prior experience playing RTS games may realise that the current course of action is unprofitable sooner by virtue of being able to read the cues discussed above, or they may pursue strategies commonly employed in RTS games, such as exploring the landscape, that increase the potential for a change in behaviour. In cases such as these, RTS experience can be considered a confounding variable.

For these reasons, Magnate was considered an ideal game to use in confirming the validity of the RTS Experience Scale (RTSES) by evaluating its ability to measure experience in playing RTS games as either a nuisance or confounding variable in Magnate as a measure of SCE. A positive relationship was hypothesised between RTS experience and game performance on the basis that unfamiliarity with the basic mechanics of the game would result in a steeper learning curve for less experienced players, and taking them more time to become proficient at the game. It was also expected, given that SCE results in wasted resources, that there would be a negative relationship between vulnerability to SCE and game performance. However, if RTS experience does confound the measurement of vulnerability to SCE, it was expected that there would be a positive relationship between RTS experience and vulnerability to SCE, but that vulnerability would still be negatively related to game performance after controlling for RTS experience.

2 Validating the Construct of RTS Experience

2.1 Method

Participants. Participants were recruited by graduate students, with a total of 506 participants completing the RTSES ($M_{age} = 43.53$, $SD_{age} = 16.75$) for use in factor analysis and 145 completing both this and the game ($M_{age} = 40.19$, $SD_{age} = 14.96$) for use in a regression model. Gender and occupation distribution is shown for both groups in Table 1.

Table 1. Gender and occupation distribution for factor analysis and regression samples

	Factor analysis	Regression
Male	164 (32.4%)	63 (43.4%)
Female	324 (64%)	79 (54.5%)
Non-binary	11 (2.2%)	2 (1.4%)
Other	2 (0.4%)	1 (0.7%)
Business	75 (14.8%)	31 (21.4%)
Education	69 (13.6%)	25 (17.2%)
Other	127 (25.1%)	41 (28.3%)
Missing	235 (46.4%)	58 (40%)

Materials. *Demographics* Survey items covering age, gender, and occupation were administered to participants.

Real Time Strategy Experience Scale (RTSES) The RTSES is a 25-item scale designed to measure a person's experience playing RTS games. The scale is divided into three subscales: general experience in playing electronic games (items 1 to 5), experience in playing strategy games (items 6 to 11), and experience in playing specific examples of RTS games (items 12 to 25). Items 1 to 5 include statements such as "I have played games" to which respondents indicate agreement using a 5-point likert scale labeled *Strongly Disagree, Disagree, Neither Agree Nor Disagree, Agree, Strongly Agree.* Items 6 to 11 include statements such as "I have played strategy games" to which respondents indicate agreement using a 5-point likert scale labeled *Never, Rarely, Sometimes, Often, Very Often.* Items 12 to 25 comprise a list of games by series title including *Age of Empires* and *Total War* to which respondents indicate their level of playing experience using a 5-point likert scale labeled *None, Low, Medium, High, Very High.* Items 4 and 9 are reverse-scored, and total scores for the whole scale and subscales are calculated by summing the numerical values of the responses, with higher scores indicating greater experience. As the purpose of this study is to validate and establish reliability for this scale, these statistics are provided in the Results section. A list of all the items can be found in the appendix.

Magnate Online Game The online RTS game *Magnate* is designed for use in studying decision-making. As it is still under development, current studies focus on implementing and testing mechanisms that are potentially useful in research. The version used in this study was designed to evaluate the use of RTS games in examining a range of decision-making phenomena, including SCE.

Like in many RTS games, the game environment in *Magnate* consists of an isometric landscape populated with resources which are collected by units directed by players. Players spend these resources on buildings and on more units, thus increasing their economy. Wood is collected solely for the purpose of creating new buildings, such as houses, from which further units are created, bridges, and resource repositories. Each unit created "belongs" to their respective house, so a unit collecting a given resource will automatically deposit the resource at the nearest appropriate repository and then visit their house before returning to collect more of the resource. Figure 1 shows the welcome screen of the game inviting players to begin the tutorial.

Fig. 1. Magnate welcome screen

The aim of the game is to amass a predetermined level of gold by collecting stone and iron and selling these at the nearest appropriate repository. Players can choose to sell either stone or iron, such that any deposited quantity of the resource selected for sale is automatically sold at a fluctuating price continually displayed to the player. If a player deposits a resource without selling it, the resource accumulates as normal, thus providing an indication of wasted labour in collecting a resource that cannot be sold or used.

The player begins by collecting and selling stone. However, each unit collecting stone or iron costs the player one gold every second, and the price of stone is so low that it is extremely difficult to attain the goal of amassing a certain level of gold. The price of iron is higher, but to collect iron, the player must explore the landscape and build a bridge to cross the river, as all of the iron is located on the other side of the river. Therefore, to attain the goal, players must demolish houses (as there is a limit of two), rebuild these on the other side of the river, and then respawn units from these again. Having already established a settlement on one side of the river that is collecting stone, it is thought that players exhibiting SCE will be reluctant to demolish this settlement and rebuild on the other side of the river, even though it will increase their chances of attaining the goal.

Following an initial tutorial explaining how to play the game, five characters are displayed on the screen from whom the player may receive advice. Characters are ordered by status, indicated by their clothing. Characters lower in status offer less useful and even misleading advice, e.g., to continue mining stone, while higher-status characters cost the player gold but offer more useful advice, with the highest status character advising the player to build a bridge and collect iron from the other side of the river. Figure 2 shows a game in which a player is collecting stone but is yet to build a bridge over the river.

The game runs for 20 min, and SCE is measured by the number of seconds taken for the player to switch from selling stone to iron, with higher values indicating greater

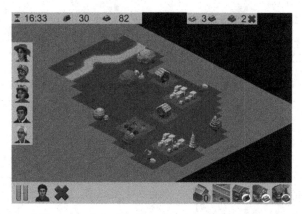

Fig. 2. A game of *Magnate* where the player is yet to build a bridge crossing the river.

vulnerability to SCE. Game performance is measured as the amount of gold held by the player at the end of the game.

Procedure. Participants were recruited by student research via word-of-mouth and through social media advertising. Advertising was also placed on Reddit and advertised in forums relating to electronic games. After reading an explanatory statement online and providing implied consent, participants completed the demographic items, followed by the RTSES and several scales related to other studies, which were administered in random order. Participants then clicked on a link to the *Magnate* game, after which they were given the option of entering a prize draw for eight Amazon gift vouchers worth 25AUD each.

2.2 Results

Factor Analysis. A principal components analysis with a direct oblimin rotation was conducted to identify factors among the RTSES items. Table 2 shows the extracted factors after rotation, with a threshold of .4 required for sufficient factor loading.

Items 1 to 11, which relate to both general gaming experience as well as experience in playing strategy games both load onto Factor 2, with the exception of item 9, which is the sole item loading onto Factor 4. Factor 2 is therefore considered to be measuring general gaming or strategy gaming experience (Gaming), while Factors 1 and 3 relate to experience in playing specific RTS game series. Items loading onto Factor 3 list games that appear to be more popular or well known, such as *Age of Empires* and *Warcraft*. Factor 3 is therefore thought to measure experience in playing popular RTS games (Popular). Factor 1 consists of more disparate and arguably less well-known games that may appeal to players with more specific preferences in game mechanics (Niche). Descriptive statistics for these scales are shown in Table 3, while correlations between the subscales and reliability statistics are shown in Table 4.

Regression Analysis. A regression analysis was conducted to determine the contribution of RTS experience to performance in *Magnate* as either a nuisance or confounding variable. This was done by firstly identifying factors related to performance in the game,

Table 2. RTSES items with a factor loading of 0.4 or greater

Item	Factor 1	Factor 2	Factor 3	Factor 4
1		.90		
2		.92		
3		.86		
4		.63		
5		.71		
6		.78		
7		.76		
8		.71		
9				.92
10		.72		
11		.79		
12			−.85	
13			−.81	
14			−.74	
15			−.41	
16	.84			
17	.75			
18	.64			
19	.87			
20	.52			
21	.87			
22	.63			
23	.55			
24			.71	
25	.74			

and then, by measuring the variance in performance accounted for by SCE after controlling for relevant factors of RTS experience. Descriptive statistics for all relevant variables are shown in Table 5, along with correlations between the factors, game performance, and SCE.

As the Popular factor was the only factor to correlate with performance, this was selected as a potential nuisance variable when conducting analyses where the independent variable, such as SCE, also correlates with the dependent variable. To determine whether this is the case in the current study, Popular was entered into a hierarchical regression model first, followed by SCE. These results are displayed in Table 6.

Table 3. Descriptive statistics for the RTSES and subscales

	Min	Max	*M*	*SD*	Skew	Kurtosis
RTSES	25	116	53.29	15.51	.80	1.11
Gaming	10	50	34.95	9.66	−.58	−.07
Popular	5	25	7.4	4.07	1.96	3.28
Niche	9	25	10.95	5.01	3.55	14.07

N = 506

Table 4. Subscale reliability statistics and correlations

	Gaming	Popular	Niche
Gaming	.94		
Popular	.52	.87	
Niche	.35	.72	.92

N = 506
All correlations are significant at the .01 level
Chronbach's alpha for each subscale is shown in the diagonal.
Chronbach's alpha for the whole scale = .94

Table 5. Descriptive statistics for the RTSES subscales, SCE, and game performance, and correlations

	RTSES	Gaming	Popular	Niche	SCE
SCE	.03	.03	−.07	.10	
Perform.	.14	.07	.24**	.11	−.18*
M	56.74	37.76	7.92	11.06	693.08
SD	14.62	8.07	4.36	4.97	366.45

N = 145
*significant at the .05 level **significant at the .01 level

The change in R^2 for both models is significant, with $F(1, 143) = 8.38, p < .05$ for Model 1 and $F(1, 142) = 4.14, p < .05$ for Model 2. The minimal difference in standardised beta between Models 1 and 2 indicates that there is little shared variance between experience with popular RTS games and SCE, and therefore the additional variance accounted for by SCE is largely unique. This, along with the lack of any correlation between SCE and experience with popular RTS games suggests that experience with popular RTS games is not a confounding variable in this instance.

Table 6. Results of a hierarchical regression model examining the ability of SCE to negatively predict game performance after controlling for Popular RTS experience.

Predictors	b	R^2	R^2 change
Model 1			
Popular	.24	.05	.05
Model 2			
Popular	.22	.08	.03
SCE	-.16		

$N = 145$

3 Discussion

3.1 Construct Validity

The aim of this study was to explore the construct of RTS experience by creating and validating a scale. The first hypothesis, that the factor structure of the scale would consist of a factor of general gaming experience, a factor of strategy gaming experience, and a factor of RTS gaming experience was not met. Instead, a single factor combining both general and strategy gaming experience was found, along with two factors of popular and niche RTS gaming experience.

Factor analysis results suggest that there is little difference in the constructs of general gaming experience and strategy-gaming experience. This may be because many gamers consider their games to incorporate an element of strategic thinking or decision-making, and items such as "I have played games that involve managing resources" are ambiguous enough for people to consider a broad range of game elements as "resources".

Furthermore, a moderate correlation between the general gaming experience scale and the popular RTS scale suggests that many people with gaming experience have experience in playing these games. Therefore, despite the wide variety of game genres and RTS titles to choose from, a limited range of RTS games are commonly played, and it appears that these may form a more definitive representation of the genre. This may be due to the fact that many game titles loading onto the Niche factor incorporate mechanics or emphasise elements that diverge from the standard collection of RTS mechanics found in titles loading onto the Popular factor. For example, *Anno* could be equally classified as a city-building or simulation game, while *Company of Heroes* relies mostly on combat mechanics. Therefore, it may be more useful to define player experience in terms of the common mechanics shared by popular games and those of the serious game.

3.2 RTS Experience as a Nuisance Variable

The hypotheses that a positive relationship would be found between experience and game performance and a negative relationship found between SCE and game performance were both met, though the relationships were weak. The lack of shared variance between SCE and experience in this instance suggests that experience can act as a nuisance variable, albeit with little influence, rather than as a confound.

These weak relationships may be due to the little real similarity in mechanics that *Magnate* has with commercial RTS games played for entertainment. These games typically include a wider range of mechanics, such as upgrades and combat, and are usually played for periods much longer than 20 min. Experience with these mechanics may result in the development of skills that are unique or definitive of the RTS genre as a fast-paced game, and these skills may not have been required for performance in *Magnate*. Therefore, in this instance, the benefits accrued to experience may have come from familiarity with more fundamental features such as the isometric environment, the point-and-click interactions with that environment, and the meaning of basic UI elements. The fact that these can be quickly learned by players in the tutorial may mean that their impact on performance is minimal, and that it may be subject to broader characteristics such as learning and general experience with digital interfaces.

3.3 Future Work

As the discussion on construct validity suggests, it may be more effective in future to determine prior learning by defining common mechanics between games rather than relying on genre classifications, which can be difficult to define due to feature overlap [16]. For example, vulnerability to SCE is defined in *Magnate* as the time taken to switch to a more profitable resource, which can only be obtained by exploring the map and building a bridge. Therefore, items such as "I play games that involve exploring a landscape", or "I play games in which problems are solved by placing objects in certain locations" might make it easier to identify prior learning that directly influences behaviour of interest to the researcher, thus providing a confound. Item format could also be expanded to include those in which participants are provided with a screenshot of a game and asked multiple-choice questions regarding their next action. Players with experience in navigating interfaces of a similar kind would therefore have an advantage in responding correctly to each item.

3.4 Conclusion

Results from this study indicate that experience playing games of a genre congruent with that of a serious game can account for around 5% of the variance in performance. However, the use of genre may not be the most effective means of measuring prior learning, and a more clearly defined overlap in the mechanics of games may increase the validity of the measure. Presenting players with items that draw on example game situations may also provide a stronger indication of prior learning.

Appendix

Initial list of RTSES items.

1. I have played games.
2. I have played games on more than one type of device.
3. I have played a lot of different games.

4. I don't know much about gaming.
5. I have a lot of experience in playing games.
6. I have played games that involve a lot of thinking.
7. I have played strategy games.
8. I have played games that require complex decision making.
9. I haven't played many games that involve strategic thinking.
10. I have played games that involve managing resources.
11. I have played games that require planning.
12. Warcraft.
13. Command and Conquer/Red Alert.
14. Starcraft.
15. Age of Empires.
16. Anno.
17. Populous.
18. Empire Earth.
19. Europa Universalis.
20. Total War.
21. Hearts of Iron.
22. Company of Heroes.
23. Supreme Commander.
24. Warhammer 40,000.
25. Stronghold.

References

1. Washburn, D.A.: The games psychologists play (and the data they provide). Behav. Res. Methods Instrum. Comput. **35**, 185–193 (2003). https://doi.org/10.3758/BF03202541
2. Chesney, T., Chuah, S., Hoffmann, R.: Virtual world experimentation: an exploratory study. J. Econ. Behav. Organ. **72**(1), 618–635 (2009)
3. Vermillion, S.D., Malak, R.J., Smallman, R., Becker, B., Sferra, M., Fields, S.: An investigation on using serious gaming to study human decision-making in engineering contexts. Des. Sci. **15**(3) (2017)
4. Good, D.: Predicting real-time adaptive performance in a dynamic decision-making context. J. Manage. Organ. **20**(6), 715–732 (2014)
5. Ahmad, M.A., Borbora, Z., Shen, C., Srivastava, J., Williams, D.: Guild play in MMOGs: rethinking common group dynamics models. In: Datta, A., Shulman, S., Zheng, B., Lin, S.-D., Sun, A., Lim, E.-P. (eds.) SocInfo 2011. LNCS, vol. 6984, pp. 145–152. Springer, Heidelberg (2011). https://doi.org/10.1007/978-3-642-24704-0_19
6. Shen, C., Monge, P., Williams, D.: Virtual brokerage and closure: network structure and social capital in a massively multiplayer online game. Commun. Res. **41**(4), 459–480 (2012)
7. Reilly, A.: A complex adaptive systems approach to personality and social psychology through design sciences. Doctoral thesis, The Australian National University, Canberra, Australia (2020)
8. Apperley, T.H.: Genre and game studies: toward a critical approach to video game genres. Simul. Gaming **37**(1), 6–23 (2006)

9. Halim, Z., Atif, M., Rashid, A., Edwin, C.A.: Profiling players using real-world datasets: clustering the data and correlating the results with the big-five personality traits. IEEE Trans. Affect. Comput. **10**(4), 568–584 (2019)

10. Roth, S., Robbert, T., Straus, L.: On the sunk-cost effect in economic decision-making: a meta-analytic review. Bus. Res. **8**(1), 99–138 (2014). https://doi.org/10.1007/s40685-014-0014-8

11. Moon, H.: Looking forward and looking back: integrating completion and sunk-cost effects within an escalation-of-commitment progress decision. J. Appl. Psychol. **86**(1), 104–113 (2001)

12. Brown, G.W., MacLean, I., McMillan, A.: A concise oxford dictionary of politics and international relations, 4th edn. Oxford University Press, Oxford (2018)

13. Friedman, D., Pommerenke, K., Lukose, R., Milam, G., Huberman, B.A.: Searching for the sunk cost fallacy. Exp. Econ. **10**, 79–104 (2007)

14. Sophis, M.J.: Temporal attention, the sunk cost effect, and delay discounting. Doctoral dissertation, University of Kansas (2018)

15. Dijkstra, K.A., Hong, Y.: The feeling of throwing good money after bad: the role of affective reaction in the sunk cost fallacy. PLoS ONE **14**(1), e0209900 (2019)

16. Lee, J.H., Karlova, N., Clarke, R.I., Thornton, K., Perti, A.: Facet analysis of video game genres. In: iConference 2014 Proceedings, pp. 125–139 (2014)

Designing Effective Playful Collaborative Science Learning in VR

Jan L. Plass(✉) ⓘ, Ken Perlin, Agnieszka Roginska ⓘ, Chris Hovey, Fabian Fröhlich,
Aniol Saurina Maso, Alvaro Olsen ⓘ, Zhenyi He, Robert Pahle, and Sounak Ghosh

New York University, New York, NY 10012, USA
jan.plass@nyu.edu

Abstract. How do we design effective immersive VR experiences? *Looking Inside Cells* is a set of collaborative immersive virtual reality science learning simulations that were designed by applying best practices for learning experience design, taking advantage of the unique affordances of VR for learning. In this paper we describe design features of immersive learning we implemented, including features related to interaction, collaboration, playfulness, and emotional design. We then describe the front-end, client-server communication, and network framework that facilitated these features. We argue that the design of effective VR learning experience requires establishing a link from learning objectives to affordances of VR and, eventually, to design features that serve specific functions in facilitating learning.

Keywords: Immersive VR · Affordances · Collaborative VR · Playful science learning

1 Introduction

The increasing availability of high quality affordable virtual reality (VR) has led to much speculation about the use of immersive, interactive environments for learning. While some consider VR a game changer for learning, research has not been consistently able to support this assertion [1]. The source of this discrepancy may be the design of VR materials for learning that does not sufficiently advantage of the unique affordances of VR for learning. To address this problem, we have developed *Looking Inside Cells*, a set of playful collaborative immersive virtual reality science learning simulations that cover middle school cell biology topics aligned to US science learning standards. These simulations were designed to take advantage of VR affordances, which will eventually allow us to verify claims for the effectiveness of VR for learning.

In this paper, we will briefly discuss VR affordances and then describe how the *Looking Inside Cells* simulations are based on design features that correspond to specific affordances of VR, and what specific function each of these features serves in support of facilitating learning. We consider this process of mapping learning objectives to affordances and design features as part of best practices of learning experience design. In the final part of the paper, we will describe technical aspects of the implementation of the collaborative VR simulations.

H. Söbke et al. (Eds.): JCSG 2022, LNCS 13476, pp. 30–35, 2022.
https://doi.org/10.1007/978-3-031-15325-9_3

2   Designing Playful Collaborative Learning Experiences in VR

2.1   Affordances of VR for Learning

Among best practices for selecting media for learning is the determination whether the specific content, learners, and contexts are a good match with the medium's unique affordances. For example, portability and locationality are affordances of mobile media, which makes mobile a good choice for learners on the move, and for learning apps that are location-aware. For immersive virtual reality, affordances include the learner's sense of presence (achieved through immersive technology), the observation of spatial relations of objects in the 3D space, the direct manipulation of 3D objects, the emotional design through visual, auditory, and haptic modes, and the collaboration through multi-user capabilities [2].

2.2   Looking Inside Cells

Looking Inside Cells is a suite of interactive cellular biology VR simulations designed for K12 classrooms. The simulations use aspects of inquiry-based learning, allowing users to find solutions to complex problems, and make and learn from mistakes, aspects of experiential learning, giving learners the opportunity to reflect after doing, and aspects of collaborative learning, where students are able to co-create, investigate, and learn from each other in exploring the simulations.

Looking Inside Cells consists of four parts. Starting with Build a Cell, students create the standard, generic model of a plant, animal, or prokaryotic cell from a toolbox of organelles. In Specialize a Cell, students transform the generic models into real world example cells including e. coli, melanocyte, blue-green algae, root hair, red blood cell, and a plant epidermal cell. In the final cell life simulation, students learn about cellular division by removing, rearranging, and replicating organelles to progress the stages of mitosis. In addition, a series of exploratory simulations shows how viruses invade a cell and take over its organelles. Students also learn about mRNA, protein synthesis, and virus replication. Below we will describe the learning experience design features we implemented to make these simulations effective learning environments.

Fig. 1. Interaction design in looking inside: cells.

2.3 Interaction Design

Looking Inside Cells allows learners to actively engage with the simulations, following the INTERACT model [3] that describes cognitive, emotional, and behavioral aspects of interactivity. Learners use 3D objects and hand tools to build cells. They can drag the organelles provided to create a cell, change generic cells into specialized cells by removing or changing organelles, and manipulate organelles to create cell division, see Fig. 1. These interactive elements, which take advantage of the 3D direct object manipulation affordance of VR, are designed to achieve learning outcomes, as research has shown that learning is an active process, and that interactions such as direct manipulations of objects foster deep learning [4]. We also optimize for viewing zones, where the main elements of the simulations on the scene are positioned within a horizontal field of view (FOV) of around 70°, and a vertical FOV of around 50°.

2.4 Collaboration Design

A central part of our VR simulations is their collaborative nature [5]. Small groups of up to 4 learners can collaborate to interact with the simulations, and changes made by one user are updated immediately in the display of the others. This feature, which takes advantage of the social collaboration affordance of VR, allows for remote collaboration of learners and fosters shared cognition. The shared features provide peripheral awareness, the ability to follow another's actions without direct communication, and facilitate more productive virtual collaboration.

An important part of collaboration design is to choose which information is shared, i.e., visible by all, and which is shown to each individual learner. Each learner has their own view of their toolbox from which they select organelles or other tasks, see Fig. 1, right panel. While users cannot view one another's toolboxes, the feedback visible there is updated across all users to maintain group cohesion in actions and progress. For example, when one user removes an organelle from the toolbox, both the availability counter and the progress bar updates across all users' toolboxes. Once it is pulled out of the toolbox, an organelle becomes visible to all. Additionally, user avatar colors are matched to active highlighting so everyone can easily discern who is moving that particular piece.

2.5 Emotional Design

Another design factor for the *Looking Inside Cells* simulations is the use of emotional design, which is the use of a range of visual, auditory, and haptic design features to induce emotional states in the learner that are conducive to learning [6]. We employ three emotional design principles that take advantage of the emotional design affordance of VR, namely playfulness design, visual design and sound design.

Playfulness Design. Playful design features are borrowed from games and have been shown to enhance learning [7]. We used the interaction design, visual design, and sound design to add playful elements such as animations to the simulations. For example, Red Blood Cells eject organelles during growth, and when users remove one from the cell at the appropriate stage, a white blood cell moves in to dispose of the unwanted material. In other instances, we substituted internal hormone-related processes for organisms, which happen beyond the cellular level, with a labeled spray bottle that triggers animations. Both of these animated interactions are playful representations of the processes they represent and can be interacted with as much as users like.

Visual Design. The visual design employs warm colors and round shapes where possible, which have been shown to induce positive emotions that lead to enhanced learning [8], see Fig. 2, left panel. Our research has shown that VR is an especially effective environment for emotion induction through visual design [9]. Visuals are designed with a futuristic look to blend with the rest of the narrative. The scene is separated into three main areas that allow for the focus of the user to change based on the scene that is loaded at any particular time, see Fig. 2, right panel. When working on any simulation, the lab (static and sky areas) is hidden so that the focus is fully on the learning materials (interactive area), thereby avoiding any distractions that could arise from having the lab be visible in the background. In contrast, when in the home menu, the lab is visible to help convey the narrative.

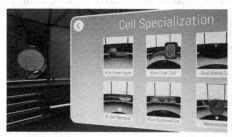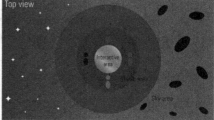

Fig. 2. Visual emotional design (left) and visual layout (right) in *Looking Inside Cells*

Sound Design. The sound design employs short loops, a tempo between 70 bpm and 120 pm, a narrow pitch range, ascending and descending melodies, no lyrical content, and short repetitions [10] and was created to reflect and support the emotional design effects of the visual design. We feature an orchestra, where each organelle is a note in a chord. As the learners assemble a cell, they also assemble a musical chord, giving closure to a task. A number of sounds for the user interface and panel presentations were also created to complement the music. These make use of notes and chords that harmonize with the background music and its instruments.

3 Technical Implementation

3.1 Game Front-End

The front-end development of Looking Inside Cells has been implemented with the Unreal Engine 4 (UE4). UE4 is one of the few free software tools that offers full support for most VR devices as well as most of the other screen devices and platforms. This flexibility and the fact that UE4 is constantly being updated made it attractive when choosing what software to use for the design of VR environments.

3.2 Client-Server Communication

Communication between clients, mediated by the NYU Corelink server, is facilitated entirely through passing of JSON encodings of generic name/value pair objects, which are sent and received via data streams, as described in Sect. 3.3. This protocol is used both to maintain shared game state and to communicate the current state of the VR headset and controllers between all participants. We note that this approach gives our network layer the potential to support interoperability between clients implemented in different engines, including WebXR, Unity and Unreal.

We considered the option of maintaining a local server at each school, but in the end we opted for a centralized networked server, for several reasons: (1) Maintaining a central server makes it far easier to perform periodic software updates and upgrades as needed, as well as to monitor any problems with the software as it is actually used in the field; (2) Passing of client data to and from a centralized server, properly anonymized for privacy, allows for research study and analysis based on actual use of the software in the field. Over time, this allows for both proper assessment and iterative improvement of the system; (3) Asking the teachers and administrators of individual schools to maintain their own local server would impose an added administrative and cost burden upon them which would be both unnecessary and unwelcome.

3.3 Corelink Network Framework

To enable Client-Server communication, the system needs to be able to exchange messages over the network. For this purpose, we are using a framework called Corelink [11] which we developed for real-time multi-user interaction. As opposed to other similar frameworks, Corelink embeds user management and allows stream processing on the fly. Corelink uses the publish-subscribe pattern to exchange data between all connected parties. Streams can be sent via Transmission Control Protocol (TCP), User Datagram Protocol (UDP) or WebSocket Secure (WSS) based on the requirements of the users for data security or availability of specific protocols. Corelink natively supports libraries for JavaScript, Browser, C++, C# and Python and enables easy use of a network layer in applications like Unreal and Unity.

Streams—in this case audio, sensor/biometrics, motion tracking and data logging streams—are injected into the system by different users and components of the system and can be received by other users or plugins subscribing to the streams. All users are authenticated and streams are secured by access control lists to prevent unauthorized access. The client-server architecture described in Sect. 3.2 builds on Corelink and makes use of the capabilities provided by the framework.

An application of Corelink is its use to connect biometric sensors, which collect physiological data from research participants while in the virtual reality simulation. These sensors have been integrated into Corelink using NodeJS. A dedicated Corelink receiver node is used to subscribe to the biometric sensor data streams. This node stores these data in a non-relational document database. The simulation contains its own Corelink sender node that orchestrates the recording of the biometric data by sending start and stop signals. In addition, the virtual reality simulation sends *event markers*, which are unique hash identifiers that represent events within the simulation used to provide contextual data to the game and biodata logs. The system uses the Empatica 4 sensor wristband device that features sensors that capture body temperature (TEMP), galvanic skin response (GSR), inter-beat interval (IBI) and blood volume pressure (BVP), which can be used for emotion detection [12].

4   Conclusion

To address the issue of mixed results of research on the effectiveness of VR for learning, we designed *Looking Inside Cells*, a series of simulations designed to take advantage of the unique affordances of VR, including the learner's sense of presence, the observation and manipulation of 3D objects, the emotional design, and the social collaboration capabilities. We described in this paper how best practices in VR design should establish a link from learning objectives to a medium's affordances and to specific design features that are grounded in theory and research. We provided examples for how this was implemented in the design of our simulations. We also described how some of these features were implemented technically. Even though we have conducted user research for this project in progress, we have not yet conducted an experimental validation of the effectiveness of these simulations. This will be the next phase of this project, and we look forward to reporting our findings shortly.

References

1. Parong, J., Mayer, R.E.: Learning science in immersive virtual reality. J. Educ. Psychol. **110**, 785–797 (2018)
2. Plass, J.L.: Growing Up Digital: Coming of Age in a Virtual World. Invited Panel, Big Ideas Series, World Science Festival (2017)
3. Domagk, S., Schwartz, R., Plass, J.L.: Interactivity in multimedia learning: an integrated model. Comput. Hum. Behav. **26**, 1024–1033 (2010)
4. Schwartz, R., Plass, J.L.: User-performed tasks and the enactment effect in an interactive multimedia environment. Comput. Hum. Behav. **33**, 242–255 (2014)
5. Plass, J.L., O'Keefe, P., et al.: Motivational and cognitive outcomes associated with individual, competitive, and collaborative game play. J. Educ. Psychol. **4**, 1050–1066 (2013)
6. Plass, J.L., Hovey, C.: The emotional design principle in multimedia learning. In: Mayer, R.E., Fiorello, L. (eds.) Cambridge Handbook of Multimedia Learning, 3rd edn., pp. 324–336. Cambridge University Press, Cambridge (2022)
7. Plass, J.L., Mayer, R.E., Homer, B.D., eds.: Handbook of Game-Based Learning. MIT Press (2020)
8. Um, E., Plass, J.L., Hayward, E.O., Homer, B.D.: Emotional design in multimedia learning. J. Educ. Psychol. **104**(2), 485–498 (2012)
9. Hovey, C., Pawar, S., Plass, J.L.: Exploring the emotional effect of immersive virtual reality versus 2D screen-based game characters. Paper presented at the Annual Meeting of the American Educational Research Association, NY (2018)
10. Hill, A.J.: Music to our ears: the effect of background music in higher education learning environments. In: Audio Engineering Society Convention 135. Audio Engin Society (2013)
11. Corelink Homepage: https://corelink.hsrn.nyu.edu/. Accessed 3 May 2022
12. Wagner, J., Kim, J., André, E.: From physiological signals to emotions: implementing and comparing selected methods for feature extraction and classification. In: 2005 IEEE International Conference on Multimedia and Expo, pp. 940–943. IEEE (2005)

Design Aspects

Academy Camp VR: Serious Game Constructions as Active Learning Experiences for Children

Kenji Saito[1,2]([✉])([iD]), Kayo Kobayashi[2], Hirotsugu Ikeya[2], Naoki Yoshioka[2], Suzuna Shibasaki[2], Asuka Takahashi[2], Atsuki Hashimoto[2], Yuma Kawanobe[2], Waki Takekoshi[2], Asuto Mano[2,3], and Tomoyasu Hirano[2,3]

[1] Waseda University, Tokyo, Japan
ks91@aoni.waseda.jp
[2] Academy Camp, Fujisawa, Kanagawa, Japan
[3] Starhouse Japan Inc., Tokyo, Japan

Abstract. We have been running children's play and learning camps since 2011, but we are withholding physical gathering after 2020 during the COVID-19 pandemic. The problem with online videoconference camps is that it is difficult to design activities that encourage children to move spontaneously and engage with the world around them. Starting in 2021, we have launched a series of VR (virtual reality) camps with each camp aiming for the construction of a VR world. We believe that by having the children actively involved in the creation of the 3D objects that make up the worlds and in game design, we are fostering a sense of efficacy that allows them to actively work on the world surrounding them and change it. In this paper, we summarize our attempts, especially our experience of constructing a VR world with children in which the immune system of the human body is turned into a serious game.

Keywords: Serious game · Virtual reality · Active learning

1 Introduction

Academy Camp[1] was started as a series of camps for children in Fukushima, Japan, in the wake of the 2011 Great East Japan Earthquake and the TEPCO Fukushima Daiichi Nuclear Power Plant accident. We are a group of university faculty, camp leaders, and many volunteers (students and adults) who carry out and support our activities. It was incorporated as a non-profit in 2012.

We have organized physical camps that include outdoor activities during long vacations and consecutive holidays at elementary to high schools in Japan. Camp activities included digital manufacturing, art making, improvisational theater, singing, orienteering, and more, including an attempt to automate school homework in 2018 and designing e-sports with ball-shaped robots in 2019. In 2020, all

---

[1] https://academy-camp.org/academy-camp-overview-in-english/.

H. Söbke et al. (Eds.): JCSG 2022, LNCS 13476, pp. 39–45, 2022.
https://doi.org/10.1007/978-3-031-15325-9_4

activities were moved online for COVID-19 measures (for this reason, we have expanded the scope of our programs to include children throughout Japan), and a videoconferencing system was used to support children's free research and other activities. However, it has been difficult to design online activities that encourage children for spontaneous actions, because of the limited (spatial) freedom that videoconferencing systems allow for children to engage with the world.

In 2021, we launched *Academy Camp VR* as a series of camps combining videoconferencing, asynchronous chat, and VR experiences. The camps are based on a *constructionist* [1] approach, and in the course of our nearly monthly activities, we have built a base on the Moon[2][3], launched two spacecraft from the lunar orbital space dock to explore for life (of our own design) in the subsurface global ocean of Jupiter's moon Europa[4], and created the microscopic world described in this paper. On average, 15 children (21 maximum) participated in each VR camp from their home, ranging from first grade to high school students, who applied for the open call on the web (we have accepted everyone). We loan out VR headsets (31 of them so far) to the children on a long-term basis.

The contributions of this short paper are as follows:

1. We present *Academy Camp VR Cells*[5], a serious-game VR world that lets players experience how the human body's immune system works.
2. We share our experience of designing this VR world with children.

2 Background

2.1 Constructionist Approach

Simply put, *constructionism* [1] is about learning by making, but in depth, it is the opposite of *instructionism*. At Academy camp, we try not to hand down knowledge to children. We do not follow a grand plan in our camps. For example, we did not plan to fly *two* spacecraft to Jupiter's moon Europa. We just advised the children to avoid deciding by majority vote, and the result was two spacecraft, which were harder to animate than one, but the presence of backup transportation was appropriate for that adventure. We learn from the children.

2.2 Tools for VR World Constructions

We use VRChat SDK3 to create our worlds, for which Unity 2019.4.31f1 is used for development as of this writing. Children are used to use Minecraft, so

---

[2] https://vrchat.com/home/launch?worldId=wrld_37674301-66c2-4b0a-9f1f-a3c084706765.

[3] https://vrchat.com/home/launch?worldId=wrld_ad05e7c3-5370-4711-a846-786f96406011.

[4] https://vrchat.com/home/launch?worldId=wrld_351134c7-9ffb-4bca-943e-6e6bb58a2600.

[5] https://vrchat.com/home/launch?worldId=wrld_2f8602af-a7ea-42a4-833b-789261f55205.

we provide two realms in the Bedrock Edition (and one in Java) to let them create 3D objects to be imported to the worlds (only 10 players can be in each realm at the same time, which is one factor limiting the number of campers). MultiBrush (derived from Tilt Brush), a 3D painting tool, is another option we use for creating 3D objects. Blender 2.92 has been used for 3D modeling with appropriate add-ons for importing Minecraft and Tilt Brush objects. Currently, children do not use Blender or Unity directly, and in fact one adult operates these tools, but we hope that this will change soon.

3   Academy Camp VR Cells

3.1   Project

Production of this VR world began in September 2021 and was approximately completed in February 2022.

The project started with our camp named *Academy Camp VR 2021.9 "You Explore! Amazing Modern & Near-Future Medicine"*, held September 18–20 with 13 children. The purpose of the camp was to let children know how the new coronavirus and mRNA vaccine against it work, and to learn about the challenges in realizing space medicine. After we reviewed DNA replication process, DNA to RNA transcription and translation to protein, we went through mRNA vaccine code according to [2]. The children then tried to express what they understood through 3D painting (Fig. 1).

Fig. 1. 3D painting DNA transcription and replication. A child wondered how the Okazaki fragments [3] are formed during DNA replication, and placed "?" mark. Like adults who have been trained to understand complex ideas by drawing diagrams, we found that children who have access to 3D painting tools can try to understand ideas by constructing their 3D models. Nicknames have been removed to protect privacy.

3.2 VR World Construction

Although we have not yet recreated DNA-level phenomena, we have begun to create a slightly larger, cellular-level virtual world. The world is measured in nanometers. We have scaled it so that 1 cm in this world represents 1 nm.

We worked with the children to create theses 3D objects in the VR world (sizes in the game world are in parentheses to give readers a sense of scale): new corona virus (120 cm), general cell (200 m), its nucleus (60 m), mitochondria (30 m), ACE2 receptor (20 cm), ribosome (20 cm), macrophage (500 m), neutrophil (140 m), red blood cell (80 m), dendritic cell (70 m), helper T cell (70 m), killer T cell (70 m), B cell (70 m), blood platelets (20 m), bacterium (10 m), antibody (15 cm), and fictitious *antibody gun* (about 150 cm) to disperse antibodies. Of these, mitochondria, neutrophil, red blood cell (three types of them because of popularity), dendritic cell, killer T cell, B cell, and antibody gun were designed by children. Macrophage was designed by the collaboration of a child and an adult. Based on their understanding of the roles of cells, the children made, for example, B cells into the shape of a giant gun and dendritic cells into the shape of a tree. Most objects were made in Minecraft (Fig. 2).

Fig. 2. 3D objects constructed in a minecraft realm.

3.3 Game Design

Basic Experience. Through discussion on Discord, the basic structure of the game was created by the end of January 2022. The world is in low gravity, and players spawn just above the cell indicated by the "You Are Here" sign in Fig. 3.

The cell above is already infected upon the start of the game, and viruses fall once in every three seconds, which might infect the cell below if they come close to the receptors on the surface, which then will lead to more reproductions of the viruses (unlike reality, the viral core can be removed from the infected cell by physical force after a player dives inside the cell). There are four antibody

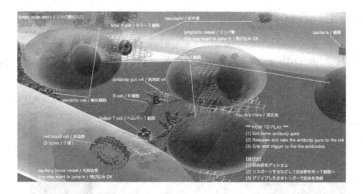

Fig. 3. This bilingual map is actually placed in the VR world. A macrophage orbits this world and prey on the infected cell above the "You Are Here" sign.

guns (we assume four or more simultaneous players) they can take from on top of the nearby B cell. Holding the antibody gun and pulling the trigger disperses antibodies at a rate of 1,000 per second. The scattered antibodies are represented by particles, and when they collide with a virus, the virus disappears.

If the players can hold on until the macrophage comes and eats the infected cell, they have won. Otherwise, players are stuck with more viruses and heavier processing on their devices.

Scoring as a Serious Game. The VR worlds we had created before this world can be considered serious games in the broadest sense, but we thought this world, with its shooting elements, was a good opportunity to think about game scores. With this in mind, yet another VR camp was held in February 2022 to finish the design of this world as a serious game and an e-sport.

The camp began by asking the children what type of game this would be. If the more viruses you make disappear, the more points you get, then this would be a shooting game. The more viruses you infect a cell with, the more viruses you can eliminate and the more points you earn. That would be odd if the goal is to maintain the health of the host human body. To this question, one child proposed to define this as a *participation game*, in which the more different experiences a player has, the more points should be scored. That was more than we expected, because we were only thinking about the shooting score issue.

In line with the proposal, we have visualized the number of times each event occurs in order for players themselves to adjust rules, whereby points are increased if the player visits various *sights* in the world (such as inside the B cell or dendritic cell) or jumps into capillaries or lymph vessels and bumps into red blood cells or other cells, while trying to keep the number of viruses always low.

3.4 Game Experiences

We were able to get the antibody guns working (Fig. 4) when we participated in a MUTEK.JP[6] hackathon in December 2021, and since then we have frequently gotten together on weekends to play the game and make adjustments.

Fig. 4. Shooting antibody guns.Nicknames have been removed to protect privacy.

Since the game design was mostly complete in February 2022, we have enjoyed several full sets of games lasting approximately 20 min, and have been able to build a team play strategy.

4 Conclusions

Through the activities described in this paper, we saw the creation of serious games with children itself as an opportunity for active learning for them.

Camps are more fun when you get to hang out with your new friends afterwards, rather than just doing certain activities in them. We get the feeling that a VR camp is similar to a physical camp in this sense, because after the program is over, children actually take their new friends with them, and go off to play in another world.

We hope that our VR camps themselves will be like such after-camp activities. As a first step, we started another series of VR camps since March 2022, where children can create various worlds based on their own ideas.

Further work includes measuring the effectiveness of the games we create with children. In any case, we hope to have a constructivist evaluation. We would like to observe what children build on their game experiences.

Acknowledgement. This work was partially supported by Palsystem Kanagawa and Palsystem Insurance Consumers' Co-operative Federation, especially for distribution of Quest 2 VR headsets to the children. We would also like to thank Public Technology Design Consortium, Keio Research Institute at SFC, Keio University, for long support for our camps.

---

6 https://tokyo.mutek.org.

References

1. Harel, I., Papert, S.: Constructionism. Ablex Publishing Corporation, New York (1991)
2. Hubert, B.: Reverse Engineering the source code of the BioNTech/Pfizer SARS-CoV-2 Vaccine (2020). https://berthub.eu/articles/posts/reverse-engineering-source-code-of-the-biontech-pfizer-vaccine/
3. Okazaki, R., Okazaki, T., Sakabe, K., Sugimoto, K., Sugino, A.: Mechanism of DNA chain growth. I. Possible discontinuity and unusual secondary structure of newly synthesized chains. In: Proceedings of the National Academy of Sciences of the United States of America, vol. 59, pp. 598–605 (1968)

Providing Applied Games Based on Didactical Structural Templates

Michel Winterhagen[1]([✉]) [ID], Benjamin Wallenborn[2] [ID], Dominic Heutelbeck[3], and Matthias L. Hemmje[1] [ID]

[1] Chair of Multimedia and Internet Applications (MMIA), University of Hagen, Hagen, Germany
{michael.winterhagen,benjamin.wallenborn, benjamin.wallenborn}@fernuni-hagen.de
[2] Center for Digitization and IT (ZDI), University of Hagen, Hagen, Germany
[3] Research Institute for Telecommunication and Cooperation (FTK), Dortmund, Germany
dheutelbeck@ftk.de

Abstract. In our previous publications, we introduced the concepts of *Course Authoring Tools* (CAT), and *Didactical Structural Templates* (DST) which are a further development of the CAT. DSTs are defined as a possibility to describe the didactical structure of a course, a study program, or an applied game in an abstract way. The idea of DSTs is based on the structure of IMS Learning Design (IMS-LD), which is a quasi-standard for modelling learning structures. We have shown what DSTs are useful for and that there is a need for an editor for DSTs which we already presented in combination with the *Didactical Structural Template Manager* (DSTM). In this paper, we will focus on how DSTs can be used as a structure for *Applied Games* (AG) as applied gaming content for an LMS course and as a stand-alone AG. We will demonstrate the possibility, of how to provide two different kinds of AGs: one that is based on a complete DST, and one that is based only on a part of a DST. Finally, this paper presents the relevant state of the art, the conceptual modeling, and the relevant implementations. The paper comes to a close with a summary and a list of the remaining challenges.

Keywords: Didactical structural template · DST · Applied game · AG · Learning tools interoperability · LTI · Learning modalities

1 Introduction

E-learning is getting more and more important. The SARS-CoV-2 pandemic lead to many problems and different first actions to slow down the pandemic, especially closing schools and as a result of this home schooling [4] and gave an upswing to e-learning provided by schools. Also at *Higher Education Institutes* (HEI), it is getting more and more important to provide learning content via e-learning for the same reason as for schools.

H. Söbke et al. (Eds.): JCSG 2022, LNCS 13476, pp. 46–57, 2022.
https://doi.org/10.1007/978-3-031-15325-9_5

The area of *Lifelong Learning* (LL) which is synonymous with continuing education, can be understood as *"Learning should be extended over the entire life span and made possible, not only the formal but also the non-formal and include informal learning"* [5] has as consequence, that the learners can learn whenever and wherever they want to. This means, that there is a need to provide learning content in this area also via e-learning.

In the area of HEIs, or in general, in the area of learning, there can be determined three actors [15] as shown in Fig. 1.

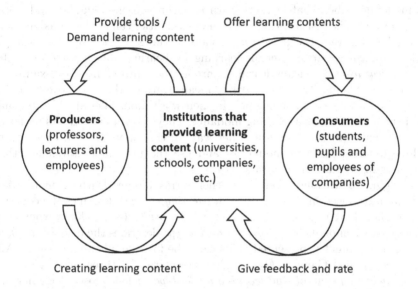

Fig. 1. Education and further training ecosystem at HEIs [15].

The producers create courses and the learning content. The consumers take part in the produced courses and the HEIs - or in general learning institutes - provide the learning content. The creation of courses and learning content normally takes place within a *Learning Management System* (LMS). To create a course, the producers have to make many settings within the LMS. To make this work easier for the producers, [15] introduced a so-called *Course Authoring Tool* (CAT).

The production of e-learning content is getting more important and is getting more in focus in the last years. Besides this, there is a parallel tendency of continuing education, respectively lifelong learning in industry, for which the production of learning content is also very important.

To provide a computational concept for standardized competencies, [13,15] introduced *Qualifications Based Learning* (QBL), which is an extension of *Competence-Based Learning* (CBL) [13]. With this QBL approach, it is possible to make a computer-readable representation of standardized *Competence*

Frameworks (CF), where a CF is a collection of all competencies which can occur in a specific context

1.1 Motivation, Problem Statement, and Approach

In the meantime, it is possible to provide learning content in different ways and for different learning modalities. According to Neil Flemming there exist four learning modalities [9], which are namely: *visual learning, auditory learning, physical learning*, and *kinesthetic learning* (the so-called VAK/VARK model). This model describes, that learners learn best through one modality and worse through others. The just mentioned learning modalities can be described in short in the following way: *visual learning* means learning by viewing (for example a video), *auditory learning* means learning by hearing (for example an audio file), *physical learning* means learning through text processing (for example a written course), and *kinesthetic learning* means learning through movement (for example by working on a real engine). In their work, Coffield et al. [2] state, that there is no such thing as a learning modality. They show, that learners prefer to learn a specific way more than another way. In this paper we will concentrate on three different learning modalities and use the just-made statement, that learners prefer to learn in a specific way.

Belonging to learning, there are other terms besides learning modalities, which are introduced in short. The term *learning content* describes the content, which learners have to learn, respectively, what learners have to know when they hold a specific competence. A *learning media type* describes the media type, and how learning content is presented. This could be for example a text-based LMS course, an Applied Game (AG), a video, et cetera. All three terms (*learning modality, learning content*, and *learning media type*) belong closely together but are all different from each other.

The fact, that learners prefer different learning modalities and that it is necessary to provide learning content not bound to a specific location and time-independent, shows that there is a need to provide learning content in different ways.

What the different learning modalities have in common is, that the learning content is based on a didactical structure in every case. The problem is, that the didactical structure has to be defined and created for every learning modality as well as for every different learning content. This is especially cumbersome, when the different learning modalities are based on the same didactical structure.

In this paper, we will focus on providing learning content in two specific learning media types:

The first learning media type will be a course in an LMS with gaming content (Edugames). The QBL approach can also be integrated into Edugames. This aspect gained special relevance through the Realizing an *Applied Gaming Ecosystem* (RAGE) project [13]. The European project RAGE will contribute a well-managed and structured repository, digital library and media archive system in the area of Applied Gaming Software Development. Not only community tools, but also training courses help to accelerate the improvement of developers and researchers of Applied Gaming even further. Through the sharing of prime knowledge resources the quality of the production process in gaming industries can be improved continuously [11]. An *Applied Game* (AG) is *"an implementation of a subject, inspired by and designed along with a context- and user-centric transfer of design concepts and qualities from the game world. Applied games consist of multimedia, digital and/or non-digital artifacts that constitute an individual and/or social perexience for their respective users"* [12]. AGs can be classified within different categories [3], which are market-based and purpose-based. The purpose-based classification shows different purposes for AGs [3]: *Edugames, Advergames, Newsgames, Activism games, Edumarket games, and Training & Simulation games.* This paper will deal with the purposes of Edugames and Training & Simulation games.

The second learning media type will be a stand-alone AG. The project *Immersive gamified learning environments for plant and machine construction* (Immerse2Learn) [8] will provide a gamified learning environment where for example the *Computer-Aided Design* (CAD) of a plant will be transformed into a *Virtual Reality* (VR)/*Augmented Reality* (AR) based game to make it possible, to train employees with different learning content in the plant environment although the plant does not exist at this time. With this procedure it will be possible to save time (and therefore money), because the employees will know the plant and its dangers and can start with their work directly, when the plant is finished. This leads to the necessity, to include the gamified learning environment into *"existing learning environments based on LMS through the identification, production and provision of appropriate learning content based on learning goals and corresponding target competence profiles"* [8]. Immerse2Learn, will provide a VR/AR based AG for learning content.

Within a wide range of domains, realizing learning activities as immersive experiences, for example, in VR, may significantly improve the learners experience and success [1].

To summarize the remainder of this paper addressing our four research questions, which we will require to work on shown below:

1. Which standard conform possibility does exist to provide a digital representation of a didactical structure of learning content?
2. Which standard conform does exist to exchange learning results between different AGs?
3. Can this standard conform exchange for learning results be used for web-based and non-web-based AGs?
4. How can the didactical structure be used for AGs?

1.2   Methodology

As the basis of our research methodology, the multi-methodological framework of Nunamaker and Chen [10] is used for the structured research and development of information systems.

The framework is divided into four phases supporting different methodological strategies: Observation, Theory Building, System Development, and Experimentation. To achieve our research goal to answer our research questions, the methodological phases can be executed repeatedly in any order. It is also possible to return to previous phases.

2 Concepts and Technologies

After describing the research methodology and the questions we want to address in this paper, we want to show in this section, which concepts already exist to provide some answers to our questions.

2.1 Didactical Structural Templates

The so-called *Didactical Structural Templates* (DST) have been introduced in [19] and extended in [17]. As described, the DSTs are based on the *IMS Learning Design* (IMS-LD) [6] and represent the didactical structure of a course and cannot only be used as didactical structure for creating courses. The DSTs can also be used as a didactical structure for a hybrid environment existing of a "classical" course with integrated applied gaming content just like a pedagogical structure for an applied game which can be a web-based computer game or a VR/AR-based game. Therefore, one DST can have different implementations.

The advantage of this approach is, that learners will be able to switch between different implementations of one DST whenever they want to and they have got the same learning progress as if they had used only one specific implementation of this DST. This means if learners like gaming, they can use the applied gaming implementation to work on the learning content. If it is easier for the learners to answer the self-tests or the final test - to stay in the exemplary stated pedagogical structure of a course - as e.g. multiple-choice quizzes, they can switch to a course within an LMS to answer the questions.

Therefore, the DSTs have the following hierarchical structure:

Method: There are many different ways a person can learn or teach. Each learning method is a sequence of learning processes.

Play: is a key part of the learning design, which represents a teaching-learning process. Similar to a theatrical play with a sequence of acts. When an act is completed, the next act begins until the completion condition is met.

Act: An Act represents a series of simultaneous activities and activity structures.

Activity: is one of the core elements of learning design, which relates to many learning environments.

Activity Structure: Activities can be combined into an activity structure with sequence mechanisms or freely select-able structuring.

To give access to the DSTs, we have provided a RESTful API, which is described in [16].

With the DSTs we can provide the didactical structure of learning content in a standard conform way, and therefore a solution for challenge 1. In the next section we will have a look into a de facto standard for exchanging learning content between applications.

2.2 Learning Tools Interoperability

Learning Tools Interoperability (LTI) is introduced in [7]. LTI supports a connection between LMSs and external applications like gaming platforms. An applied game prototype based on the *Unity Game Engine* (Unity) [14] has been introduced in [18]. This prototype is used later as an example for implementing an LTI connection.

However, this only works for web applications and not for desktop applications. To enable this also for desktop applications, the solution presented in [18] has to be extended.

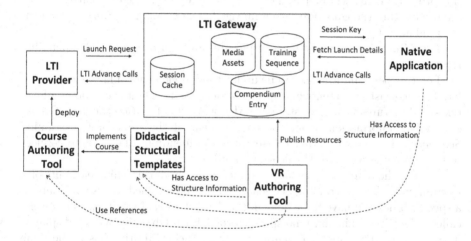

Fig. 2. LTI gateway and VR authoring tools

This needed extension has been provided in [16] as shown in Fig. 2. In short, the approach works as follows: a desktop application sends a request for an LTI session key to the so-called LTI Gateway, which is a web application. The LTI Gateway asks the LTI provider for a session key and sends this session key to the desktop application. With this session key, the desktop application can send LTI data to the LTI provider.

Having this, we have a standard conform solution to exchange learning data between web applications and - with the extension of the LTI-Gateway - non-web applications and therefore a solution for challenges 2 and 3. In the next subsection we will have a look into how an AG in the context of Immerse2Learn based on a DST can be provided.

2.3   Provide an Applied Game Based on a Complete DST

An AG can base on a complete DST or just a part of it. Therefore challenge 4 has to be divided into two parts: the one, where an AG is based on a complete DST and the other one, where an AG is based on a part of a DST.

In this section, we will describe an example, of how an AG which is based on a complete DST can be designed.

In both cases, a DSTs structure has to be mapped to the elements of an AG. This mapping has to be done individually.

As described before, in the Immerse2Learn project a plant is designed with the help of a CAD program. To train the employees for the new plant and to save time, the training should take part via e-learning.

Training means in this context, that the employees will know all dangerous zones within the new plant as well as the closest emergency exits from different points in the plant.

To give this training more structure, a DST has to be designed. In the case of this project, an AG will be based on the complete DST. The components which are used within the game are shown in Fig. 2. The meaning of every component is as follows [16]:

The *Media Assets* can be texts or pictures and can be used by Compendium Entries.

The *Compendium Entries* can be understood as elements of knowledge transfer. They consist of contents in a specific order. Each content is composed of e.g. texts and pictures which are stored as Media Assets. The *Compendium Entries* e.g. deliver information about the environment of the game or the Training Sequences. To access the Media Assets, the Compendium Entry has to connect to the content server and download it from there.

At last, the *Training Sequences* can be understood as learning elements of a learning path. These Training Sequences consist of so-called *Tasks* which are in a specific order and have to be done in the defined order. Each Task contains so-called *Objectives* which have no specific order. Each Objective will be displayed in a menu in the game. To complete a task, each Objective has to be done completely.

The mapping of the DST elements to the AG components has been presented also in [16] and is displayed in Table 1.

Table 1. Exemplary mapping IMS-LD - applied game

IMS-LD element	Applied game element
Method	Applied game
Play	Levels
Act	Training sequence
Activity structure	Task
Activity	Objective

With the just described solution we have a concept for an AG which is based on a complete DST and therefore a solution for one part of challenge 4.

The second part of challenge 4, where an AG is based on a part of a DST remains open at this time. We will show a conceptual model in the next section.

3   Conceptual Work

After describing the already existing concepts and technologies in the previous section, this section will present conceptual modeling for the second part of challenge 4. This is namely to provide an AG which is based only on a part of a DST.

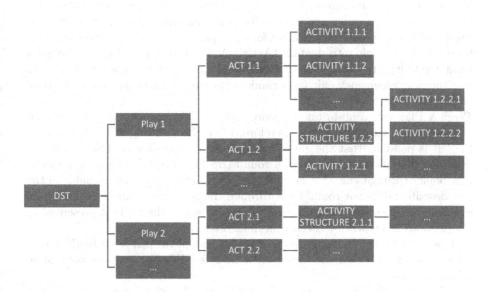

Fig. 3. Hierarchy of an exemplary DST.

Figure 3 shows the hierarchy of a DST in an example. This shows, that an AG, which is based on a part of a DST, can be based on a Play, an Act, an Activity Structure, or a single Activity.

Therefore, we have four possibilities to give structure to an AG based on a part of a DST. In the following we will show how the different possibilities can be used as structure. There will also be given some examples to every possibility. These examples will be placed within the context of Immerse2Learn.

Activity: This means, that the game is based on the smallest element of a DST. Therefore, this game can only be small. This can be for example a round trip through a plant.

Activity Structure: An Activity Structure can be understood as a summary of different Activities. There exist two possibilities for an Activity Structure to handle the containing Activities: The first one is, that every containing Activity has to be done completely in the given order to complete an Activity Structure, or that a given percentage of Activities has to be done completely in any order to complete an Activity Structure. This means, that these different possibilities also have to be taken into account. Therefore, the resulting AG can contain more small games described before. This can be for example, that the AG contains different round trips through a plant, whereby every round trip has a different focus. This focus can be for example a single round trip, one with hints for dangerous places within a plant, or a round trip where the nearest emergency exits will be shown from different starting points in the plant.

Act: An Act can contain different Activities and Activity Structures. An Act implies, that the containing elements have to be executed one after another. This is to say for the resulting AG, that also for an Act, the specification has to be taken into account. For the resulting AG, an Act can be understood as a single level in a game. This can be for example, that the single level contains for example a simple introduction (Activity), a bunch of round trips through a plant (Activity Structure), and a time-based game where the learners have to find the next emergency exit for a random starting point in the plant (Activity or Activity Structure).

Play: A Play can contain one or more Act(s). The Acts have to be executed in the given order of the Play. Therefore, when the resulting AG is based on a Play, it is possible, that the game contains one or more levels. This can be for example, that the first level gives a round trip (and everything that belongs to this point) through the area around the plant. The second level could be the just described different round trips through the plant itself, and the third level could be for example a learning success check, where the content presented in the previous levels will be checked in different ways.

One can imagine, that it is easily possible to adopt the just described different structures for AGs that are based on a DST for different learning content in different areas.

It is necessary, that an AG implements the LTI API to make it possible to send the learning result back to the caller, if this is the use case. Implementing the LTI API would make it possible for example that the AG can be included in an LMS course in the way, that the course can call the AG and the AG returns the learning result to the LMS.

Implementing an AG based on a part of a DST is an open challenge and will not be presented in this paper.

4   Prototypical Implementation

As mentioned in Sect. 2.3, we already have a working AG based on a specific DST which has been produced in the Immerse2Learn project. The following figures show some screenshots of the VR application (Figs. 5 and 6).

In this VR application, the learners can move in the new plant. During the learning phase, the way to the next emergency exit will be pointed with a green line, that fades away (see Fig. 4).

Fig. 4. Pointing the way to the next emergency exit [8].

Fig. 5. Person in panic reached during moving through the plant [8].

Fig. 6. Pointing to the emergency exit [8].

During the game it is possible, that a reached emergency exit is closed or a barrier prevents the learners to reach a specific emergency exit. Therefore, the learners have to move to another emergency exit.

While the learners move through the plant, they reach also persons in panic, which can prevent the learners from reaching an emergency exit.

An emergency exit is pointed with a green half-circle in the game. When learners reach an emergency exit, they can try to open it. When the exit opens, the learners have reached the end of the AG.

Summarized is to say, that the developed game works as wanted and is based on a specific DST. An open challenge at this point is to evaluate, whether the AG returns the learning results via LTI correctly.

5 Conclusion

In this paper, we have shown, how a digital representation of didactical structures in a standard conform way can look like with the representation of DSTs.

Afterward, we resented LTI as a de facto standard for exchanging learning content between applications. Due to the fact, that LTI only works for web applications, we provided a solution for how desktop applications can also via LTI.

To show, how an AG can be based on a DST, we had to divide this challenge into two parts: the first one, where an AG is based on a complete DST and the second one, where an AG is based on a part of a DST (e.g. to embed this AG into a course in an LMS). To solve the first part of this challenge, we have shown a solution of an AG that has been implemented and designed within the Immerse2Learn project. To solve the second part of this challenge, we have shown a conceptual model, how this could look like.

5.1 Future Work

A prototypical implementation of an AG based on a part of a DST is still an open challenge. When this prototypical implementation exists, an evaluation has to be done for this AG.

Also, an evaluation of the complete system, where it is possible to switch between different implementations of the same DST without loosing the learners learning progress in combination with the both presented AG is also an open challenge.

Acknowledgement. This publication has been produced in the context of the RAGE and Immerse2Learn projects. The projects have received funding from the European Union's Horizon 2020 Research and Innovation Action under grant agreement No 644187 and from European funds for regional development (EFRE). However, this paper reflects only the authors' views and the European Commission is not responsible for any use that may be made of the information it contains.

References

1. Allcoat, D., von Mühlen, A.: Learning in virtual reality: effects on performance, emotion and engagement. Res. Learn. Technol. **26** (2018). https://doi.org/10.25304/rlt.v26.2140, https://journal.alt.ac.uk/index.php/rlt/article/view/2140
2. Coffield, F., Mosley, D., Hall, E., Eccelstone, K.: Learning styles and pedagogy in post 16 education: a critical and systematic review (2004). www.researchgate.net/publication/232929341_Learning_styles_and_pedagogy_in_post_16_education_a_critical_and_systematic_review
3. Djaouti, D., Alvarez, J., Jessel, J.P.: Classifying serious games: the g/p/s model. www.ludoscience.com/files/ressources/classifying_serious_games.pdf
4. Friedrich-Ebert-Stiftung: Schule in zeiten der pandemie empfehlungen für die gestaltung des schuljahres 2020/21 (2020)
5. Gruber, E.: Erwachsenenbildung und die leitidee des lebenslangen lernens. Magazin erwachsenenbildung.at, p. 13 (2007). https://nbn-resolving.org/urn:nbn:de:0111-opus-75469
6. I.G.L.-Consortium: Learning design specification (2003). www.imsglobal.org/learningdesign/index.html
7. I.G.L.-Consortium: Lti v1.3 and lti advantage (2019). www.imsglobal.org/activity/learning-tools-interoperability
8. Immerse2Learn: Immersive gamifizierte lernumgebungen für den anlagen- und maschinenbau (2020). https://immerse2learn.de/
9. Leite, W.L., Svinicki, M., Shi, Y.: Attempted validation of the scores of the vark: learning styles inventory with multitrait-multimethod confirmatory factor analysis models (2009). https://journals.sagepub.com/doi/10.1177/0013164409344507'

10. Nunamaker, J.F., Chen, M., Purdin, T.M.D.: System development in information systems researchs (1990). https://gkmc.utah.edu/7910F/papers/JMIS
11. RAGE: Rage - realising an applied gaming ecosystem (2018). https://rageproject. eu/
12. Schmidt, R., Emmerich, K., Schmidt, B.: Applied games – in search of a new definition. In: Chorianopoulos, K., Divitini, M., Hauge, J.B., Jaccheri, L., Malaka, R. (eds.) ICEC 2015. LNCS, vol. 9353, pp. 100–111. Springer, Cham (2015). https:// doi.org/10.1007/978-3-319-24589-8_8
13. Then, M.: Supporting qualifications-based learning (QBL) in a higher education institution's IT-infrastructure. Ph.D. thesis, FernUniversität Hagen (2020). https://ub-deposit.fernuni-hagen.de/receive/mir_mods_00001608
14. Unity: Unity technologies. https://unity3d.com/de
15. Wallenborn, B.: Entwicklung einer innovativen Autorenumgebung für die universitäre Fernlehre. Ph.D. thesis, FernUniversität Hagen (2018). https://ub-deposit. fernuni-hagen.de/receive/mir_mods_00001428
16. Winterhagen, M., Heutelbeck, D., Wallenborn, B., Hemmje, M.: Integration of pattern-based learning management systems with immersive learning content. In: CERC 2020 Proceedings, pp. 211–221 (2020). https://ceur-ws.org/Vol-2815/ CERC2020_paper13.pdf'
17. Winterhagen, M., et al.: Supporting structural templates for multiple learning systems with standardized qualifications. In: EDULEARN20 Proceedings, pp. 2280–2289. 12th International Conference on Education and New Learning Technologies, IATED, 6–7 July 2020. https://doi.org/10.21125/edulearn.2020.0705, http://dx. doi.org/10.21125/edulearn.2020.0705
18. Winterhagen, M., et al.: Lti-connections between learning management systems and gaming platforms: integrating a serious-game prototype into moodle courses. J. Inf. Technol. Res. **13**, 47–62 (2020). https://doi.org/10.4018/JITR.2020100104
19. Winterhagen, M., Then, M., Wallenbrn, B., Hemmje, M.: Towards structural templates for learning management systems taking into account standardized qualifications. Technical Report, FernUniversität Hagen (2019). https:// www.researchgate.net/publication/340601087_Towards_Structural_Templates_for_ Learning_Management_Systems_taking_into_account_Standardized_Qualifications

Couch Fitness Heroes - Examining Fitness Exergame Motivational Concepts and Player Monitoring

Thomas Tregel[1,2](✉) ⓘ, Philipp Niklas Müller[2] ⓘ, Ayumi Lara Bischoff[2], Josef Kinold[2], and Stefan Göbel[2] ⓘ

[1] Multimedia Communications Lab - KOM, Technical University of Darmstadt, Darmstadt, Germany
thomas.tregel@tu-darmstadt.de
[2] AG Serious Games, Technical University of Darmstadt, Darmstadt, Germany

Abstract. In recent years, sports and fitness apps have become increasingly popular. In a 2018 survey, 60% of respondents aged 18–69 years old reported using a fitness app several times a week [1]. Moreover, it is expected that the use of these offers will continue to increase in the future. By 2024, 18.3 million users are predicted to use the service. Due to the COVID-19 pandemic, with restrictions on team sports and the closure of gyms, many people try to compensate for the lack of exercise by doing workouts.

There are many different programs and apps that motivate the user to do sports at home. Systems like Nintendo's Switch Ring Fit Adventure try to animate the user playfully. Other apps, such as Adidas Training by Runtastic and 7-min Workout, on the other hand, motivate the user through instructions, challenges and customizable workout plans for body-weight exercises.

This paper aims to analyze the current market situation of digital fitness applications. The applications are to be categorized and evaluated concerning their application area and structure. The focus of the analysis is, on the one hand, on the possibilities and methods for recording sport sessions and, on the other hand, on the applications' approach to motivate the users to exercise in the long term.

Keywords: Exergames · Workout apps · Health effects · Player motivation · Player monitoring

1 Introduction

While some industries are suffering greatly from the economic impact of the Corona pandemic, sports apps, fitness games, and other applications are currently experiencing a boom. After all gyms were forced to close in mid-March 2020, free workout videos on YouTube saw millions of clicks on YouTube. Nintendo's *Ring Fit Adventure* game was in high demand and sold out in many

H. Söbke et al. (Eds.): JCSG 2022, LNCS 13476, pp. 58–72, 2022.
https://doi.org/10.1007/978-3-031-15325-9_6

places, sometimes selling for many times its actual price. There are also numerous apps for Android or iOS in the AppStore or on GooglePlay with training plans, tracking functions and other features.

Fitness applications such as those mentioned are becoming increasingly popular, and not just in the age of Corona. In particular, less ambitious athletes can be motivated to exercise more with push notifications or the option to increase their high scores. Due to the wide range of applications, fitness training is now possible anytime and anywhere.

Exergames are an example of the positive effects of digitization: according to the World Health Organization (WHO), around one-third of adults and two-thirds of adolescents exercise too little [2]. In Germany, around 42.2% of the population did not reach the minimum threshold defined by the WHO, which is 150 min of moderate-intensity physical activity or 75 min of vigorous-intensity exercise per week [3]. Physical inactivity is considered one of the most common causes of diseases such as diabetes mellitus [2], cardiovascular diseases, and various cancers [4]. Therefore, it is responsible for many deaths or at least a significant loss of quality of life.

Individuals affected by physical inactivity often lack the time and desire to do so. Sports applications in the form of apps or digital games are a good starting point and help in various ways to maintain and help to maintain motivation in the long term.

Our goal is to categorize these applications, followed by selecting and analyzing current best practice examples for each category. The focus of the analysis is, on the one hand, on the possibilities and methods for exercise tracking and verification and, on the other hand, on the applications' approach to motivate the users to exercise in the long term. In such (playful) fitness applications, our analysis further considers applications for users with different needs, e.g. in terms of exercise intensity, duration, focus on specific body parts, and fitness goals.

2 Basic Aspects of Serious Games in Sports

- *User Motivation:* The aim of developing a fitness application is to arouse the interest of potential users with the help of an innovative and fun game idea with a specific athletic demand. For the success of such an application, it is also relevant that users remain motivated over an extended period of time. Serious games in sports and health should promote the fitness and thus the health of the players. This cannot be achieved in one or two training sessions but is a long-term process. For a perceptible training effect, users are sometimes dependent on support. For example, push notifications as training reminders on the cell phone or advancement to a higher level through successful completion of the training sessions can have a motivating effect.
- *Social component:* The presence of a social component is often closely related to the aspect of user motivation mentioned above. Interaction with other players in multiplayer modes or even online leaderboards can promote long-term motivation. This can be achieved through competitions and rankings

and through the fun of playing together, ranging from strictly singleplayer games to games in which the multiplayer mode forms the basis of the game idea.

– *Individualisation:* In order to achieve good results, it is necessary to adapt the training to the individual characteristics, goals and needs of the users. In principle, it is assumed that the degree of individualization and the effectiveness of the training correlate positively. For example, sufficient individualization can be related to the long-term motivation of a user. Motivation can counteract the users' under- or overstraining. For example, the degree of personalization of fitness apps and games varies greatly from application to application. In one workout app, for example, users go through a rigid sequence of exercises. In contrast, in a different app, the training plan is put together individually depending on the training goal, available time or experience.

– *Training theory approach* For fitness training to lead to the desired goals, it is necessary that proven training methods are used and that users do not perform randomly selected exercises. The latter can reduce the training's success, and carries the risk of injuries. Particularly with strength training, the risk of injury due to overload or incorrect execution is high. A rough guideline for the design of training sessions is provided by the eight common training principles [5]:
   1. Progressive Overload
   2. Individualization
   3. Regularity
   4. Specificity
   5. Reversibility
   6. Variation and Adaptation
   7. Rest and Recovery
   8. Periodization

Furthermore, there is a trend toward more specialized training methods such as *Functional Training* or *Tabata*. This trend is often represented in the development of fitness applications.

– *Exercise verification and tracking:* Due to the technical progress, modern sensor technology allows for precise tracking of user movements. In this way, applications try to ensure, for example, that specified movements are executed correctly. In addition, the measurement of vital parameters - which is usually limited to tracking heart rate - is a reasonable basis for individualized training. The heart rate usually increases linearly with the power output [6] and provides information about the training intensity. Therefore, it can help to target the training and determine the optimal load. Furthermore, the resting heart rate can provide information about the development of the personal fitness level and thus strengthen the users' motivations.

3 Categorization and Selection of Representative Applications

There are many ways to categorize fitness applications based on their different properties. In principle, each criterion to separate and evaluate an application can be used for classification. The work aims to evaluate the applications concerning the motivation and exercise tracking component, leading to a subdivision according to the type of exercise, resulting in the following categories:

- Outdoor cardio training
- Indoor training - workout apps
- Indoor cardio training - exergames

The category of indoor cardio training thereby includes many of the currently popular exergames, primarily designed for entertainment purposes since they require a camera-based setup or a virtual reality headset. Individual mobile apps fit into more than one category as their usage is not bound to a place and, depending on exercise selection, can focus on cardio or strength training.

The following representative applications are chosen based on their popularity, measured by downloads and user ratings for mobile applications and by reviews and ratings for games available on platforms like Steam or the Nintendo eShop, and further promising applications based on an extensive search for these platforms. For each selected application, the adherence to the principles presented in Sect. 2 is elaborated if applicable for the given application.

3.1 Outdoor Cardio Training

Most applications in the outdoor cardio category measure the user's movements with the aid of GPS or acceleration sensors Table 1. The data is used to identify the type of movement. The applications often differentiate between walking, running, cycling and hiking. A typical app for this category is the *adidas Running - Run Tracker* [24] application. From the recorded data, the exercise time and distance, as well as the calorie consumption, are determined. For calorie consumption calculation, users must enter their height and weight. All obtained data is stored so that statistics can be displayed subsequently.

The *Samsung Health* [20] and *Fitbit* [19] app are aimed at daily and permanent use of the app. The user's activities are detected with the help of the smartphone's acceleration sensors. The app records the movement in everyday life, i.e. they measure, among other things, how many steps are taken per day with an optional configurable step goal. *Fitbit* includes continuous data on the user's heart rate due to being limited to Fitbit wrist devices. This enables the categorization into different training zones based on the user's estimated maximum heart rate. These zones are for fat burning, cardio training and maximum performance, allowing for motivational features and statistics utilizing the time spent in each active zone to, e.g. introduce weekly challenges. Additionally, the app estimates the user's VO2max value, which is an indicator of a person's general fitness level [12] and their performance during endurance exercise [13]. The value is based on the user's resting heart rate, age and weight. Training or weight loss can positively change the cardio fitness index.

The applications *Running App - GPS Run Tracker* [21], *Runnin'City* [23] and *adidas Running - Run Tracker* focus on the consciously performed sporting activities. The respective activity or sport must be selected manually to record the activity. Target time or distance for a defined period can be set as targets depending on the application.

Run an Empire [22] is a building game where new terrain and castles can be conquered through movement. If a player already owns these fields, the building production is accelerated, and the player gains an advantage over the opponents. Castles are conquered by placing knights, a virtual unit in the game. These knights are sent by visiting a terrain square with a castle, where in the end, the player with the largest force of knights in the castle receives a reward (Fig. 1).

(a) Fitbit   (b) Run An Empire

Fig. 1. Examples for outdoor cardio training applications.

3.2 Indoor Training - Workout Apps

Unlike the outdoor cardio apps, the indoor workout apps do not use any sensors and the exercises are not recorded. Instead, the execution of the exercises is

Table 1. Outdoor cardio: recorded data ("rec") and provided statistics ("stat") '

Parameter & Investigated application	Running app - GPS run tracker		Samsung health		Fitbit		Runnin' city		Adidas running - Run tracker		Run an empire	
	Rec.	Stat.	Rec.	Stat.	Rec.	Stat.	Rec.	Stat.	Rec.	Stat.	Rec.	Stat.
Training time	✓	✓	✓	✓	✓	✓	✓	✗	✓	✓	✓	✓
Body weight	✓	✓	✓	✓	✓	✓	✗	✗	✗	✗	✗	✗
Distance	✓	✓	✓	✓	✓	✓	✓	✗	✓	✓	✓	✗
Calories	✓	✓	✓	✓	✓	✓	✓	✗	✓	✓	✗	✗
Step count	✗	✗	✓	✓	✓	✓	✗	✗	✗	✗	✗	✗
Altitude	✗	✗	✗	✗	✗	✗	✗	✗	✓	✓	✗	✗

visualized in the application, and by switching to the next exercise, it is assumed that the described exercise has been performed. If applicable, the time for an exercise is limited by a countdown. The user is given instructions by an audio guide so that he or she does not have to have the smartphone in sight at all times Table 2.

One specific niche in this area are applications for strength training, which we do not distinguish from the general workout apps as most of these apps we considered can be configured to work as a cardio training application or a pure strength training application. One representative of a strength-focused application developer is the *Leap Fitness Group* [18].

7 min Workout. The fitness app *7 min Workout* [7], shown in Fig. 2a, is based on High-Intensity Circuit Training (HICT). Each workout consists of approximately 12 30-second exercises, each followed by a 10-s rest. One training session lasts about seven minutes. Therefore, the application is ideal for people with little time whose daily routine leaves little time for exercise. Due to this app's promise to provide an efficient, effective and safe method for improving one's muscle strength and aerobic fitness, the app gained popularity with many similar apps being released.

HICT typically combines endurance and strength exercises, often alternating between intense and less intensive exercises performed alternately. This type of training is usually a combination of exercises with the body's own weight, with no additional needed equipment.

A desirable side effect is the Excess Post-Exercise Oxygen Consumption (EPOC), which is strongly emphasized in strength endurance training with high intensity. After great physical exertion, more oxygen is required than at rest. As a result, energy consumption is increased, which is why EPOC is essential in weight loss [8]. According to Klika and Jordon, seven-minute workouts can reduce body fat, increase insulin sensitivity and maximal oxygen capacity (VO2max) and improve muscle fitness [9].

In the app, users can choose between predefined workouts for each body area, each consisting of a fixed selection of exercises. It is possible to complete the exercises in a random order to avoid boredom possibly. A computer voice guides users through the various exercises, giving instructions and correcting common mistakes. A link is provided with a detailed video to increase understandability if the individual movements are unclear despite the animation and explanations.

Although the app provides a fixed framework for the workout, there are some options to customize the workout. If the workout was not intense enough or if the seven minutes are not sufficient, the round can be repeated or modified in duration according to one's preferences.

For motivational aspects, an exercise reminder is available and a 30-day program of adjustable difficulty. While the former feature aims to establish a habit at a fixed time of day and prevent forgetting to exercise, the 30-day program aims to provide a diversified set of workouts over a month. All completed sessions of the previous 30 d are available for statistical evaluation providing detailed information about each session.

(a) 7-Minute workout   (b) Adidas Training by Runtastic

Fig. 2. Examples for indoor training workout applications.

Adidas Training by Runtastic. A similar prominent workout app is *Adidas Training by Runtastic* [10] (see Fig. 2b, which primarily emphasizes the personalization aspect of training sessions. The user is asked about training goals, usual everyday activity and available time during registration. During startup, a selection of, e.g. short or guided workouts is presented, whereby the answers given during registration are addressed. The spectrum ranges from HIIT to yoga and endurance training to more balance and stability exercises. Depending on the workout, the focus is on strength, cardio or balance exercises, where strength exercises are diversified regarding of the stressed muscle group. They equally include isometric, eccentric and concentric [11] movements.

All guided workouts consist of videos. A coach guides users through the various exercises, virtually exercising alongside the user and communicating about the workout to establish a more personal setting. All other workouts are compilations of different exercises, each of which begins with a skippable warm-up. In addition, short videos help users to perform the exercise correctly. Further information about most exercises can be accessed within the app with more detailed videos.

For personalization aspects, the app provides personalized training plans and individual workout creation to allow workout customization. Since a sound training plan would require expert knowledge, it is automatically generated based on the user's desired weekly training activity, current fitness level and cardio goal.

The app introduces individual challenges for motivational aspects, e.g. to reach a specific daily training duration and ranks them in a leaderboard system introducing a social component. Additionally, detailed statistics for every previous training are available for the user, which potentially affects the user's self-awareness and training effectiveness.

3.3   Indoor Cardio Training - Exergames

Ring Fit Adventure. *Ring Fit Adventure* [14] for the Nintendo Switch is an exergame - a mixture of game and fitness training. The training is embedded in a story: a bodybuilder dragon wants to achieve total fitness and destroys the world around him. The players move through the game world by means of fitness exercises and other movements and fight against various opponents in many levels.

The adventure mode is the core singleplayer mode in which players fight a dragon, whose appearance is strongly based on that of a bodybuilder. For personalization, the players are questioned to determine the optimal training intensity out of 30 intensity levels, which influence the number of repetitions to be performed or the health points of the opponents. The fine gradation makes it possible to adapt to the individual fitness level.

The users move around in the game by executing actual running movements, tracked by the controllers' sensors. In this way, items can be collected, stairs climbed, and ditches jumped over on the running tracks. It is possible to buy clothes and drinks in a small store, increasing life energy and character power in a small role-playing-game fashion. The gameplay is guided by quests given by villagers allowing players to earn items or coins.

The enemies that regularly appear in the game must be defeated by performing fitness exercises. The animated character "Flexi" shows movements that have to be imitated by the players to inflict damage on the opponents and defeat them (see Fig. 3). Essential for success are correct execution and good timing, for which the accuracy is determined with the help of the controllers. There are more than 40 exercises in four different categories, each particularly effective on different

Fig. 3. Ring fit adventure fight against enemies. "Flexi" shows the correct exercise execution on the left side. (https://www.netzpiloten.de/wp-content/uploads/2019/10/Ring-3.jpg, last accessed: 01. May 2022.)

types of enemies. Due to the variety of exercises, monotony and potential boredom are avoided, especially since the players' concentration is on fighting the opponents. Thus they are distracted from physical exertion. Experience points can be earned to advance to the next level by defeating enemies and completing missions. This positively affects attack and defense abilities and unlocks new attacks represented by a new exercise.

After each level, an informative workout summary is displayed, which includes data on, among other things heart rate, fitness and activity level, training time, calories burned, and distance run.

Fitness Boxing. *Fitness Boxing* [15] is an exergame for Nintendo Switch offering boxing-inspired workouts to matching music. In this exergame, players choose between daily and free training.

The daily training consists of a recommended exercise compilation adapting to the player's requirements. Players can configure their fitness goal (cardio, cardio/strength, general fitness), body focus (e.g. chest, legs, full body) and the workout duration. Thus, the daily training aims to reach the designated fitness goal.

On the other hand, the free training chooses a more game-like approach. Players can choose to play in parallel with other players, initiate duels or compete by reaching a preferably long series of successful punches. For the singleplayer game modes, players choose focus-training, where a body region focus is selected or song-training. For the latter, players choose one of the game's included songs and exercise at their own speed and select individual exercises based on their intensity and required technique. This game mode allows players to unlock more songs to increase the song repertoire, which can have a motivating collection effect.

Fig. 4. Fitness boxing gameplay where the trainer shows the movement's correct execution [15].

The core gameplay of *Fitness Boxing* consists of the box training where symbols move upwards on the left and right side to their respective "target square". When one of the symbols reaches this target square, the corresponding movement must be performed on the correct side (see Fig. 4). Depending on the accuracy of the execution and timing, each movement is scored.

After a warm-up phase, the players are slowly introduced to more complex punch sequences, so-called"combos". Depending on the selected difficulty, the side is changed once or three times to ensure an even training load on both body halves. At the end of each training section, the combo to be learned is performed four or eight times in succession to consolidate the learned combo.

At the end of the training, the performance is evaluated by converting the successful hits into a maximum of three stars. Furthermore, the training duration and the calorie consumption based on age, weight and height are displayed.

With growing experience, further exercises can be unlocked, making the game varied and bit by bit more challenging and demanding, so that the training load is progressively increased.

Depending on the selected intensity, age, weight and height, the calorie consumption is about 450–550 calories per 45 min. Fitness Boxing offers both strength and cardio training, for which the physical stress and requirements grow with the user's abilities due to the gradual increase in speed and complexity of each movement. The application can positively influence the training condition of the user if used regularly. For users with a high level of fitness, the training intensity is possibly too low and not sufficient for a noticeable training effect.

The application cannot correct incorrect, unclean strokes, so the risk of poor execution is relatively high. In addition, hand-only tracking cannot accurately capture leg movements and the overall posture. Therefore, the responsibility to ensure the correct execution of movements to maximize the effectiveness of the training is with the players.

Fig. 5. Beat saber view with an overview over the player's current score

Beat Saber. *Beat Saber* [16] is a game for VR devices shown in Fig. 5. By default, the game is played with a red and a blue lightsaber, which the players see instead of the controllers. To the beat of the music, red and blue blocks appear in different frequencies and arrangements, which have to be cut up with the matching lightsaber. Arrows can be seen on the blocks, which indicate the direction of the strike. If there is only one point on a block, it can be cut in any direction. In addition to these blocks, bombs and walls can appear, which the players must avoid with their swords or bodies.

The more blocks the players cut, the more points they get. The score also depends on how much momentum - before or after the hit - is used to cut a block, and how centered the lightsaber hit it. For each consecutive block are hit, a combo multiplier is gained, drastically increasing the gained points while it is active.

Depending on the played song or level, the arm and shoulder muscles are stressed by the cutting movements. Hand-eye coordination is trained through the rapid execution of movements in response to visual stimuli, which is also essential in other sports or everyday life.

Many users report weight loss successes that they have achieved through Beat Saber. The Virtual Institute of Health and Exercise confirms that playing the game burns about 8–10 calories per minute. In terms of calories burned and physical activity, Beat Saber is comparable to tennis and is suitable for endurance training. With increasing difficulty and growing experience of the user, energy expenditure increases [17].

Since the songs and thereby levels playable in Beat Saber are highly diverse, the physical exertion depends on different factors. Due to the cognitive challenge of perceiving the expected cutting movements combined with the hand-eye coordination challenge not every level is suitable for every player. For that reason, we are planning to investigate the efficacy of Beat Saber in a future study by providing players with selected levels based on their abilities and measuring their physical exertion levels.

Table 2. Indoor training/cardio: individualization and motivation

Application	Individualization	Motivation
Workout apps		
7-Minute training	Duration	30-day program, notifications, statistics
Adidas training by runtastic	Trainingplans, recommended Workouts, Workout modification	Challenges, notifications, statistics, health facts
Exergames		
Ring fit adventure	Own fitness plan, Difficulty	Experience points, unlocking exercises, storytelling, game modes, highscores
Fitness boxing	Fitness goal, focus, duration, intensity	Unlocking songs, unlocking exercises, multiplayer, statistics
Beat saber	Difficulty, large amount of different levels	Gameplay-focused, game modes, multiplayer, highscores, large community

4   Discussion, Summary, and Final Remarks

Unlike most exergames, smartphone apps usually do not require any additional equipment. Especially the purchase of a game console or even a pair of VR glasses is associated with considerable costs, while today, a large part of society owns a smartphone. In addition, many fitness apps are available free of charge in the respective app stores and are therefore less expensive overall than many exergames. At the same time, however, the options for exercise verification are severely limited by the lack of sensors or the like, as is the case with *7-Minute Workout* and *Adidas Training*, for example. As a result, tracking is inaccurate or non-existent, so the correct execution of movements cannot be verified. As a further consequence, it is not possible to individualize the training based on objective data such as heart rate.

The training adjustment through subjective feedback or manual settings is nevertheless possible. The possibilities for individualization are limited in the case of *7-Minute Workout* is limited to the adjustment of the countdown/break/training duration, while *Adidas Training* offers far more options for personalization.

Since fitness applications can be used at home, the workout can be started independently of fixed opening hours or bad weather. In addition, there is no travel distance. The users are independent, which facilitates the integration of sport into everyday life. Once again, it is that lack of time is a frequent cause of insufficient exercise in everyday life.

On the other hand, exergames are characterized by making sports more accessible to users, by embedding it in a game. *Ring Fit Adventure* stands out in this respect. Players experience a story, while the other applications consist of individual units.

A game like *Beat Saber* is not a typical fitness app. Its effectiveness bases on the addictive effect that motivates users to exercise. It differs from the other applications, especially in the individualization of the workout, which is only possible by changing the difficulty level. In addition, it does not offer the option of targeted strength training.

One of the main advantages of exergames like the ones considered in the analysis is users' motivation through playfulness. The training aims not to be perceived as a strenuous sport but to be fun and be remembered positively, which is crucial for long-term motivation and thus the effect of the training. With the help of modern technology such as VR, imaginative, unrealistic worlds can be created, and training forms and environments can be developed for different target groups with different preferences.

While conventional sports require additional effort for a workout to be monitored and analyzed, tracking is comparatively easy to integrate into fitness applications. Controllers already integrated into the application can be used to record movements or measure the heart rate. Based on such information, automatic individualization of training sessions is theoretically possible. However, training personalization has not become the standard yet, as it has to take many aspects into account where individual data might not be available. In addition, heart rate, for example, is not reliable and meaningful enough as a sole reference value to make extensive adjustments to the training. Nevertheless, it is advantageous that fitness applications can automatically register every workout. With the help of statistics generated in this way, users can gain an overview of their training behaviour and benefit from long-term progress monitoring.

Although fitness applications can motivate users to exercise regularly, they do not force fixed training times, as usual in club sports. It is undoubtedly desirable for athletes to find sufficient motivation on their own. In terms of training effectiveness, however, set, fixed dates can be helpful, making it easier to ensure the regularity of training.

Further, it is problematic to integrate strength training into a game. The load in weight training is usually very high. Thus, it is challenging to integrate it into a game while retaining a game's entertainment aspect, which is central to motivating users. The investigated exergames reflect this problem insofar as the focus of all applications is more on endurance training than strength training. The latter takes place, if at all, almost exclusively with the user's body weight. There is always a certain amount of endurance, even in training sessions where strength is specifically trained. In strength training, the correct execution is of particular importance. Because the player's attention is focused on the game, the risk of errors is high. Such execution errors cannot be identified and corrected precisely enough by fitness applications due to insufficient tracking.

This problem is particularly severe in aesthetic sports such as dancing. Providing feedback is challenging since the applications usually only record the swing or the direction of a movement, but not its detailed design and physical expression. In such a context, the presence of a human trainer is required.

Even team sports cannot be fully mapped by fitness applications. In multiplayer mode, players rarely interact and mostly play independently. In most cases, the winner is determined based on scores. Virtual avatars are not capable of fully depicting people's facial expressions and body language nor act as a source of possible physical collision. Fitness applications do not have a sufficient social component and are therefore not a suitable alternative to team sports.

Fitness applications are well suited to make workouts appealing to users and facilitate regular sports access. In the process, their general fitness can be improved. Depending on the user's individual goals and fitness level, fitness applications can be suitable as a stand-alone workout. However, the focus of most applications is clearly on the fun of the game rather than on the theoretical foundation of the training units. The possibility, feedback and the social component are not equivalent to training in a team or under the guidance of a trainer.

Based on comparing the advantages and disadvantages of fitness applications, it can be concluded that although they cannot replace traditional sport, they can complement it and enrich it with new possibilities.

References

1. Statista: Sport & Fitness 2018, May 2018. https://de.statista.com/statistik/studie/id/53817/dokument/sport-und-fitness/. Accessed 01 May 2022
2. World Health Organization Europe: Physical inactivity and diabetes'. https://www.euro.who.int/en/health-topics/noncommunicable-diseases/diabetes/news/news/2015/11/physical-inactivity-and-diabetes. Accessed 01 May 2022
3. World Health Organization: Global recommendations on physical activity for health. WHO Press, Switzerland (2010)
4. Lynch, B.M.: Sedentary behavior and cancer: a systematic review of the literature and proposed biological mechanisms. Can. Epidemiol. Prev. Biomark. **19**(11), 2691–2709 (2010)
5. Kraemer, W.J., Ratamess, N.A., French, D.N.: Resistance training for health and performance. Curr. Sports Med. Rep. **1**(3), 165–171 (2002). https://doi.org/10.1007/s11932-002-0017-7
6. Such, U., Meyer, T.: Die maximale herzfrequenz. Deutsche Zeitschrift für Sportmedizin **61**(12), 310–311 (2010)
7. Vistra Corporate Services. 7-Minute Workout (1.363.110) (Mobile app). Published by Simple Design Ltd. (2020). Android
8. Jéquier, E., Bielinski, R., Schutz, Y.: Energy metabolism during the postexercise recovery in man. Am. J. Clin. Nutr. **42**(1), 69–82 (1985)
9. Klika, B., Jordan, C.: High-intensity circuit training using body weight: maximum results with minimal investment. ACSM's Health Fitness J. **17**(3), 8–13 (2013)
10. Runtastic. adidas Training by Runtastic Trainingsplan Workout (5.4.11) (Mobile app). Android/iOS. Published by Runtastic (2019)
11. Jonath, U.: Lexikon Trainingslehre, pp. 165–167. Rowohlt Taschenbuch Verlag GmbH (1986). ISBN: 3499176386
12. Wagner, P.D.: New ideas on limitations to VO2max. Exerc. Sport Sci. Rev. **28**(1), 10–14 (2000)
13. Balady, G., et al.: Clinican's guide to cardiopulmonary exercise testing in adults. Am. Heart Assoc. **122**, 191–225 (2010)
14. Nintendo Entertainment Planning & Development: Ring Fit Adventure. Published by Nintendo, Nintendo Switch (2019)

15. Imagineer. Fitness Boxing. Nintendo Switch. Published by Nintendo (2018)
16. Beat Games/Oculus Studios. Beat Saber (v1.20.0). Oculus Quest/PlayStation 4/Steam. Published by Beat Games/Oculus Studios (2018)
17. Virtual Reality Institute of Health and Exercise, Beat Saber. http://vrhealth. institute/portfolio/beat-saber/. Accessed 01 May 2022
18. Google Play, Leap Fitness Group. http://play.google.com/store/apps/developer? id=Leap+Fitness+Group. Accessed 01 May 2022
19. Fitbit, Inc., Fitbit (3.58) (Mobile app). Android/iOS. Published by Fitbit
20. Samsung Electronics Co., Ltd., Samsung health (6.21) (Mobile app). Android. Published by Samsung
21. Leap Fitness Group, Running App - GPS Run Tracker (1.3.0) (Mobile app). Android. Published by Leap Fitness
22. Location games, Run An Empire (3.0.13) (Mobile app). Android. Published by Run An Empire
23. Mile Positioning Solutions, Runnin' City (JOOKS Sport Tourism Experience) (6.0.5) (Mobile app). Android. Published by Runnincity
24. Adidas Runtastic, adidas Running - Run Tracker (Mobile app). Android/iOS. Published by Runtastic

Game Design

Design Considerations of Learning Resources: Improving Learning and Engagement of Students with Visual Impairments

Sundus Fatima[1] and Jannicke Baalsrud Hauge[1,2(✉)]

[1] BIBA- Bremer Institut Für Produktion Und Logistik GmbH, Hochschulring. 20, 28359 Bremen, Germany
{fat,baa}@biba.uni-bremen.de
[2] KTH-Royal Institute of Technology, Kvarnbergagt.12, 15134 Södertälje, Sweden

Abstract. There is an increasing trend to use digital and interactive tools in classrooms. There are different types of resources like serious games, gamified applications, learning platforms and many other means of interactive learning and educational tools that are being used in classrooms. However, it is quite challenging to engage students with certain impairments in this interactive learning, since the tools are often not designed for their needs. Therefore, there is a need to make design considerations flexible enough to accommodate specific requirements and needs that could influence the playing experiences for these groups. The paper explores and discusses design considerations of a digital learning environment. These are the initial design considerations with the focus on improving player experience. In this context, the emphasis is on engagement factors mainly that could support learning, keeping under consideration the target group of visually impaired students.

Keywords: Design considerations · Accessibility · Player experiences

1 Introduction

Digital and interactive learning is gaining attention and popularity in educational sectors [1]. Students are getting more used to of this interactive learning using educational platforms in the classrooms [2].

The main challenge in such a learning environment is the inclusiveness and attractiveness for students with certain impairments. The focus of this research is on visual impaired students which include a wide range of sight problems with different levels of severity. In the paper, we discuss design consideration with the aim to provide visual impaired students with the same opportunity like other students, by providing them the possibility to gain knowledge in an inclusive learning environment where they face no or minimal difficulties, accessing same information as all other students [3]. There are several interactive and inclusive learning platforms available for this purpose [4]. However, it is still challenging to design a flexible platform/application that could accommodate needs of all visual impaired users. It is hardly possible to address all sorts of sight

H. Söbke et al. (Eds.): JCSG 2022, LNCS 13476, pp. 75–83, 2022.
https://doi.org/10.1007/978-3-031-15325-9_7

impairments optimal in one design which could support learning. This challenge and limitations in terms of designing constitute research question (**RQ**): Which design considerations need to be under taken for improving playing experience that could support learning of students with visual impairments?

For designing considerations, accessibility features are being discussed which could improve player experiences in terms of learning and engagement. Visual impairment comprises any kind of vision loss, whether it is someone who cannot see at all or someone who has partial vision loss. Some people are completely blind, and some face trouble in seeing colors blindness, fully or partially [24]. This may involve several factors: target group age, type of impairment, severity of the type of impairment [24] etc. Designing a platform considering different types of visual impairments is one biggest challenge and limitation. What is being proposed in this paper are the initial theoretical design considerations.

To be compatible with external assistive software such as screen readers and eye gaze, providing alternative text tags for images and consistent keyboard navigation. For this, the interfaces need to be programmed following the Web Content Accessibility Guidelines (WCAG 2.1) to achieve at least AA standard [5].

The paper focuses on proposing design consideration as a part of an Erasmus + project (INCLUDEME) is co-funded by the European Commission.

2 Research Approach and Methodology

In order to address the research question, we have used the following research approach:

- A literature review to identify the relevant standards in games accessibility research for visual impaired students to identify guidelines, challenges and recommendations.
- Theoretical proposition of initial design considerations in terms of accessibility features influencing player experiences supporting learning
- Discussion on proposed design consideration, limitations, potential influence of identified guidelines in critical aspects and next steps.

3 Literature Review

This work aims to propose and discuss design considerations that improve playing experience of visual impaired students. The literature review is being conducted in that context to observe and analyze guidelines and challenges explained in literature to consider while coming up with the design for such target group. The selection and inclusion criteria for the articles included in literature review is based on the challenges and recommendations on game accessibility research and guidelines for designing visual impaired students.

"Computer Games and Visually Impaired People" (2007) [19], explains accessibility in games can be defined as the ease of playing a game or using a platform, even with limiting conditions, permanent or temporary disabilities such as blindness, deafness and less mobility [19]. Accessibility in games deals with a more complex problem than accessibility in other types of software [19]. This paper gives an overview of accessibility and its challenges, approaches, and guidelines for designing and development of accessible games and content. Several accessibility and playability recommendations and guidelines are available in the literature to guide the accessible game designing. Most of these guidelines are the result of research into the methods of designing, implementing and evaluating accessible games. A group composed of studios, specialists and academics proposed the Game Accessibility Guidelines (GAG, 2019), which discussed a complete list of guidelines, divided by disabilities and subdivided into basic, intermediate and advanced guidelines, according to the complexity of its compliance and feasibility within the project [20, 21]. GAG presented a reference for inclusive game design for different target group with other impairments [20, 21]. IGDA(2004) [23] is a paper published by Game Accessibility Special Interest Group (GAG-SIG) of the IGDA (The International Game Developers Association) has developed a set of accessibility recommendations for games considering different types of disabilities. Among these, 16 recommendations are specific to people with visual impairment (IGDA Game Access S.I.G. 2019) [23]. Another article "Hamlet on Holodeck: The future of Narrative in Cyberspace" explains about keeping and maintaining playful and enjoyable aspects of playing games without losing essence of being objects of fun and entertainment [22]. The paper includes the collection of guidelines and approaches on accessible games. Moreover, there is a collection of accessible games with short descriptions and categorization of different impairments supported for these games, which serve as a source of guideline for designing an accessible game for people with different impairments especially for visual impaired.

The literature review presented four articles and contributions. Their selection and inclusion are in such a manner, which provides an overview of defining accessibility, accessibility standards in computer games, accessible game guidelines, challenges and solution in terms of designing for visual impaired. Since, in this paper, initial design proposition are made this literature review plays a vital role in connecting to what is being proposed in terms of designing after visualizing standards and guidelines, which are discussed in literature for specific target group.

4 Player Experiences

Playing experiences includes and analyses all aspects of behaviors and feelings of player [11]. It defines and explains how a player/user feels when interacting with learning environment/platform in terms of performing tasks, motivation, learning, ease of use and engagement. There are certain factors influencing player experiences, which includes mechanics, rewards system, interfaces, quality of graphics and sounds, responsiveness, controls and intensity of interaction.

The design considerations in terms of accessibility features to improve engagement experience which could support learning of visually impaired learners are being discussed and proposed in the paper, which could undergo minor or major changes during development phase of first or initial prototype.

4.1 Learning

For visually impaired students, it is challenging to be involve in learning process [11] as lack of proper accessible tools and applications would not provide them with enough opportunity to involve into learning. As when these students play games which are intend for learning lacks various customizable accessibility features (i.-e.: not been able to magnify text, changing font size or colour, image and screen colour and could be several features etc.) and students face difficulties to see information or elements properly and being unable to customize it according to their needs it effects somehow their learning [11].

Gaming accessibility [20, 21] which include features such as: being able to choose font size which suits their preferences are effective when reading text over screen, to provide with the possibility to change or use different colour in text (Fig. 1.) is beneficial for those who are unable to see colour properly, customizing the amount of background, colour and images, providing high contrast between text/UI and background and a range of different control methods (mouse, keyboard, and switches) would contribute effectively towards improving learning experience. In order to achieve, an improved, flexible and customizable (to some extent according to needs of target group) learning experiences of visually impaired students is one of the aspect of this proposed design consideration.

This digitally enabled play-learn in everyday spaces fostering cross subject learning [12], facilitated by personified mini games where educational resources and ad-hoc learning [13] in the surrounding environment can be triggered. Such a pervasive approach would increase flexibility for learners [14] and expands the boundaries of anytime, anywhere learning, enriching their learning experience.

Fig. 1. A screen interface with possibility to choose colour [18]

4.2 Engagement

Inclusion of accessibility features with which students would be able to customize learning environment according to their needs and requirements to some extent could be effective to engage [15], as it would provide them an opportunity to use/play with more ease and to reduce difficulties and problems in using them which would somehow improve engagement to use such platforms or applications which proposed design consideration intend to achieve.

With the possibility to customize interface in terms of fonts, colour, background text/image and ensuring about the elements and contents on the screen are well spaced particularly at small or touch screen [20, 21] are appropriate and these are the basic considerations to be taken when designing for visual impaired [20, 21] as these features will provide them with the ability to customize according to their needs in order to see contents and elements on the screen. These accessibility features which will provide easiness to use the learning resources along with content itself within mini games, platform and application etc. would improve engagement factors among players that would support their learning effectively.

To fully customize interface according to the needs and requirements of target group is challenging and that is the limitation when designing such platforms/applications as it is difficult in terms of designing and implementation point of view. As visual impairment includes several sorts of disabilities considering other factors like: age, budget to develop and design such platform and applications and proper hardware and tools etc. could be challenging. There are other challenges and weaknesses, which are important to point out as considering our target group, it would include many types of sight problems and severities. Designing a platform or application in terms of accessibility features that would accommodate needs and requirements of all specially in terms of engagement is still a big challenge and quite hard to achieve.

5 Proposed Design Considerations

5.1 Accessibility Features

Accessibility is represented by what we need or intend to do, our interactions with the environment and our personal preferences [6].

Students who are unable or have difficulties in reading textual information on screens or seeing colors could be of several types and intensities of sights problems. These students when use educational interactive learning platforms they face difficulties and it could be challenging for them because of the lack of accessibility options, which is the main hindrance that resist them being involved in learning with engagement.

Accessibility should be adaptable enough which could allow players to manipulate the interfaces of the portal [7] to suit the individual needs of target and user groups as shown in (Fig. 2.). For the text may be too small, the wrong colour, difficult to read elements on the page, wrong language or the interface is too busy with images and flashing content [8].

With accessibility features to customize these aspects could make a huge difference [9]. There are similarities in the types of features required for accessible content [10], such as font sizing options, colours [20, 21], and text to speech and also gaming accessibility [20, 21] which includes other factors such as being able to change the speed and difficulty, customising the amount of background and images, practice mode and tutorials as well as range of different control methods (mouse, keyboard, and switches) are the

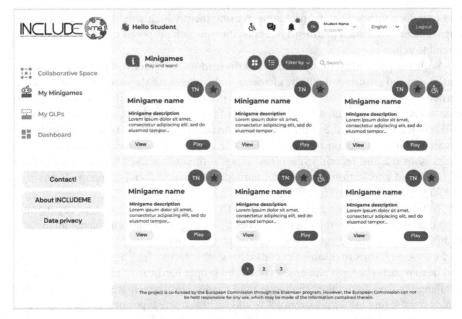

Fig. 2. Mini games interface (Accessibility Features) [18]

proposed initial design considerations in terms of accessibility features in accordance with gaming guidelines [20, 21] and needs of our target group.

The platform with such accessibility features would enable visual impaired students to customize the screen according to their needs. Since, students who are not been able to view information properly provided to them on screen for several reasons due to blindness, colour blindness, weak eye sight etc. proposed features and gaming guidlines [20, 21] like: font sizing, colour adjustments, text to speech would contribute significantly towards ease of using it which could help improving their engagement and experiences influencing learning.

6 Discussion and Conclusion

The proposed design consideration intend to achieve features in accessibility which would enable its players to customize interfaces according to their needs and requirements which in result would improve player experience.

Proposed design considerations show potential strengths with possible limitations and challenges in terms of designing. It has three strengths: it will provide more means of representation, presenting information and learning content in different ways; will provide more means of action and expression, so that all learners can demonstrate and express what they know. It will offer more means of involvement, stimulating interest and motivation and engagement for learning. However, visual impairment includes different sorts of problems with different levels of intensities which include factors like: types and intensity of impairment, age of target group etc. accommodating all in one design is where it limitations are taken into account.

With the proposed design considerations main challenge would be scalability and adaptability related to the severeness of a specific impairment. For instance, ability to customize font size could be helpful but then providing options for the availability of different fonts is important as there are certain fonts which are not easy on the eyes for visual impaired people specially those who have blur vision and have difficulty to distinguish and see letters it would be challenging for them to read texts or information which in result could effect their engagement and motivation to play or use such platform as if player could not read properly it will effect learning factor too. One more aspect, by customizing size of text over screen, it should take into account that game interface should be flexible enough to accommodate accordingly keeping other gaming elements appearing on the screen in consideration. Proposed guidelines in terms of changing colour of text could be challenging for those who have typical green/red colour blindess resulting into seeing everything in grey. This could effect somehow engagement as providing options for the contrast colour scheme for text or background image could be challenging as well while designing and for engagement point of view as not providing sufficient contrast options or visualizing colourful text or elements in grey would effect their ability to learn which might reduce their interest to be engage in such a learning environment. The accessibility feature of text-to-speech is presented which could be beneficial. However, those visual impaired people suffering from hearing issues too which involves dual impairment it would be difficult for them to hear instructions properly that could result in facing difficulties to understand which might could effect their experience in terms of being engaged into this digital form of learning. These are the potential critical aspects of proposed general guidelines for specific sorts of visual impairments. However, our target group is of broad spectrum and what is being proposed in this paper are the general guidelines considering visual impaired students on wider spectrum.

This research work is carried out to put focus on about inclusion of visual impaired students in digital learning environment that could improve player experience in terms engagement supporting learning. In order to answer the research question, design considerations in terms of accessibility features following game accessibility guidelines such as: being able to manage the size of text font and colour on the screen which could help learners to read properly who are unable to see textual information clearly, being able to customize background colour for those who have problems to see colours and text-to-speech option to help those who are unable to visualize elements on screen. These accessibility features of customizing fonts size, colour and text-to-speech mainly would be effective for visual impaired people as it would provide them with an opportunity to customize an interface according to their needs. These proposed features are achieved after the reviews of research papers and what is explained in literature for accessibility. However, it is important to highlight these features could not make a learning resource complete accessible to all visual impaired. It is important to understand the level and type of one's impairment when applying accessibility.

These are the proposed design considerations keeping one aspect of design process (accessibility) with one focused target group (visual impaired students). However, the proposed design considerations and guidelines could be changed during the development phase of the first initial prototype based on this initial design. These are the initial design considerations that are being proposed after analyzing what is explained in literature. This work is a part of an Erasmus + project. There would be development (implementation) of this platform in coming phase where pilots would be setup. One of the aspect would be in order to test the design consideration including visually impaired students with other range of target groups, to test if design considerations fulfilling needs and requirements of target group and to visualize how well platform is being designed and proposed guidelines are fitting in order enhance player experience in terms of engagement and learning.

Acknowledgements. The work presented herein is partially funded under the Erasmus+ Project (INCLUDEME) and Program of the European Union.

References

1. Lenihan, D.: Health games: a key component for the evolution of wellness programs. Games Health J. **1**(3) (2012). https://doi.org/10.1089/g4h.2012.0022
2. Iten, N., Petko, D.: Learning with serious games: is fun playing the game a predictor of learning success? Br. J. Edu. Technol. **47**(1), 151–163 (2016)
3. All, A., Nuñez Patricia Castellar, E., Van Looy, J.: Digital game-based learning effectiveness assessment: reflections on study design. Comput. Educ. **167** (2021). ISSN 0360-1315. https://doi.org/10.1016/j.compedu.2021.104160
4. Mayo, M.: Games for science and engineering education. ACM Commun. **50**(7), 30–35 (2007)
5. Stefan, I.A., Hauge, J.B., Sallinen, N., Stefan, A., Gheorghe, A.F.: Accessibility and education: are we fulfilling state of the art requirements? The 17th International Scientific Conference eLearning and Software for Education 2021, eLse, Bucharest (2021)
6. Torrente, J., Freire, M., Moreno-Ger, P., Fernández-Manjón, B.: Evaluation of semi-automatically generated accessible interfaces for educational games. Comput. Educ. **83** (2015). https://doi.org/10.1016/j.compedu.2015.01.002
7. Hildén, A., Hammarlund, J.: Can all young disabled children play at the computer? In: Miesenberger, K., Klaus, J., Zagler, W. (eds.) ICCHP 2002. LNCS, vol. 2398, pp. 191–192. Springer, Heidelberg (2002). https://doi.org/10.1007/3-540-45491-8_41
8. Barlet, M.C., Spohn, S.D.: Includification: A Practical Guide to Game Accessibility. The Ablegamers Foundation, Charles Town (2012)
9. Hitchcock, C., Stahl, S.: Assistive technology, universal design, universal design for learning: improved learning opportunities. J. Spec. Educ. Technol. **18**(4) (2003). https://doi.org/10.1177/016264340301800404
10. Bocconi, S., Dini, S., Ferlino, L., Martinoli, C., Ott, M.: ICT educational tools and visually impaired students: different answers to different accessibility needs. In: Stephanidis, C. (ed.) UAHCI 2007. LNCS, vol. 4556, pp. 491–500. Springer, Heidelberg (2007). https://doi.org/10.1007/978-3-540-73283-9_55
11. Smeddinck, J., Gerling, K.M., Tiemkeo, S.: Visual complexity, player experience, performance and physical exertion in motion-based games for older adults. In: The 15th ACM SIGACCESS International Conference on Computers and Accessibility (ASSETS 2013), Bellevue, WA, USA (2013). https://doi.org/10.1145/2513383.2517029
12. Domínguez, A., Saenz-de-Navarrete, J., de Marcos, L., Fernández-Sanz, L., Pagés, C., Martínez-Herráiz, J.-J.: Gamifying learning experiences: practical implications and outcomes. Comput. Educ. **63** (2013). https://doi.org/10.1016/j.compedu.2012.12.020

13. Pereira, P., Duarte, E., Rebelo, F., Noriega, P.: A review of gamification for health-related contexts. In: Marcus, A. (ed.) DUXU 2014. LNCS, vol. 8518, pp. 742–753. Springer, Cham (2014). https://doi.org/10.1007/978-3-319-07626-3_70
14. Burzagli, L., Emiliani, P.L., Graziani, P.: Accessibility in the field of education. In: Stary, C., Stephanidis, C. (eds.) UI4ALL 2004. LNCS, vol. 3196, pp. 235–241. Springer, Heidelberg (2004). https://doi.org/10.1007/978-3-540-30111-0_19
15. Archambault, D., Olivier, D., Svensson, H.: Computer games that work for visually impaired children. In: Stephanidis, C. (ed.) Proceedings of HCI International 2005 Conference (11th International Conference on Human-Computer Interaction), Las Vegas, Nevada, July 2005, 8 p. (Proceedings on CD-Rom) (2005). https://doi.org/10.1145/1178477.1178578
16. Buaud, A., Svensson, H., Archambault, D., Burger, D.: Multimedia games for visually impaired children. In: Miesenberger, K., Klaus, J., Zagler, W. (eds.) ICCHP 2002. LNCS, vol. 2398, pp. 173–180. Springer, Heidelberg (2002). https://doi.org/10.1007/3-540-45491-8_38
17. Archambault, D., Burger, D.: TIM development and adaptation of computer games for young blind children — Interactive Learning Environments for Children — ERCIM WG U14ALL & i3Spring Days 2000, Athens (2000)
18. INCLUDEME Project: D4.1 INCLDUEME Design Specifications (2022)
19. Archambault, D., Ossmann, R., Gaudy, T., Miesenberger, K.: Computer games and visually impaired people. Upgrade **8**(2), 43–53 (2007)
20. GAG Game Accessibility Guidelines (2019). http://gameaccessibilityguidelines.com. Accessed 24 Aug 2019
21. Gee, J.: Good Video Games + Good Learning: Collected Essays on Video Games, Learning, and Literacy. Peter Lang Publishing, New York (2007)
22. Murray, J.H.: Hamlet on the Holodeck: The Future of Narrative in Cyberspace. The Free Press, New York (1997)
23. IGDA Game Access S.I.G. (2019). https://igda-gasig.org/about-game-accessibility/guidelines/visual/
24. Dela Torre, I., Khaliq, I.: A study on accessibility in games for the visually impaired. In: 2019 IEEE Games, Entertainment, Media Conference (GEM) (2019). https://doi.org/10.1109/GEM.2019.8811534

Resilient IN: Design of an Interactive Narrative HRV-Biofeedback Game to Develop Stereotype and Social Identity Threat Resilience

Katherine Picho[1], Ethan Osborne[2], Fatyma Camacho[2], Aaja Ouellette[2], Mason Woodford[2], and Edward Melcer[2](✉)

[1] Howard University, Washington, D.C., USA
katherine.picho@howard.edu
[2] University of California, Santa Cruz, CA, USA
{etosborn,fcamach1,aaouelle,mwoodfor,eddie.melcer}@ucsc.edu

Abstract. Stereotype threat and social identity threat are social phenomena that adversely affect underrepresented groups within STEM (i.e., women and people of color). While there are existing programs and techniques for training resiliency against these threats, the use of biofeedback and serious games may prove useful to enhance the efficacy and engagement of such training. In this paper, we present the work in progress on our interactive narrative biofeedback game (Resilient IN) that utilizes resonant frequency heart rate variability to train player resilience to stereotype and social identity threat as they move through a mock interview at a tech company within the game. Specifically, we discuss the design of the game in detail—focusing on how specific elements of the design draw from existing literature to evoke and train resilience during play, as well as design and validation of the game narrative/script with individuals in the technology and engineering industry. Finally, we provide future directions for the work, such as upcoming studies to validate the game's efficacy in evoking and training resiliency to different kinds of threats.

Keywords: Social identity threat · Stereotype threat · Serious games · Heart rate variability · Biofeedback

1 Introduction

Women and people of color are grossly under-represented in engineering and computer science. Blacks and Hispanics constitute only 6% and 7% of the Science and Engineering workforce relative to their participation in the U.S. workforce as a whole i.e. 15% and 16%, respectively [59]. Similarly, women account for only 27% of computer and mathematical scientists and 16% of Engineers [59]. They

H. Söbke et al. (Eds.): JCSG 2022, LNCS 13476, pp. 84–101, 2022.
https://doi.org/10.1007/978-3-031-15325-9_8

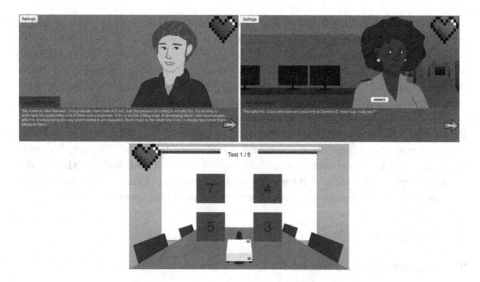

Fig. 1. Three scenes from Resilient IN. The first scene (left) is an interaction with one of the interns. The second scene (right) is the player's interaction with the receptionist. The third scene (bottom) is the working memory task that the players will attempt.

also exit these domains at higher rates than men—over 32% leave STEM degree programs in college [13] and those who graduate are less likely than their male counterparts to work in a STEM occupation [67].

Research suggests psychosocial factors such as stereotypes about gender roles, and intellectual abilities of women and people of color [64,65] with beliefs that brilliance is integral to success in certain STEM fields [5,20,34,36] contribute to these disparities. Indeed, stereotypes linked to racial and gender social identities have been shown to degrade the performance of some individuals belonging to under-represented groups [1,64,65]—a phenomenon called social identity threat.

Conversely, biofeedback trains individuals to consciously elicit a parasympathetic response (e.g., achieve a state of rest and relaxation) [2,10,21]. This can effectively repattern physiological responses to stimuli [43], with lasting effects on psychological well-being, socio-emotional function [41,42] and performance [9,10]. There is also evidence to suggest that biofeedback training controls responses to anger inducing stimuli [21], and aids in emotional intelligence and regulation [70].

In a related vein, serious games are used in many different contexts to help teach resilience [7,31,38,57] and have been utilized in combination with biofeedback to help train emotion regulation [52–54] and stress management [7]. However, to our knowledge, there has never been a game developed that utilizes biofeedback and is concerned with stereotype threat.

In this paper, we present our work in progress creating a Resonant Frequency Heart Rate Variability-Biofeedback (HRV-Biofeedback, hereafter) game to address stereotype and social identity threat. Specifically, we will discuss the design and development of our serious game, Resilient IN, for training resilience towards stereotype and social identity threat in a non-laboratory environment (see Fig. 1). Specifically, the game is designed to investigate physiological responses to stereotype and social identity threat-i.e., possible relations between resonant frequency heart rate variability and working memory, as well as changes in cardiovascular reactivity from rest to task (reactivity) under stereotype and social identity threat. In order to achieve this, the game integrates HRV-Biofeedback to facilitate emotion regulation training. Notably, this is the first serious game to address stereotype and social identity threat through biofeedback, allowing for novel future empirical inquiry and research findings that could inform a new generation of interventions that leverage biofeedback training in serious games to attenuate various stereotype and social identity threats.

2   Background

2.1   Stereotype and Social Identity Threat

Social Identity Threat (SIT) is a psychosocial phenomenon where members of stereotyped groups experience concern and anxiety over confirming, as a self-characteristic, a negative stereotype about the group [66]. When examined solely in testing or evaluation contexts, social identity threat is referred to as stereotype threat. Thus, the former concerns outcomes other than performance, and the latter, which falls under the larger umbrella of social identity threat, pertains to the negative impact of stereotypes relative to performance or evaluation outcomes.

For instance, the stereotype that 'women aren't good with numbers', can impede their performance on quantitative tasks in environments where these stereotypes are made salient. In typical experiments, members of marginalized groups complete challenging tasks in stereotype-relevant domains under one of two conditions: (a) non-threatening contexts, where no stereotypes are highlighted, or (b) contexts where negative stereotypes alleging intellectual inferiority in the domain are made salient. A stereotype threat effect is observed when members of stigmatized groups exposed to negative stereotypes about their group under-perform relative to their counterparts who have not been exposed to the stereotype. A long-term consequence of chronic exposure to social identity threat is domain disidentification and attrition from the domain [65].

The stereotype threat process model [62] identifies three distinct but interrelated processes by which ST disrupts performance: a physiological stress response that impairs prefrontal processing, active self-monitoring which affects regulation of attention, and efforts to suppress negative thoughts and emotions that arise during cognitive tasks [62]. Although negative emotions set off a cascade of neural and physiological responses that interfere with task performance, under-performance due to social identity threat is less a function of these emotions than it is how they are regulated. Both theory and research implicate emotion suppression as maladaptive and a primary mechanism through which social identity threat impedes performance [61]. There is converging evidence that social identity threat depletes executive resources (i.e., working memory) via emotion-suppression [32], which impairs the phonological aspects of working memory responsible for supporting complex cognitive activities [4], and leads to inefficient cognitive processing [48,68] that under social identity threat, individuals from stereotyped groups (i.e. women, and people of color) frequently use emotion suppression as an emotion regulation strategy, to the detriment of working memory [32] and hence task performance; and that cognitive reappraisal can successfully reverse the performance deficits observed when emotion suppression is used to downregulate emotions under threat [32,37].

2.2 Techniques for Developing Resiliency

Several interventions to counteract stereotype threat exist e.g., self-affirmation [8,63], adopting a malleable view of intelligence [22], and teaching about ST [32,58]. So far, only one intervention has addressed emotion regulation, which is a key pathway to mediating the phenomenon: The Stereotype Threat Reduction Intervention Program (STRIP, hereafter). STRIP [55] is an evidence and skills-based intervention designed to reverse stereotype threat induced performance deficits among women and students of color. It provides metacognitive monitoring and emotion regulation skills-training to combat two major and related pathways critical to the stereotype threat process: active self-monitoring, which affects regulation of attention, and the suppression of negative thoughts and emotions that arise during cognitive tasks [61].

The STRIP emotion regulation intervention protocol supplants maladaptive emotion regulation strategies like emotion suppression responsible for impairing cognitive processing under social identity threat [62], with a combination of adaptive emotion regulation skills like cognitive reappraisal, psychological distancing, and attentional regulation, which that exert little to no cognitive cost to these cognitive processes. Here, participants learn to increase or decrease their psychological distance from an emotional event (psychological distancing), mentally re-frame the meaning of emotionally charged stimuli to change the trajectory of negative emotions (cognitive reappraisal), and consciously direct attention to focus on selective information to magnify the experience of select stimuli (attentional regulation).

The metacognitive skills component of STRIP re-directs self-monitoring to focus on problem solving strategies which facilitate rather than impede efficient cognitive processing. Specifically, it focuses on honing metacognitive monitoring skills to improve student calibration by imparting skills necessary to (a) accurately judge task performance, (b) identify gaps in their knowledge (c) develop strategies to close these gaps (d) assess their own monitoring skills during task performance will be taught and practiced. Here, attentional regulation is deployed to train students to focus on the elements, which would help redirect focus from concerns over the threatening stereotype to the task at hand.

Our game is designed to support and enhance STRIP's emotion regulation protocol specifically by integrating it with HRV-Biofeedback training to improve

(a) HRV (b) performance, (c) working memory, executive functions and affective control, all of which are typically impaired under SIT.

2.3 Biofeedback in Serious Games

Biofeedback trains individuals to consciously elicit a parasympathetic response (achieve a state of rest and relaxation) [2,10,21], which can effectively repattern physiological responses to stimuli [43], with lasting effects on psychological well-being, socio-emotional function [41,42] and performance [9,10]. Through biofeedback, newly learned response patterns become increasingly familiar to the brain and feed-forward neurological connections to a new set point [43].

There is evidence to suggest that biofeedback training controls responses to anger inducing stimuli [21], and aids in emotional intelligence and regulation [70]. Students who receive biofeedback training are also more effective at self-activating the optimum (desired/trained) psychophysiological state under stressful conditions, which has been directly linked to reduced anxiety and improved test performance [2,9,10]. Specifically, HRV training influences brain and emotion function with lasting positive outcomes [39].

Fig. 2. Background art that was created for each scene of Resilient IN.

3   Design of 'Resilient IN' Game

Resilient IN is an interactive narrative HRV-Biofeedback game designed to train resilience towards stereotype and social identity threat through emotion regulation training. This is achieved by having players role-play through an authentic scenario where they would encounter situations that elicit stereotype and social identity threat. As players progress through the game, they are provided with continuous HRV-Biofeedback to visibly show them how stereotype and social identity threat situations are impacting them physiologically. These biofeedback signals are also monitored by the game and explicit in-game feedback is given to the player if their RF-HRV becomes too high in order to facilitate further emotion regulation training. The game is designed to measure HRV at rest (prior to) and during gameplay in order to identify substantial changes and differences in player physiology. In this way, Resilient IN offers a safe medium for players to encounter instances of stereotype and social identity threat and practice emotion regulation techniques to combat their impact.

Resilient IN is built for Windows machines using Unity and the ink plugin[1] to script the game's interactive narrative. We chose the interactive narrative genre for Resilient IN's design since interactive narratives are a highly accessible genre of games due to a low demand on player actions, focus on storytelling, and role-playing elements all helping to engage a larger audience [11,69]. This accessible aspect of interactive narratives has made them highly popular with men, women, and even novices to games [12], as well as for educational/training purposes both commercially and in academia [11,18,46,50]. Furthermore, the role-playing nature of interactive narratives has been shown to be highly effective at improving player attitudes [24,25], motivation [23], knowledge [45], and skills [44]. This makes the use of interactive narrative games an ideal approach for training resiliency as it easily and intuitively enables learners to role-play through various stereotype and social identity threat scenarios.

The core design focus of Resilient IN is context as social identity threat is a highly contextual phenomenon. Specifically, context (both physical and social) is not only central to the activation of social identity threat [65], but also a key moderator of outcomes related to the phenomenon [55,56]. In our game, players are invited to a technical interview for a highly competitive software engineering internship at a non-existent brand name technology company (see Fig. 2 for in-game background art of the company). This setting was chosen since technology companies (such as those within the Silicon Valley tech industry) are notorious for being male-dominated environments [30].

Contextual elements in the game are also manipulated to make negative gender stereotypes and implicit bias of the same accessible to the player, i.e., to elicit gender related social identity threat. These elements are manipulated at two levels: (a) physical context, and (b) social interactions with others before and during the interview. Examples of the manipulating physical context include but are not limited to sexist posters in the hallway that simultaneously accentuate gender stereotypes and downplay the ability of women to compete in the tech environment, and numeric (under) representation with respect to interview candidates. The player also finds themself in the minority group of a candidate pool dominated by White men. Finally, there is a working memory task for the player to complete at the end of the interview which doubles as both (1) a diagnostic of ability and key determinant of admissions into the in-game internship program [65], and (2) a quantitative task for accessing social identity threat impact on the player's working memory. Notably, a leaderboard is present during the working memory task that shows the scores of top candidates, all of whom are male and White or Asian.

Examples of manipulating social context include the player's interactions with other candidates, staff, and the interview panel of five, which is littered

---

[1] https://www.inklestudios.com/ink/.

with micro-aggressions rooted in assumptions that stem from implicit gender or race bias. For instance, one of the interviewers confuses the player for a secretary and asks her for an update on back ordered office supplies, and company staff who assumes that the player is there for a different interview (to fill an entry low-level administrative assistant position) and is very surprised to learn that the player is there for the software engineering internship.

Fig. 3. Two posters that will be lining the hallways of the company as the player makes their way to the interview room. These posters are based on real world posters that have made the news in recent years due to gender stereotyping (see Footnote 2 and 3).

3.1 Environmental Biases

Even small aspects of a physical environment can have a significant impact on individuals. For instance, small decisions such as having stereotypically masculine posters (e.g., Star Wars) displayed on the wall can lower women's sense of belonging in computer science domains [14,15]. Additionally, these studies also show that the setup of classrooms in computer science courses can influence the engagement and interest of female students, and classroom arrangements that display stereotypically male artifacts diminish women's desire to enter the field relative to classrooms with artifacts that are regarded as neutral [14,15]. For this reason, we line the hallway leading up to the interview room with sexist posters (see Fig. 3 for example posters). Notably, these posters are based on real world posters that made the news in recent years for gender stereotyping[2,3]. With this we intend to further elicit social identity threat through blatant ambient sexism that draws from real world equivalents.

---

[2] https://www.bbc.com/news/business-51032631.
[3] https://www.theguardian.com/society/2015/aug/11/look-like-a-girl-think-like-a-man-bic-outrage-south-africa-womens-day.

Fig. 4. Character designs for Resilient IN.

3.2   Character Designs

How characters are designed also impact how they are perceived by the players. In [19], it was found that stereotypes for video game characters exist, and they are very distinct across the gender line. It is important to note these inherent stereotypes when designing characters in a game. For example, female characters were labeled mostly as provocatively dressed, thin but curvy, sexual, and subservient while male characters were labeled as powerful, aggressive, athletic, and superhero in [19]. Regarding female self-efficacy and general attitudes about women, [3] found evidence that playing a sexualized character can have a negative impact on both female self-efficacy as well as attitudes toward women in general. However, it was noted by the authors that this result was not the strongest and additional research should be done to further qualify these findings. Other research also shows that interacting with sexist men triggers social identity threat among female engineers resulting in performance deficits on quantitative tasks [36]. With our character art, we have attempted to play with the stereotypes of what a person in that job function would be. Figure 4 shows two of our interns, both white, one is an engineer, and the other is in finance. To denote the difference, the engineer is in a much more casual outfit where the finance intern is much more formally dressed. The rest of our characters also follow stereotypes to increase the stereotypes being encountered throughout the game.

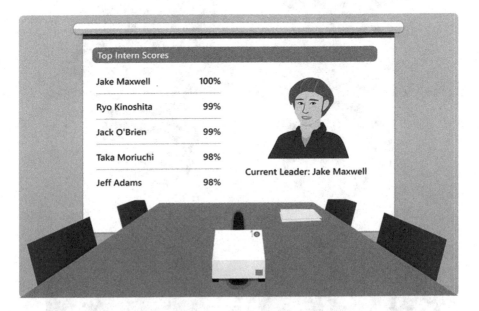

Fig. 5. The leaderboard that is present for players during their interview showing white and Asian males as the top performers.

3.3 Gamification of Leaderboards

A subset of educational gamification literature is concerned with the additional pressure that leaderboards can put on women regarding their belief in their math abilities. The stereotype that women are worse than men at math already exists, and [16] notes that the inclusion of a leaderboard is a means to making the stereotype that much more salient. Results from these researchers indicated that, in contrast with extant literature, women performed worse when in the all-women leaderboard condition as compared to all men leaderboard condition. This was attributed to a "social comparison" that researchers believed was more salient than the inherent stereotypes. Other studies have noted gamification can lead to better learning [28] and learning performance [51] and help individuals with goal setting [35], i.e., "I want to be number one on the leaderboard". However, a literature review noted that "some underlying confounding factors exist" across a multitude of gamification studies, including the "the role of the context being gamified" [27]. To investigate the effects of leaderboards on stereotype threat and resilience, we have created a leaderboard in our game that contains only males who are either white or Asian (see Fig. 5). This leaderboard is present during the entire working memory task at the end of the in-game interview.

3.4 Biofeedback Training

Biofeedback has been utilized in a variety of contexts within the serious games field. For example, researchers have studied its effectiveness for training stress management skills [7,52,53,68] and others have studied if it can improve problem-solving ability in individuals with chronic brain injury [33]. A study has also been done on teaching emotion regulation in financial traders [31]. These studies exemplify a few of different types of biofeedback that can be utilized, including heart rate [7], heart rate variability [70] and skin conductance/breathing rate [52,53]. These studies also share a common outcome: biofeedback training led to better decision-making skills and emotion regulation.

Stereotype threat and SIT in particular are marked by increases in blood pressure [6] and sympathetic activation, i.e., increased heart rate and beta electroencephalography (EEG) activation [47]. To explore the impacts of our HRV-Biofeedback training, the signals that we intend to assess during gameplay are: *mean arterial blood pressure, pre-ejection period*—a near pure measure of sympathetic nervous system activation of the heart—and players' *HRV*. More specifically, emotional regulation capacity will be assessed using HRV, which will be computed from electrocardiography (ECG) by analyzing the variability in timing between R-R intervals. Emotion suppression, which is the primary mediating pathway for stereotype threat to occur, is characterized by decreased heart rate [17,26], increased mean arterial blood pressure [17], and lower cardiac output and ventricular contractility in combination with higher temperature, pulse, and respiration [40]. Therefore, in addition to heart rate, these additional physiologic signals of reactivity to stereotype threat and SIT will be assessed using impedance cardiography during gameplay.

Fig. 6. The HRV-Biofeedback UI. It is shown on the top of the screen during gameplay, and provides both numeric feedback of the player's current resonant frequency HRV as well as iconic feedback of how that value relates to the player's baseline resonant frequency HRV range.

We are also approaching our design similar to [70], where it was determined that the addition of a visual representation of biofeedback in the game helped players to breathe better. Therefore, the HRV-Biofeedback will be displayed on screen for players to see real time feedback during gameplay (see Fig. 6). Specifically, the HRV-Biofeedback UI displays both numeric feedback of the player's current resonant frequency HRV as well as iconic feedback of how that value relates to the player's baseline resonant frequency HRV range. As a player's resonant frequency HRV value goes up, the UI will change color to reflect one of four different states: 1) *Within Baseline* where the player's HRV is within their normal baseline; 2) *Above Baseline Warning* where the player's HRV is within one-half of one standard deviation above their normal baseline; 3) *Above Baseline* where the player's HRV is above one-half of one standard deviation of their normal baseline but below one full standard deviation; and 4) *Way Above Baseline* where the player's HRV is more than one full standard deviation above their normal baseline. Additionally, when a player's HRV reaches the *Above Baseline* level or higher, the game will pause and prompt players to employ one of the STRIP emotion regulation protocols (such as cognitive reappraisal) [55].

3.5 Design and Validation of Interactive Narrative Script

Resilient IN features an individual invited to a technical interview at a competitive company. It is designed to elicit gender-related social identity threat, which is achieved by manipulating context at two levels: (a) physical context, (b) social interactions with others before and during the interview. The script, written by the 1st Author, was grounded in empirical studies which show that elements in the physical context, such as numeric representation [29,49], as well as sexist social interactions [37,60] can trigger and exacerbate social identity threat. In this way, the dialog and interactions within the script are written to subtly evoke SIT. For instance, certain characters assume the player is interviewing for a non-technical position upon first meeting, some interviewers will show disapproval of the player's university, all interviewers and company executives are male and predominately white, and conversely most female characters are in non-technical or lower ranking positions. Importantly, we wanted to ensure that these interactions were authentic to real world scenarios and interactions encountered by individuals within the technology and engineering industry. Therefore, we validated the script for authenticity with professionals in that industry.

Participants. The authenticity of the script was validated with 20 individuals in the technology and engineering industry. The sample constituted 10% White women, 30% minority (Black/Hispanic) men and 60% minority women. Additionally, 90% of the sample held mid to senior level executive positions in their careers. Companies like Google, Riot games, JP Morgan, IBM, and Amazon were represented in the sample.

Procedure. Respondents read the script and completed a short survey where they were asked to rate the authenticity of the script and qualitatively share what elements of the script were most authentic and/or inauthentic. Authenticity ratings were anchored on a 10-point Likert scale ranging from 1 (not authentic at all) to 10 (very authentic).

Results. The script received very high authenticity ratings, with mean, median and mode scores of 8.5, 7 and 10, respectively. Overall, respondents were able to identify incidents of microaggression in the script, and find them very relatable, given their own personal experiences in the workforce. The parts of the script that respondents found most authentic were incidents where the player was mistakenly assumed to have stereotypical job roles, and the surprise others expressed when they found out that the player was in a role counter to the stereotype. These incidents were most relatable to the content validators because at some point in their careers, they too had experienced implicit messages that devalued their intellectual contributions, based on others' views that they did not belong and that they needed to be grateful just to be "a part of the room". There were hardly any suggestions regarding how to improve the authenticity of the script, except for one that suggested increasing more scrutiny of the play with security prior to being let into the main building.

4   Discussion

The purpose of validating the script was to ensure that the game feels like a real-life situation in order to increase the likelihood of transfer of emotion regulation from the game to the real world. Utilizing our combination of HRV-Biofeedback training and a serious game, the authentic environment will enable players to train emotion regulation at low-stakes and ultimately reduce the impact from stereotype and social identity threat they will experience in the real world.

4.1   Need for Game-Based Tools to Develop Resiliency

As aforementioned, to our knowledge there does not exist a game with the intentions of teaching resilience for those that are experiencing stereotype and social identity threat. We believe this is an area that could greatly benefit from a game of this nature. Games for helping teach resiliency already exist in different contexts, including low-income community risk resilience [38], industrial safety resilience training [54], and general academic resilience [57]. In each of these instances, the researchers utilized the game to simulate reality. For example, in one study the research goal was to determine what was needed for the community to create better plans in the future to help become more resilient in the face of adversity. In this work, three different games were developed that enabled players to gradually gain an understanding into how complex scenarios regarding risk can be as well as allow them to practice developing strategies to mitigate risk. In Resilient IN, we similarly intend to utilize an interactive narrative role-playing game to authentically simulate real world stereotype and social identity threat and allow players to practice mitigating their effects to prepare for the real-life scenarios they will encounter.

5   Future Work

Moving forward, we plan to conduct multiple studies of the game to examine if (1) the game appropriately elicits stereotype and social identity threat, and (2) the utility of incorporating the HRV-Biofeedback in training emotion regulation in players as well as if this results in them developing stronger resiliency. We also plan to continue researching and identifying additional aspects where we can include more liminal or subliminal messaging.

6   Conclusion

In this paper, we present the design of Resilient IN—a novel HRV-Biofeedback game that integrates resonant frequency heart rate variability for training resilience to stereotype and social identity threat. We discuss the design of the game in detail—focusing on how specific elements of the design draw from existing literature to evoke and train resilience during play, i.e., through the use of environmental biases, character designs, gamification of leaderboards, and HRV-Biofeedback training. We also discuss the design and validation of the authenticity of the game narrative/script with individuals in the technology and engineering industry. Notably, to our knowledge, this is the first serious game to address stereotype and social identity threat through HRV-Biofeedback, allowing for novel future empirical inquiry and research findings that could inform a new generation of interventions that leverage biofeedback training in serious games to attenuate various stereotype and social identity threats.

References

1. Armenta, B.E.: Stereotype boost and stereotype threat effects: the moderating role of ethnic identification. Cult. Divers. Ethn. Minor. Psychol. **16**(1), 94 (2010)
2. Aritzeta, A., Soroa, G., Balluerka, N., Muela, A., Gorostiaga, A., Aliri, J.: Reducing anxiety and improving academic performance through a biofeedback relaxation training program. Appl. Psychophysiol. Biofeedback **42**(3), 193–202 (2017)
3. Behm-Morawitz, E., Mastro, D.: The effects of the sexualization of female video game characters on gender stereotyping and female self-concept. Sex Roles **61**(11), 808–823 (2009)
4. Beilock, S.L., Rydell, R.J., McConnell, A.R.: Stereotype threat and working memory: mechanisms, alleviation, and spillover. J. Exp. Psychol. Gen. **136**(2), 256 (2007)
5. Bian, L., Leslie, S.-J., Cimpian, A.: Gender stereotypes about intellectual ability emerge early and influence children's interests. Science **355**(6323), 389–391 (2017)
6. Blascovich, J., Spencer, S.J., Quinn, D., Steele, C.: African Americans and high blood pressure: the role of stereotype threat. Psychol. Sci. **12**(3), 225–229 (2001)
7. Bouchard, S., Bernier, F., Boivin, É., Morin, B., Robillard, G.: Using biofeedback while immersed in a stressful videogame increases the effectiveness of stress management skills in soldiers. PloS One **7**(4), e36169 (2012)
8. Bowen, N.K., Wegmann, K.M., Webber, K.C.: Enhancing a brief writing intervention to combat stereotype threat among middle-school students. J. Educ. Psychol. **105**(2), 427 (2013)
9. Bradley, R.T., McCraty, R., Atkinson, M., Arguelles, L., Rees, R.A., Tomasino, D.: Reducing test anxiety and improving test performance in America's schools. Boulder Creek: Institute of Heart-Math (2007)
10. Bradley, R.T., McCraty, R., Atkinson, M., Tomasino, D., Daugherty, A., Arguelles, L.: Emotion self-regulation, psychophysiological coherence, and test anxiety: results from an experiment using electrophysiological measures. Appl. Psychophysiol. Biofeedback **35**(4), 261–283 (2010)
11. Camingue, J., Carstensdottir, E., Melcer, E.F.: What is a visual novel? Proc. ACM Hum. Comput. Interact. **5**, 1–18 (2021)
12. Camingue, J., Melcer, E.F., Carstensdottir, E.: A (visual) novel route to learning: a taxonomy of teaching strategies in visual novels. In: International Conference on the Foundations of Digital Games, pp. 1–13 (2020)
13. Chen, X.: STEM attrition: college students' paths into and out of STEM fields. Statistical Analysis Report. NCES 2014-001. National Center for Education Statistics (2013)

14. Cheryan, S., Meltzoff, A.N., Kim, S.: Classrooms matter: the design of virtual classrooms influences gender disparities in computer science classes. Comput. Educ. **57**(2), 1825–1835 (2011)
15. Cheryan, S., Plaut, V.C., Davies, P.G., Steele, C.M.: Ambient belonging: how stereotypical cues impact gender participation in computer science. J. Pers. Soc. Psychol. **97**(6), 1045 (2009)
16. Christy, K.R., Fox, J.: Leaderboards in a virtual classroom: a test of stereotype threat and social comparison explanations for women's math performance. Comput. Educ. **78**, 66–77 (2014)
17. Dan-Glauser, E.S., Gross, J.J.: The temporal dynamics of two response-focused forms of emotion regulation: experiential, expressive, and autonomic consequences. Psychophysiology **48**(9), 1309–1322 (2011)
18. Diez, J.D.S., Melcer, E.F.: Cookie mania: a serious game for teaching internet cookies to high school and college students. In: Ma, M., Fletcher, B., Göbel, S., Baalsrud Hauge, J., Marsh, T. (eds.) JCSG 2020. LNCS, vol. 12434, pp. 69–77. Springer, Cham (2020). https://doi.org/10.1007/978-3-030-61814-8_5
19. Dill, K.E., Thill, K.P.: Video game characters and the socialization of gender roles: young people's perceptions mirror sexist media depictions. Sex Roles **57**(11), 851–864 (2007)
20. Elmore, K.C., Luna-Lucero, M.: Light bulbs or seeds? How metaphors for ideas influence judgments about genius. Soc. Psychol. Pers. Sci. **8**(2), 200–208 (2017)
21. Francis, H.M., Penglis, K.M., McDonald, S.: Manipulation of heart rate variability can modify response to anger-inducing stimuli. Soc. Neurosci. **11**(5), 545–552 (2016)
22. Good, C., Aronson, J., Inzlicht, M.: Improving adolescents' standardized test performance: an intervention to reduce the effects of stereotype threat. J. Appl. Dev. Psychol. **24**(6), 645–662 (2003)
23. Grasse, K.M., Kreminski, M., Wardrip-Fruin, N., Mateas, M., Melcer, E.F.: Using self-determination theory to explore enjoyment of educational interactive narrative games: a case study of academical. Front. Virtual Reality (3), 1–14 (2022)
24. Grasse, K.M., Melcer, E.F., Kreminski, M., Junius, N., Ryan, J., Wardrip-Fruin, N.: Academical: a choice-based interactive storytelling game for enhancing moral reasoning, knowledge, and attitudes in responsible conduct of research. In: Bostan, B. (ed.) Games and Narrative: Theory and Practice. ISCEMT, pp. 173–189. Springer, Cham (2022). https://doi.org/10.1007/978-3-030-81538-7_12
25. Grasse, K.M., Melcer, E.F., Kreminski, M., Junius, N., Wardrip-Fruin, N.: Improving undergraduate attitudes towards responsible conduct of research through an interactive storytelling game. In: Extended Abstracts of the 2021 CHI Conference on Human Factors in Computing Systems, pp. 1–8 (2021)
26. Gross, J.J., Levenson, R.W.: Emotional suppression: physiology, self-report, and expressive behavior. J. Pers. Soc. Psychol. **64**(6), 970 (1993)
27. Hamari, J., Koivisto, J., Sarsa, H.: Does gamification work?-A literature review of empirical studies on gamification. In: 2014 47th Hawaii International Conference on System Sciences, pp. 3025–3034. IEEE (2014)
28. Huang, B., Hew, K.F.: Do points, badges and leaderboard increase learning and activity: a quasi-experiment on the effects of gamification. In: Proceedings of the 23rd International Conference on Computers in Education, pp. 275–280. Society for Computer in Education, Hangzhou (2015)
29. Inzlicht, M., Ben-Zeev, T.: A threatening intellectual environment: why females are susceptible to experiencing problem-solving deficits in the presence of males. Psychol. Sci. **11**(5), 365–371 (2000)

30. Jarvie, D.: Organizational social networks and implications for inequality in silicon valley tech. In: Papa, R. (ed.) Handbook on Promoting Social Justice in Education, pp. 1641–1662. Springer, Cham (2020). https://doi.org/10.1007/978-3-319-74078-2_152-1

31. Jerčić, P., et al.: A serious game using physiological interfaces for emotion regulation training in the context of financial decision-making. In: 20th European Conference on Information Systems (ECIS 2012), Barcelona, pp. 1–14. AIS Electronic Library (AISeL) (2012)

32. Johns, M., Inzlicht, M., Schmader, T.: Stereotype threat and executive resource depletion: examining the influence of emotion regulation. J. Exp. Psychol. Gen. **137**(4), 691 (2008)

33. Kim, S., Zemon, V., Cavallo, M.M., Rath, J.F., McCraty, R., Foley, F.W.: Heart rate variability biofeedback, executive functioning and chronic brain injury. Brain Inj. **27**(2), 209–222 (2013)

34. Kirkcaldy, B., Noack, P., Furnham, A., Siefen, G.: Parental estimates of their own and their children's intelligence. Eur. Psychol. **12**(3), 173–180 (2007)

35. Landers, R.N., Bauer, K.N., Callan, R.C.: Gamification of task performance with leaderboards: a goal setting experiment. Comput. Hum. Behav. **71**, 508–515 (2017)

36. Lecklider, A.: Inventing the Egghead: the Battle Over Brainpower in American Culture. University of Pennsylvania Press, Philadelphia (2013)

37. Logel, C., Iserman, E.C., Davies, P.G., Quinn, D.M., Spencer, S.J.: The perils of double consciousness: the role of thought suppression in stereotype threat. J. Exp. Soc. Psychol. **45**(2), 299–312 (2009)

38. Marome, W., Natakun, B., Archer, D.: Examining the use of serious games for enhancing community resilience to climate risks in Thailand. Sustainability **13**(8), 4420 (2021)

39. Mather, M., Thayer, J.F.: How heart rate variability affects emotion regulation brain networks. Curr. Opin. Behav. Sci. **19**, 98–104 (2018)

40. Mauss, I.B., Cook, C.L., Cheng, J.Y.J., Gross, J.J.: Individual differences in cognitive reappraisal: experiential and physiological responses to an anger provocation. Int. J. Psychophysiol. **66**(2), 116–124 (2007)

41. McCraty, R., Atkinson, M., Tomasino, D., Bradley, R.T.: The coherent heart heart-brain interactions, psychophysiological coherence, and the emergence of system-wide order. Integr. Rev. Transdisc. Transcult. J. New Thought Res. Prax. **5**(2) (2009)

42. McCraty, R., Atkinson, M., Tomasino, D.: Impact of a workplace stress reduction program on blood pressure and emotional health in hypertensive employees. J. Altern. Complement. Med. **9**(3), 355–369 (2003)

43. McCraty, R., Tomasino, D.: Emotional stress, positive emotions, and psychophysiological coherence. In: Stress in Health and Disease, pp. 342–365 (2006)

44. Melcer, E.F., et al.: Getting academical: a choice-based interactive storytelling game for teaching responsible conduct of research. In: International Conference on the Foundations of Digital Games, pp. 1–12 (2020)

45. Melcer, E.F.: Teaching responsible conduct of research through an interactive storytelling game. In: Extended Abstracts of the 2020 CHI Conference on Human Factors in Computing Systems, pp. 1–10 (2020)

46. Melcer, E., Nguyen, T.-H.D., Chen, Z., Canossa, A., El-Nasr, M.S., Isbister, K.: Games research today: analyzing the academic landscape 2000–2014. In: Foundations of Digital Games (2015)

47. Mendes, W.B., Major, B., McCoy, S., Blascovich, J.: How attributional ambiguity shapes physiological and emotional responses to social rejection and acceptance. J. Pers. Soc. Psychol. **94**(2), 278 (2008)
48. Muraven, M., Baumeister, R.F.: Self-regulation and depletion of limited resources: does self-control resemble a muscle? Psychol. Bull. **126**(2), 247 (2000)
49. Murphy, M.C., Steele, C.M., Gross, J.J.: Signaling threat: how situational cues affect women in math, science, and engineering settings. Psychol. Sci. **18**(10), 879–885 (2007)
50. Nguyen, T.-H.D., Melcer, E., Canossa, A., Isbister, K., El-Nasr, M.S.: Seagull: a bird's-eye view of the evolution of technical games research. Entertainment Comput. **26**, 88–104 (2018)
51. Ortiz-Rojas, M., Chiluiza, K., Valcke, M.: Gamification through leaderboards: an empirical study in engineering education. Comput. Appl. Eng. Educ. **27**(4), 777–788 (2019)
52. Parnandi, A., Gutierrez-Osuna, R.: Partial reinforcement in game biofeedback for relaxation training. IEEE Trans. Affect. Comput. **12**(1), 141–153 (2018)
53. Parnandi, A., Gutierrez-Osuna, R.: Visual biofeedback and game adaptation in relaxation skill transfer. IEEE Trans. Affect. Comput. **10**(2), 276–289 (2017)
54. Patriarca, R., Falegnami, A., De Nicola, A., Villani, M.L., Paltrinieri, N.: Serious games for industrial safety: an approach for developing resilience early warning indicators. Saf. Sci. **118**, 316–331 (2019)
55. Picho, K., Rodriguez, A., Finnie, L.: Exploring the moderating role of context on the mathematics performance of females under stereotype threat: a meta-analysis. J. Soc. Psychol. **153**(3), 299–333 (2013)
56. Picho, K., Stephens, J.M.: Culture, context and stereotype threat: a comparative analysis of young Ugandan women in coed and single-sex schools. J. Educ. Res. **105**(1), 52–63 (2012)
57. Pusey, M.: The effect of puzzle video games on high school students' problem-solving skills and academic resilience. In: Proceedings of the 2018 Annual Symposium on Computer-Human Interaction in Play Companion Extended Abstracts, pp. 63–69 (2018)
58. Rivardo, M.G., Rhodes, M.E., Camaione, T.C., Legg, J.M.: Stereotype threat leads to reduction in number of math problems women attempt. North Am. J. Psychol. **13**(1), 5–16 (2011)
59. Rivers, E.: Women, minorities, and persons with disabilities in science and engineering. National Science Foundation (2017)
60. Seron, C., Silbey, S.S., Cech, E., Rubineau, B.: Persistence is cultural: professional socialization and the reproduction of sex segregation. Work. Occup. **43**(2), 178–214 (2016)
61. Schmader, T., Johns, M.: Converging evidence that stereotype threat reduces working memory capacity. J. Pers. Soc. Psychol. **85**(3), 440 (2003)
62. Schmader, T., Johns, M., Forbes, C.: An integrated process model of stereotype threat effects on performance. Psychol. Rev. **115**(2), 336 (2008)
63. Schmiedek, F., Hildebrandt, A., Lövdén, M., Wilhelm, O., Lindenberger, U.: Complex span versus updating tasks of working memory: the gap is not that deep. J. Exp. Psychol. Learn. Mem. Cogn. **35**(4), 1089 (2009)
64. Spencer, S.J., Steele, C.M., Quinn, D.M.: Stereotype threat and women's math performance. J. Exp. Soc. Psychol. **35**(1), 4–28 (1999)
65. Steele, C.M., Aronson, J.: Stereotype threat and the intellectual test performance of African Americans. J. Pers. Soc. Psychol. **69**(5), 797 (1995)

66. Steele, C.M.: A threat in the air: how stereotypes shape intellectual identity and performance. Am. Psychol. **52**(6), 613 (1997)
67. Tompkins, J.E., Lynch, T., Van Driel, I.I., Fritz, N.: Kawaii killers and femme fatales: a textual analysis of female characters signifying benevolent and hostile sexism in video games. J. Broadcast. Electron. Media **64**(2), 236–254 (2020)
68. Wenzlaff, R.M., Wegner, D.M.: Thought suppression. Annu. Rev. Psychol. **51**(1), 59–91 (2000)
69. Yin, L., Ring, L., Bickmore, T.: Using an interactive visual novel to promote patient empowerment through engagement. In: Proceedings of the International Conference on the Foundations of Digital Games, pp. 41–48 (2012)
70. Zafar, M.A., Ahmed, B., Gutierrez-Osuna, R.: Playing with and without Biofeedback. In: 2017 IEEE 5th International Conference on Serious Games and Applications for Health (SeGAH), pp. 1–7. IEEE (2017)

Designing an Anti-Bullying Serious Game: Insights from Interviews with Teachers

Elaheh Sanoubari[1]([⊠]), John E. Muñoz Cardona[1], Andrew Houston[1], James Young[2], and Kerstin Dautenhahn[1]

[1] University of Waterloo, Waterloo, Canada
{esanouba,jmunozca,houston,kdautenh}@uwaterloo.ca
[2] University of Manitoba, Winnipeg, Canada
young@cs.umanitoba.ca

Abstract. Bullying in schools is a widespread problem with serious and long-lasting consequences. We explore designing *RE-Mind* – an anti-bullying serious game that uses social robots to foster bystander intervention against bullying of peers among school-age children. To ground the design of *RE-Mind* in how bullying happens between peers at local schools, we conducted semi-structured interviews with 13 elementary teachers. Insights from this study highlight a need for novel anti-bullying interventions that (i) are relevant to children's present-day experiences, (ii) are designed by children and, thus, are relatable for them, and (iii) lessen the burden on teachers. In this work, we present an overview of our methodology and qualitative findings and discuss how this research informs the design of the game elements in *RE-Mind*. This work demonstrates the first steps towards designing an anti-bullying serious game involving social robots and contributes insights for designers of pedagogical robots and anti-bullying interventions for children.

Keywords: Serious games · Peer bullying · Social robots

1 Introduction

Peer bullying in schools is a universally prevalent problem with serious consequences and long-term implications on one's well-being [6]. Despite an abundance of research, traditional anti-bullying interventions often fall short of effectively reducing bullying in schools [18,32,52]. Interventions mediated by Information and Communication Technologies (ICTs) have shown promising results in supporting pedagogical objectives and promoting children's well-being [44]. Motivated by this, we explore the design of *RE-Mind*[1]: a drama-based serious game that employs social robots and aims to encourage bystander children to intervene and take action against bullying of their peers.

---

[1] Short for **R**obots **E**mpowering **Mind**s.

H. Söbke et al. (Eds.): JCSG 2022, LNCS 13476, pp. 102–121, 2022.
https://doi.org/10.1007/978-3-031-15325-9_9

It is important for the engagement of peers in such games, that they include realistic depictions of bullying and avoid stereotypical narrative design [26]. Teachers play an integral role in identifying and intervening against peer bullying in schools [21]. Research shows that supportive teachers are an important factor for contributing to a positive school climate and reducing bullying [5]. They can offer an *adult perspective* on how bullying happens among peers, and their experience in navigating this sensitive topic can be an invaluable resource to researchers. However, literature also indicates that teachers are prone to underestimating the scale of bullying, being unaware of it, or being desensitized to it [17,35,42]. This is exacerbated by the fact that victimized students often avoid reporting bullying to teachers in fear of escalating it [63]. It is important for researchers and designers of anti-bullying tools to explore the perspectives of both children and teachers to gain a well-rounded understanding.

In this study, we have interviewed teachers from local elementary schools as stakeholders to inform the design of *RE-Mind*. This research extends a previous work in which we conducted a co-design study with children and prompted them to design fictional robotic characters and write stories about them [57]. This study helped us understand how children conceptualize a phenomenon such as bullying in the context of social robots. The present work complements this by grounding children's creative and fantastical designs in teachers' account of how peer bullying happens in schools. To that end, we administered semi-structured interviews with 13 teachers of grades 3–6. The interviews focused on anti-bullying protocols and programs currently used in schools and their effectiveness, how bullying happens in school, and peers' reactions to it.

We transcribed the interviews and qualitatively analyzed the data. Qualitative insights emerging from this analysis suggest that: (i) teachers find the anti-bullying programs commonly used in schools outdated, and there is a need for novel interventions relevant to children's present-day experiences with bullying; (ii) teachers believe that children do not *buy into* the scenarios described in the anti-bullying interventions, and it is important to involve them in designing programs that are relatable to them; (iii) it is common for schools to put the burden of detecting and dealing with bullying almost entirely on teachers, and as such, technology-based interventions that reduce teachers' workload may be desirable. Emerging themes from this data shed light into the contemporary dynamics of peer bullying and interventions that teachers find helpful.

In this paper, we overview related literature to motivate our approach and focus on bystander intervention, briefly review the co-design study with children, outline the methodology for current work, present qualitative observations, and explore how this research informs the design of game dynamics in *RE-Mind*. In particular, we propose game design elements for serious games involving social robots and discuss lessons learned in light of prior work.

2   Related Work

Traditionally, research on developing strategies against bullying has focused on victims, or bullies; whereas the majority of people present in a bullying incident belong to neither group [50]. While few interventions target the bystanders, those that do have shown promising results in reducing bullying [60]. Children that are bystanders to bullying, typically find it morally wrong [31]. However, motivating them to take action against it remains challenging [54]. While bystanders are present in more than 85% of bullying incidents, they only intervene in 10% [16,30]. Meanwhile, bullying stops in more than 50% the cases after a bystander intervenes [50]. This makes bystanders a key demographic in bullying prevention.

Researchers suggest fostering peer intervention by using techniques such as role-playing and interactive drama [4,55]. Meta-analysis reviews on drama-based pedagogy suggest that it can improve a range of social skills in children including the ability to make friends, resolve conflicts, and recognize emotions in others [37]. These skills are highly relevant to empowering children to confront difficult social situations such as bullying. Also, as more programs are incorporating the modalities offered by ICTs, researchers have recognized their benefits in fostering active learning, providing equal opportunities, making education more descriptive and enjoyable for peers, and most importantly, promoting *skills beyond learning* [24]. Serious games can support learning through self-exploration and provide an attractive setting for children to acquire skills [12,25]. In the context of bullying, serious games can offer tailored education while providing a buffer to let children safely explore "emotionally hot" topics [58]. However, ICT tools are generally underused in anti-bullying interventions [44].

A notable example of a prior anti-bullying serious games is FearNot! – a game in which children act as an invisible friend to an animated character and use a chatbot to give advice about the bullying that the character is experiencing [23,27]. Another prominent example is Kiva – a game in which children role-play as a virtual student and test their knowledge and strategies about bullying through puzzles and quizzes [33]. In addition, several others have used simulations of virtual worlds with animated characters [64], virtual reality [14], conversational agents [66], interactive narratives [36] and similar mechanisms to increase children' knowledge of bullying and promote bystander intervention. We argue for using robots as a role-playing vehicle in anti-bullying games, instead of animated characters. Prior studies show that robots are substantially more effective in improving learning and resulting in behavioral changes [7], compared to virtual agents. Also, research shows that children can envision robots assuming fictional roles of victims, bullies, and bystanders [57]. *RE-Mind* is, to the best of our knowledge, the first anti-bullying serious game to employ robots.

3   Research Questions

We set out to gain a deeper understanding of how bullying happens in local elementary schools, to support designing *RE-Mind*. In particular, we are interested in the following research questions, and their implications for the design of *RE-Mind*: (i) what anti-bullying programs and protocols are used; (ii) how does bullying take place among peers; and (iii) how do children react to or intervene in the bullying of their peers? Given that school-age children tend to *legalize* bullying as they grow up, it is recommended that anti-bullying interventions begin at the age that bullying behaviours start to emerge [40]. As such, our research questions focus on grades 3–6 of schools in Canada (i.e., ages of 8–12).

4   Co-design with Children

This research extends our previous work: a co-design study in which we investigated how 8–12 year old children envision a "student robot" about their age and its various social interactions [57]. 22 children followed a step-wise process to design the looks and personality of the robot and make stories and animations of its different social interactions (see Fig. 1). We avoided mentioning the term "bullying" to children in this study to protect them from any potential emotional harm from explicitly associating their own lived experiences with bullying, and avoid biasing them to use clichés in their designs (e.g., a character designed as a stereotypical victim, rather than an average peer). We qualitatively analyzed data from children's brainstormed ideas, sketches, low-fidelity prototypes of robots, story-planners, story-boards, animations and interview transcriptions. Findings suggested that children had no difficulty envisioning robots as fictional students, and even though unprompted, they elaborated on various bullying-related scenarios in which robots took on the roles of aggressors, victims, or bystanders; supporting using robots in the context of bullying (see Fig. 2).

Fig. 1. Examples of children's ideas, sketches, and prototypes in the co-design study.

5   Interviews with Teachers

5.1   Recruitment

We promoted the study on media groups and asked interested teachers of grades 3 to 6 in local schools to contact us. Teachers digitally signed a consent form prior to the interview, and we thanked them with a $15 e-gift card afterwards. This protocol was approved by our institutional Research Ethics Board.

Fig. 2. Frames from a child's stop-motion animation (1): The robot (A) notices that a peer (B) is excluded from games that other students (C) are playing. (2): The robot (A) intervenes by inviting the excluded peer (B) to play basketball.

5.2   Participants

We recruited 13 teachers with experience of teaching grades 3–6 in Canadian elementary schools (with almost equal distribution of an average of 4.75 teachers experienced with each grade). Participants had 2–32 years of teaching experience (M = 12.3 years, SD = 9.1). Among them, 7 teachers taught in public schools, 2 in private schools, 2 in religious schools and 2 in French-Immersion schools. This distribution is in approximate accordance with the number of schools in Canada.

5.3   Procedure

The interviews were conducted online or over the phone. At the beginning, teachers briefly described their teaching experience and if they had also taught classes outside of our grades of interest, we asked them to only draw on their experiences with grades 3–6 for answering the questions. We explained that bullying is typically a repeated behavior and offered a definition from Olweus [48]: *"We say a student is being bullied when another student, or several other students say mean and hurtful things or make fun of him or her or call him or her mean and hurtful names; completely ignore or exclude him or her from their group of friends or leave him or her out of things on purpose; hit, kick, push, shove around, or lock him or her inside a room; tell lies or spread false rumors about him or her or send mean notes and try to make other students dislike him or her and other hurtful things like that."*. We conducted the interview revolving around the research questions and asked probing questions whenever appropriate to gain in-depth information (e.g., can you tell me more about it?). The interviews were audio-recorded and lasted about 45 min.

5.4   Analysis

We transcribed the interviews and used the NVivo software [28] to conduct thematic analysis [11]. Since this was an exploratory research, we used inductive coding to code excerpts from the interviews. The codes were later collapsed into the categories that best reflected the analyses. We discussed the categories as a group, refined them, and determined the overarching emergent themes.

6   Qualitative Observations

6.1   Anti-Bullying Programs in Schools

Bullying Prevention. The majority of our participants stated that their school has no specific anti-bullying programs (10/13). Among those, some mentioned general strategies (2/10), a zero-tolerance policy for bullying (2/10), or curriculum support to teachers instead (3/10). Only three teachers (3/13) cited school-wide programs; although bullying was not the specific focus of any of them (e.g., *Buddy Bench*: a designated bench in school that a child can sit on when they need a friend). Several teachers (7/13) explained that their schools hold one-off events, such as presentations (5/13) or assemblies (2/13). Overall, teachers found the anti-bullying protocols unsatisfactory and pointed to insufficient education, and lack of organizational strategies and repercussions for bullying (4/13). *"We try to keep everything done in the classroom, because as soon as we try and go higher up, we know that the students are being sent back and that the issues are going to keep repeating themselves."* [T10]. This observation confirmed that there is a need for novel anti-bullying interventions in local elementary schools.

Focus of Strategies. The majority of participants believed that schools delegate dealing with bullying to teachers (9/13). The focus of the teachers' strategies against bullying can be categorized into three themes: (i) mediation strategies (6/13, e.g., providing an intervention script), (ii) education about bullying (e.g., discussing what is bullying, 3/13), and (iii) fostering social skills and values (e.g., inclusion 5/13). For example, T4 explained that they teach children: *"...to keep the friends together, to stand up for each other, to include the ones that someone else has excluded, just to prove to the bully that they are valued."* *[sic]*. This guides our intervention approach and narrative design in *RE-Mind*.

Effectiveness of Programs. Participants' opinions about the effectiveness of the programs varied. A few teachers (3/13) speculated about the reasons behind ineffective programs include: (i) scenarios being created by adults, (ii) scenarios being outdated and irrelevant to children, (iii) isolated lessons, rather than ongoing interventions, (iv) researchers not being in-tune with the reality of classrooms and designing generic programs. *"I would get the kids to help come up with scenarios, not just the run of the mill program that they did in 1990, which is very outdated now."* [T19]. This validates our approach of co-designing with children, and interviewing teachers to ground our designs in reality of the classrooms rather than traditional definitions. Also, this theme indicates a need for longitudinal interventions (e.g., serious games), rather than one-off lessons.

Protocols Against Bullying. If bullying happens in the classroom, teachers often address it themselves (13/13) by investigating the incident and solving the issue or to giving children choices to resolve their problem (e.g., "this needs to stop or parents will be notified"). Sometimes teachers intervene by taking away privileges (e.g., disabling chat in a virtual classroom). If it is a serious or repeated instance, they notify the parents and ask the school social worker or the principal's office to intervene (13/13). At this point, some schools discuss a behavior plan that outlines how they will react should the student continue the problematic behavior. Teachers mentioned that in serious cases, the principal's office may do an "in-school suspension" (4/13); *"they basically just in a room in the office. They were just basically doing nothing, which in my opinion, is not super helpful."* [T14]. This highlights that even when anti-bullying strategies exist, a great deal of work is put on the teachers. So, they may benefit from stand-alone intervention approaches that lessen this burden.

Peers' Knowledge of Bullying. The majority of teachers agreed on two points: (i) children know the basics about bullying (7/13), and (ii) children, especially at younger grades, often overly report or label conflicts as bullying, when it is in fact teasing or joking (9/13). *"We have kind of a mix of children's ideas of what bullying is. I find the younger they are, 'oh, so and so took my pencil, they're bullying me', and it's like, no, that's not really what bullying is."* [T3] *[sic]*. RE-Mind could demonstrate the fine line between bullying and teasing; for example, by leveraging various scenarios with nuanced differences and encouraging children to reflect and determine what constitutes bullying.

6.2   Peer Bullying in Schools

Frequency and Intensity. More than half of the teachers believed that bullying happens "all the time", or on a daily basis (7/13), and several mentioned that it happens frequently (6/13)– *"I would probably say it happens daily, but the amount of times that teachers actually get told about it, not as often. They just keep it to themselves, they're not telling adults."* [T14] *[sic]*. Also, several teachers highlighted that even though bullying happens frequently, it is typically committed by very few peers who target many people (5/13). Several added that sometimes bullying can last as long as several years (7/13). This reaffirms that despite an abundance of research, bullying is still a prevalent problem and exploring novel interventions against it remains relevant.

Types of Bullying. Among the types of bullying listed in the definition offered by Olweus [48], (i) Exclusion (12/13), mean remarks (8/13), spreading rumors (8/13), and name-calling (5/13) are still very common in local schools. However, physical bullying and stealing happen very rarely – *"I remember when I first started teaching... every couple of weeks, there was a schoolyard fight. Like, in the 90s! Punching, kicking, pulling hair, you know, the whole thing. And I haven't seen a fight like that happen in... wow, I don't even know."* [T22] *[sic]*. It is evident that dynamics of peer bullying have changed drastically over the past decades, which may challenge the contextual validity of traditional interventions.

Where it Happens. There was a consensus among the participants that in-person bullying typically happens in unsupervised environments (11/13, e.g., recess, cafeteria) or unstructured times (5/13, e.g., break time) where it is difficult for staff to supervise everyone – *"anywhere where there's not a teacher or an adult visible?"* [T1] *[sic]*. The majority (9/13) pointed to cyberbullying as one of the common types of bullying not listed in the definition. A few (2/13) believed that it is uncommon because phones are banned on the premises and school devices are monitored, whereas several pointed that online bullying is not confined to school (4/13). The majority of teachers (7/13) were concerned that cyberbullying is becoming increasingly common due to online classrooms, social media, access of young children to technology, and the invisibility offered by a virtual world. *"Cameras were on for all the students for a while. So then the kids would tell each other 'oh look what you're wearing, look what your room looks like'... all these students have cell phones, they will take a picture of someone, they will go online and make a meme out of it. And then they take the meme and share within their social media platform."* [T20]. This provides input for designing scenarios for *RE-Mind* that reflect children's present day experiences.

Why it Happens. According to the participants, the common reasons of peer bullying includes bad parenting (5/13, e.g., little supervision of online activities) and personal trauma (5/13, e.g., having been bullied themselves). Teachers cited differences in ones appearance (6/13, e.g., different physique or fashion), being a minority, or having immigrant or refugee status (5/13, e.g., different food or accent), or a low socioeconomic status (4/13), as factors that could lead to a child's victimization. This observation supports exploring role-play as a medium to help children take various perspectives, reflect, and build empathy.

Gender Differences. All teachers had noticed gender differences in bullying; they explained that girls tend to do more "social bullying" such as exclusion (7/13), are more verbal (6/13), subversive (6/13) – *"Oh, they can be nasty and it's very subtle. Girls are definitely more the emotional strains. They are the social type."* [T4] *[sic]*. Whereas boys tend to exhibit more physical bullying (e.g., pushing) than girls (6/13), and they typically resolve conflicts faster after an incident (4/13). Teachers mentioned that it is more common for boys to bully someone over their athletic abilities (6/13)– *"boys will make fun of other boys athletic ability, 'you're not fast runner, don't play soccer.', and then they'll bring that point across by choosing that person last for the team or just not letting them play at all."* [T22]. This observation informs *RE-Mind*'s narrative design.

Age Differences. Several teachers expressed that that bullying gets worse among older children (9/13). They explained that as children age and get more access to technology, online bullying becomes more common. Also, their problems get more complicated; for example, as their bodies develop, issues related to gender and sexuality begin to unearth. Their social circles get more established and social exclusion becomes more common. Also, pre-mediated and psychological bullying take place more often. Finally, peer intervention becomes more frowned upon and happens less frequently. Teachers pointed that younger children often resort to teasing and physical bullying (4/13), because they "do not know better", are more emotional, less socially-aware, and do not know how to do psychological bullying (3/13). Also, younger children are often more open to intervening in bullying of a peer (2/13) – *"[when a young child intervenes] teacher says good for you, thank you for standing up for your friend; that means the world to them. Whereas nobody wants that kind of attention as they get older, because then it just makes you look like a wimp or, it's just not a favorable look."*

[T22]. Learning from this, serious games like *RE-Mind* can be designed to provide tailored experiences that address peers' age-specific needs.

Effects of the Pandemic. Finally, even though we did not bring up COVID-19, several teachers pointed out to the diverse effects of pandemic on peer bullying. Some thought that pandemic has decreased bullying (especially physical bullying) because there is less interaction among children (4/13). Others thought that the pandemic has worsened the situation by decreasing social skills among kids, or making bullying harder to detect (3/13) – *"I think kids are internalizing it. It's harder to detect the bullying, and kids are not as forthcoming that they're being bullied, especially if they have other priorities to deal with."* [T19] *[sic]*. This contributes to the contextual-validity of *RE-Mind*, by shedding light on the nuanced and underexplored impacts of the pandemic on peer relationships.

6.3   Peers' Reactions to Bullying

Bystander Presence. The majority of teachers believed that bystanders are often present when bullying takes place (8/13) – *"I personally haven't come across or heard that it was just the person who was getting bullied and the person who was bullying in a corner. It's more of a group because they want attention."* [T20] *[sic]*. This suggests that bystanders remain the majority in most bullying incidents and reaffirms the relevance of bystander-focused interventions.

Bystander Feelings. Several teachers believed that bystanders often feel empathetic towards the victims (4/13), and know that what is happening is wrong (4/13) – *"I'm sure what goes through their head is boy I'm happy it's not me. To be able to say, I am glad it's not me, they'd have to have some sort of empathy to kind of translate those feelings to how they wouldn't want to be in that situation."* [T1] *[sic]*. This supports that there is negative bias towards bullying amongst bystanders, which makes them easier to influence via interventions.

Frequency of Interventions. Several teachers stated that the frequency of bystander intervention can vary, depending on factors such as the culture of the classroom, which side they support (i.e., whose friend they are), and their age (5/13). A few mentioned that bystander intervention is uncommon in their school (3/13). Only one teacher indicated that it happens frequently (1/13). The majority of teachers had observed peer intervention by getting a teacher (sometimes in confidence) (7/13), or telling their parents (2/13). Teachers had also observed students directly intervening by calling the bully out (3/13), or pulling the victim away (2/13) – *"On a very very rare occasion another student will stand up and be like hey, this is wrong. The majority of them will just laugh at it. There will be very few who will be strong enough to go and say that hey, you know, whatever you're doing is wrong. Stop!"* [T20]. Thus, interventions should aim to build confidence and encourage peers to do what they feel is right.

Intervention Effectiveness. The majority of teachers found peer interventions at least somewhat effective and believed it usually stops the bullying (7/13). Others believed that intervention results in escalating the bullying (3/13) or directing it to the bystander (2/13). *"Most of the times, they'll back off. Or they'll start bullying the bystander who is standing up for them."* [T18] *[sic]*.

While encouraging, this emphasizes the importance of not over-promising outcomes.

Why Bystanders Avoid Intervention. The common reasons for avoiding interventions included (i) fear of victimization (5/13), (ii) interventions not being seen favourably in the peer group (4/13), (iii) having a limited understanding of bullying (e.g., thinking it was for fun, 3/13), or (iv) being friends with the bully (4/13). Others mentioned shyness, getting used to bullying, or diffusion of responsibility (3/13) – *"A child couldn't go tell the teacher if something happened because they would be made fun of for being a tattletale or being a snitch. Nobody wants to be the one."* [T22] *[sic]*. Given that otherwise passive bystanders are the main target of our intervention, it is important that *RE-Mind* aims to explore all the reasons that children may hesitate to intervene.

Victim's Reactions. Common themes in victims' reactions as described by teachers include covering up the incident, or staying silent about it (5/13), avoiding it or walking away (3/13), or crying (3/13). Sometimes victims tell parents who inform the school (4/13). T17 explains that if a child that is bullied looks upset and gets teacher's attention, *"The conversation that usually comes after the teacher walks away is that you can't hide it from your face that you're upset, or you got us in trouble because you look upset. It's not always the best scenario, obviously, for the victim."*. This provides input for designing realistic stories about victims' experiences of bullying, to support bystander perspective-taking.

Ideal Reactions. Several teachers thought the ideal reaction for a victimized peer is to get help (e.g., tell a teacher). Others thought that victims should address the incident themselves (4/13) – *"I think standing up for yourself is always a good strategy to try. But that can backfire in a lot of ways."* [T22]. Also, teachers believed the best reaction for bystanders is to address it themselves, for example, by "de-escalating" the bullying [T4] or having a mediation script (5/13). While several teachers argued for reporting the bullying (6//13), a few thought that going to adults should be the last course of action (2/13). Others suggested strategies such as "being friends" [T15] by building empathy and defusing the bully's power (3/13), or removing the victim from the situation (3/13) – *"I think it's more effective when it comes from the peer group. Everybody wants to belong to that peer group."* [T22]. We take inspiration from teachers' intuitions of *what works* to set the objectives of *RE-Mind*.

7   Serious Game Design Involving Social Robots

In this section we discuss how insights from this research can inform our design and present a preliminary exploration of game design elements of *RE-Mind*. We bring in some of children's ideas about social robots in a fictional school from our previous co-design study [57] and incorporate the insights into this discussion. Related work recommends an initial matching stage indicating how game design elements can be linked to learning objectives to start off the creative process [3]. Thus, we conducted ideation sessions to discuss game ideas in light of the qualitative insights. The scenario we envision for the game can be implemented by using multiple social robots with scripted behavioral routines (e.g., conversations, reactions) in a fictional school setting. The story can be designed based on realistic bullying scenarios described in the two studies. A child will play the game by watching a dramatic segment where two robots (assuming roles of bully and victim) are interacting, while using a computer with a Wizard of Oz (WoZ) setup [19] to control a third robot (acting as a bystander) to intervene and impact how the story unfolds. The other robots will be programmed to react accordingly based on the player's interventions. As the story develops, new situations will arise and the child will have several opportunities to intervene. This game will enable children to practice their anti-bullying strategies and watch how their decisions impact the narrative. With this as a starting point, we identify some Human-Robot Interaction (HRI) and game design elements that can be integrated in *RE-Mind* architecture (see Fig. 3). We used the *Robo Ludens* taxonomy to identify relevant elements for designing games involving social robots (e.g., game mechanics, robot role) [43]. Figure 3 distinguishes conventional game design elements from ones unique to involvement of social robots in *RE-Mind*.

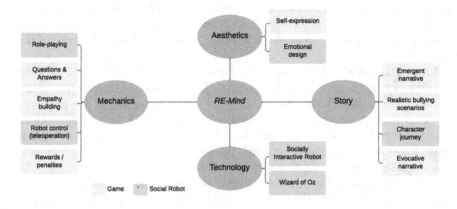

Fig. 3. Game design elements brainstormed for the *RE-Mind*.

7.1 Game Design Elements

RE-Mind is an interactive pedagogical tool aiming to foster peer support against bullying. We discuss the game design elements in terms of the elemental tetrad previously described by Schell [59], where mechanics, story, technology, and aesthetics are deconstructed to create a game experience.

Game Technology. i) Socially interactive robots: physically-embodied agents that are capable of social interactions offer great potentials as game partners. Our research demonstrated that children could imagine social robots taking roles related to bullying [57] and interviews with teachers revealed that ICT-based interventions may benefit their workload. As a key aspect, *RE-Mind* will use social robots as vehicle for role-playing to engage children in a safe situated learning.

ii) Wizard of Oz (WoZ): as a commonly used technique in HRI studies, WoZ [19], refers to a (typically hidden) experimenter remotely operating a robot and controlling aspects of its behavior (e.g., movement, speech). Using this technique, *RE-Mind* can allow children to direct the robot in a general sense (e.g., telling the robot to leave). This may endow them with a sense of agency and psychological ownership which elicits an emotional game-play experience. In reality, children's open-ended input will be interpreted and realized by the 'wizard', giving them the impression that the robot understands and follows their advice.

Game Mechanics. i) Role-play: unlike real-life bullying, or a re-enactment of it using actors, role-playing with robots lets participants engage through a proxy, and as such, they may see, experience, and act on violent behavior safely [15]. Our research showed that many existing interventions and approaches focus on taking perspective and building empathy. A role-playing game can realize these objectives by enabling the players to take various roles and experience the narrative from different perspectives. Teachers indicated that sometimes a peer resorts to bullying because they have been bullied themselves (also mentioned by others [22]). *RE-Mind* can enable the player to see the dramatic segment from the eyes of the 'victim' (i.e., the robot's camera), which may promote empathy.

ii) Questions & answers: trivia-like quizzes allow players to interact with games via selecting responses and progressing in game levels. Using quizzes in serious games can foster thinking skills and enhance knowledge acquisition [3]. Teachers indicated that children know the basics about bullying, but they sometimes confuse bullying with teasing or joking. *RE-Mind* can use game-like quizzes to help children learn about such nuances in an engaging setting.

iii) Empathy building: a recently trending game mechanic [53] proposes creating a mutual feelings between the player and the game character in order to progress and play the game. Similarly, *RE-Mind* can build challenges around empathetic tests, such as asking children how they envision a character feels to progress in the game to promote building empathy.

iv) Robot control – teleoperation: this game mechanic has been widely used by roboticists and HRI researchers [46]. It will allow children to quite literally put themselves in someone else's shoes, to encourage perspective-taking [51].

v) Rewards and penalties: this is an extensively used game element that allows players to be rewarded or penalized based on their game performance, evoking a Pavlovian principle of learning. Rewarding players keeps them motivated to continue the game and conduct tasks even if they are repetitive [59]. Teachers mentioned that while intervention is usually effective, it does not guarantee success and highlighted that ideally, such interventions should be *the norm*. Using this mechanism in conjunction with an emergent narrative, *RE-Mind* can reinforce bystander intervention as a good behavior, without over-promising positive outcome. *RE-Mind* may reward children with points or badges for consistently choosing good strategies, de-escalating, or solving empathy challenges, and penalize them for bad strategies or failing quizzes by stalling the narrative progress.

Game Story. i) Emergent narrative: while the individual dramatic segments of *RE-Mind* will be scripted, the narrative will emerge from child's decisions in the game. That is, when a child makes a decision in the role-play, the emergent narrative chooses the next dramatic segment non-deterministically. This calls for a spontaneous unscripted response from the child to deal with the new situation. Related work in psychodrama posits that such a process enables children to adapt general principles to their own abilities, and prepares them for unforeseen situations by helping them "work out the inevitable *bugs*" of the system [9]. Such safe and playful exploration of a range of possible situations empowers young people to review and revise their own assumptions [10].

ii) Realistic bullying scenarios: teachers highlighted that children often do not find the scenarios described in anti-bullying programs realistic, as the stories are often outdated or irrelevant to their lived experiences. we aim to create believable and ecologically-valid scenarios related to bullying by taking inspirations from qualitative evidence we have gathered by this research. For instance, *RE-Mind* scenarios should reflect the impacts of COVID-19 on peer bullying [62].

iii) Character journey: as a cornerstone of narrative building, "the hero's journey" is a template of stories that describe the character evolution of a hero that goes on adventures [59]. *RE-Mind* can incorporate this element by allowing the character controlled by the child to evolve as it faces challenging situations such as being a bystander to rumours, exclusions and cyberbullying in the fictional school, and tries to interact and build empathy with other fictional characters.

iv) Evocative narrative: in our co-design study with children, we noticed that they seem to draw on their own experiences to craft relatable stories, even when fantastical characters (such as *student robots*) are involved. *RE-Mind* will aim to foster connections between the fictional character and the player by building the narrative around evoking emotions, elaborating on characters' feelings and experiences, and appealing to player's preferences (see examples in [38]), which may lead to a more engaging play, and a more effective learning experience [41].

Game Aesthetics. i) Self-expression: game aesthetic elements may include any sensory phenomena that the player experiences in the game which define how the game is sensed by players [59]. We learned from the interviews that lack of *buy in* from children limits the effectiveness of conventional anti-bullying programs. To mitigate this, *RE-Mind* aims include features to foster children's self-expression, such as customizing the appearance and personality of their robot.

ii) Emotional design: games aesthetics can use a range of features to elicit emotions and influence players in behavioral, introspective and visceral level [45], positively influencing the state of flow (being in the zone) in serious games [1] which can enhance learning [39]. Social robots are capable of using a range of communication modalities, such as speech, facial expression, body movements and gestures that can support the emotional design of *RE-Mind*.

8   Discussion

We presented qualitative observations and lessons learned from semi-structured interviews with 13 elementary teachers about peer bullying in local schools. The interviews were conducted to support the design of an anti-bullying serious game, *RE-Mind*. Our findings highlight a need for novel anti-bullying interventions that are relatable by children and reduce teachers' workload. Some of our observations confirmed prior work on anti-bullying interventions; the frequency and intensity of bullying and limited effects of anti-bullying programs aligned with our expectations. Our study also aligns with related work about gender and age differences in peer bullying. Teachers also confirmed that bystanders are frequently present in bullying scenarios, and although they seldom intervene, they usually find it morally wrong. This is in line with prior work on the behavior of bystanders, and it re-affirms that they are a key demographic for anti-bullying interventions and their existing negative attitudes towards bullying makes them a more realistic target for impacting behavioral change [29].

However, several findings were contrary to our expectations. For example, we were surprised to find that anti-bullying interventions are generally underused in local schools, and the responsibility is mostly placed on teachers. It was reported that schools mostly rely on monitoring and disciplinary methods to combat bullying, rather than interventions aimed at shaping children's attitudes and changing their behaviors. Even when interventions are used, they are typically one-time events rather than ongoing programs. *"If it's integrated into the year, it just becomes the norm as to how they stand up for each other. Isolated lessons are great for awareness, but they don't encourage practice."*, T4 explained.

8.1   Promoting Situated Learning and Meta-Cognition

Teachers' insights on reasons why bystanders avoid intervention (e.g., fear of losing social status) highlight that it is not rooted in a lack of knowledge about bullying; rather, intervening against someone holding (perceived) power is a skill, and skills go beyond mere knowledge of facts. We argue that practicing a drama-based serious game enables *situated learning* [56], because thoughts are embedded in experiences and learning emerges from building new structures of knowledge through partaking in actions to solve a problem in the real world [2, 20]. Role-play develops a capacity for *meta-cognition*, the ability to think about one's own thinking process [8]. This ability plays an integral role in helping young people become skilled thinkers. Similarly, researchers argue that serious games incorporate meta-cognitive strategies with gaming, which often leads to higher engagement in learning and better pedagogical outcomes [65]. *RE-Mind* aims to go beyond increasing knowledge, and promote intervention skills in children.

8.2   Direct vs. Indirect Bullying

During the interviews, we cited a commonly-used definition of bullying by Olweus (2001 [48], built on his earlier work in 1994 [47]) to establish common ground

with respect to the characteristics of bullying behavior (see Sect. 5.3). This definition includes several forms of direct bullying such as physical aggression (e.g.,
kicking, pushing), locking someone in a room, and stealing or damaging one's
property. However, qualitative evidence from our study suggest that nowadays
direct bullying happens scarcely in local elementary schools and this definition
may no longer apply. *"A lot of bullying nowadays is exclusion, and social control.
It's not the traditional beat a kid up kind of thing. That's really, really rare."*, one
participant (T4) emphasized. Another teacher (T22) explained *"I think there's
been a lot of education around solving your problems with words... Even thinking
of myself growing up, people thought it wasn't a big deal. Whereas now, somebody
might be appalled. If you say I pushed that person, somebody will be like, WOW,
you put your hands on someone?!"*.

Prior work has reported gender differences in types of bullying behavior, with
indirect bullying (e.g., excluding from friend groups) being more prevalent among
girls while direct bullying is more common with boys [13]. However according to
our participants, even though gender-related differences still exist, they are less
pronounced these days. That is, while all the teachers we interviewed reported
having noticed gender differences such as girls being more subtle, they also highlighted that gender differences are not necessarily conspicuous – *"I mean, to say
boys never spread rumors or gossip, they do."* [T22] *[sic]*.

8.3   Contemporary Dynamics of Peer Bullying

In the course of the study, teachers unpromptedly discussed several contemporary issues related to bullying. For instance, they elaborated on the adverse
effects of the pandemic on the dynamics of peer bullying in their online or in-
person classes. Teachers also talked about bullying incidents based on cultural
or ethnic differences among peers, such as negative remarks based on minority
skin color or hair style, immigrant or refugee status, different food preferences
or accents. This is an important issue in local elementary schools as Canada is
a multicultural and highly diverse country and Ontario is home to more than a
hundred thousand new immigrants every year. Finally, the majority of teachers
emphasized the prevalence of cyberbullying and raised alarm about its extensive increase over the recent years as technologies such as social media have
become more and more available to younger children (which is in lines with
prior work, e.g., [34]). *"Back when I was a kid, a long long time ago, once we
left school, like we were turned off from there, right? We didn't have social media
like we do now. So now our kids are connected 24/7 whether they want to be or
not. There's always ways for people to reach out"* *[sic]*, T18 highlighted. Others brought up many examples of children using social networks, media sharing
platforms, memes, and anonymous messaging apps for bullying peers.

We argue that commonly-used traditional bullying definitions fall short of
reflecting such contemporary dynamics of peer bullying. This is particularly
noteworthy as the majority of our participants stressed that children often do
not find the scenarios described in the anti-bullying interventions relatable and
do not *buy into* them. *"They tend to be scenarios that kids listen to and laugh*

at because it has nothing to do with them, you know? The scenario doesn't connect to them and it doesn't reflect and sell them in 2020 way of skills and kids being with each other", T19 explained. Along the same lines, in 2021, a video[2] was trending on TikTok (a social media platform popular among the youth with roughly one third of users between ages of 10–19 [49]) that mocked the unrealistic and wishful thinking outcomes of anti-bullying intervention strategies that are commonly taught in elementary schools. This video was liked by over 1.2 M users and more than 2 K users were inspired to make their own TikTok videos using the original sound. In fact, previous work on effectiveness of anti-bullying programs underlines the importance of "buy in" from all the stakeholders, including teachers and students, and warns that "no violence prevention program can or will work in any school" without the presence of this factor [61]. In addition to the evident disconnect from the students, teachers in our study also had mixed opinions about best anti-bullying practices. Overall, we believe the qualitative evidence demonstrates a lack of buy in for anti-bullying interventions, and highlight that conducting elicitation studies are ever so important for ensuring the ecological validity of such programs and grounding their designs in contextual dynamics such as local culture and contemporary challenges.

9 Conclusion

This paper reported on results from a semi-structured interview study with 13 teachers about bullying in local elementary schools. This research was conducted to support the design of *RE-Mind*, an anti-bullying serious game that involves role-playing with social robots and aims to encourage bystander children to intervene against bullying of their peers. We present qualitative findings and discuss how the lessons learned from this research inform the design of the narrative and game dynamics used in *RE-Mind*. This work contributes insights for designing pedagogical serious games and novel anti-bullying interventions.

References

1. Alexiou, A., Schippers, M.C., Oshri, I., Angelopoulos, S.: Narrative and aesthetics as antecedents of perceived learning in serious games. Information Technology & People (2020)
2. Andersen, C.: Learning in "as-if" worlds: cognition in drama in education. Theory Pract. **43**(4), 281–286 (2004)
3. Arnab, S., et al.: Mapping learning and game mechanics for serious games analysis. Br. J. Edu. Technol. **46**(2), 391–411 (2015)
4. Aylett, R.S., Louchart, S., Dias, J., Paiva, A., Vala, M.: FearNot! – an experiment in emergent narrative. In: Panayiotopoulos, T., Gratch, J., Aylett, R., Ballin, D., Olivier, P., Rist, T. (eds.) IVA 2005. LNCS (LNAI), vol. 3661, pp. 305–316. Springer, Heidelberg (2005). https://doi.org/10.1007/11550617_26

---

[2] https://bit.ly/32Ay8wG.

5. Baek, H., Andreescu, V., Rolfe, S.M.: Bullying and fear of victimization: do supportive adults in school make a difference in adolescents' perceptions of safety? J. Sch. Violence **18**(1), 92–106 (2019)
6. Bauman, S., Toomey, R.B., Walker, J.L.: Associations among bullying, cyberbullying, and suicide in high school students. J. Adolesc. **36**(2), 341–350 (2013). https://doi.org/10.1016/j.adolescence.2012.12.001
7. Belpaeme, T., Kennedy, J., Ramachandran, A., Scassellati, B., Tanaka, F.: Social robots for education: a review. Sci. Robot. **3**(21), eaat5954 (2018)
8. Blatner, A.: Drama in education as mental hygiene: a child psychiatrist's perspective. Youth Theatre J. **9**(1), 92–96 (1995)
9. Blatner, A.: Role playing in education. Disponibile all'indirizzo: https://www.blatner.com/adam/pdntbk/rlplayedu.htm (2009)
10. Blatner, A., Blatner, A.: The art of play: helping adults reclaim imagination and spontaneity. Rev. Brunner/Mazel (1997)
11. Braun, V., Clarke, V.: Using thematic analysis in psychology. Qual. Res. Psychol. **3**(2), 77–101 (2006)
12. Cai, Y., van Joolingen, W., Walker, Z. (eds.): VR, Simulations and Serious Games for Education. GMSE, Springer, Singapore (2019). https://doi.org/10.1007/978-981-13-2844-2
13. Carbone-Lopez, K., Esbensen, F.A., Brick, B.T.: Correlates and consequences of peer victimization: gender differences in direct and indirect forms of bullying. Youth Violence Juv. Justice **8**(4), 332–350 (2010). https://doi.org/10.1177/1541204010362954
14. Carmona, J.A., Espínola, M., Cangas, A.J., Iribarne, L.: Mii school: new 3D technologies applied in education to detect drug abuses and bullying in adolescents. In: Lytras, M.D., et al. (eds.) TECH-EDUCATION 2010. CCIS, vol. 73, pp. 65–72. Springer, Heidelberg (2010). https://doi.org/10.1007/978-3-642-13166-0_10
15. Chaim, D.B.: Distance in the Theatre. UMI Research Press, Ann Arbor, Mich (1984)
16. Cowie, H.: Understanding the role of bystanders and peer support in school bullying. Int. J. Emot. Educ. **6**(1), 26–32 (2014)
17. Crothers, L.M., Kolbert, J.B., Barker, W.F.: Middle school students' preferences for anti-bullying interventions. Sch. Psychol. Int. **27**(4), 475–487 (2006)
18. Cunningham, C.E., et al.: What limits the effectiveness of antibullying programs? A thematic analysis of the perspective of teachers. J. Sch. Violence **15**(4), 460–482 (2016). https://doi.org/10.1080/15388220.2015.1095100
19. Dahlbäck, N., Jönsson, A., Ahrenberg, L.: Wizard of Oz studies—why and how. Knowl.-Based Syst. **6**(4), 258–266 (1993)
20. Davidson, J.: Embodied knowledge: possibilities and constraints in arts education and curriculum. In: Bresler, L. (eds) Knowing Bodies, Moving Minds. Landscapes: the Arts, Aesthetics, and Education, vol. 3. Springer, Dordrecht (2004). https://doi.org/10.1007/978-1-4020-2023-0_13
21. Dedousis-Wallace, A., Shute, R.H.: Indirect bullying: predictors of teacher intervention, and outcome of a pilot educational presentation about impact on adolescent mental health. Aust. J. Educ. Dev. Psychol. **9**, 2–17 (2009)
22. Dulmus, C.N., Sowers, K.M., Theriot, M.T.: Prevalence and bullying experiences of victims and victims who become bullies (bully-victims) at rural schools. Veictims and Offenders **1**(1), 15–31 (2006)

23. Enz, S., Zoll, C., Vannini, N., Schneider, W., Hall, L., Paiva, A., Aylett, R.: emotional learning in primary schools: FearNot! an anti-bullying intervention based on virtual role-play with intelligent synthetic characters. Electron. J. e-Learn. **6**(2), 111–118 (2008)
24. Foutsitzi, S., Caridakis, G.: ICT in education: benefits, challenges and new directions. In: 2019 10th International Conference on Information, Intelligence, Systems and Applications (IISA), pp. 1–8. IEEE (2019)
25. Freire, M., Serrano-Laguna, A., Manero, B., Martinez-Ortiz, I., Moreno-Ger, P., Fernandez-Manjon, B.: Game learning analytics: learning analytics for serious games. In: Spector, M.J., Lockee, B.B., Childress, M.D. (eds.), Learning, Design, and Technology, pp. 1–29. Springer (2016). https://doi.org/10.1007/978-3-319-17727-4_21-1
26. Goodwin, J., Bradley, S.K., Donohoe, P., Queen, K., O'Shea, M., Horgan, A.: Bullying in schools: an evaluation of the use of drama in bullying prevention. J. Creat. Ment. Health **14**(3), 329–342 (2019)
27. Hall, L., Jones, S., Paiva, A., Aylett, R.: FearNot!: providing children with strategies to cope with bullying. In: Proceedings of the 8th International Conference on Interaction Design and Children, pp. 276–277. ACM (2009)
28. QSR International: NVivo (2021). www.qsrinternational.com/nvivo-qualitative-data-analysis-software/home
29. Isaacs, J., Hodges, E.V., Salmivalli, C.: Long-term consequences of victimization by peers: a follow-up from adolescence to young adulthood. Int. J. Dev. Sustain. **2**(4), 387–397 (2008)
30. Jeffrey, L.R.: Bullying bystanders. Prev. Res. **11**(3), 7–8 (2004)
31. Jennifer, D., Cowie, H.: Listening to children's voices: moral emotional attributions in relation to primary school bullying. Emot. Behav. Difficulties **17**(3–4), 229–241 (2012). https://doi.org/10.1080/13632752.2012.704314
32. Jimenez-Barbero, J.A., Ruiz-Hernández, J.A., Llor-Zaragoza, L., Pérez-Garcia, M., Llor-Esteban, B.: Effectiveness of anti-bullying school programs: a meta-analysis. Child Youth Serv. Rev. **61**, 165–175 (2016)
33. Kärnä, A., Voeten, M., Little, T.D., Poskiparta, E., Kaljonen, A., Salmivalli, C.: A large-scale evaluation of the KiVa antibullying program: grades 4–6. Child Dev. **82**(1), 311–330 (2011)
34. Katz, I., Lemish, D., Cohen, R., Arden, A.: When parents are inconsistent: parenting style and adolescents' involvement in cyberbullying. J. Adolesc. **74**, 1–12 (2019)
35. Khanolainen, D., Semenova, E., Magnuson, P.: 'Teachers see nothing': exploring students' and teachers' perspectives on school bullying with a new arts-based methodology. Pedagogy Cult. Soc. **29**(3), 469–491 (2021)
36. Konstantopoulou, A.G., Nikolaou, E.N., Fessakis, G.N., Volika, S.P., Markogiannakis, G.M.: Designing interactive digital storytelling as a strategy of raising children's awareness of bullying in preschool education: implications for bullying prevention. Andreas Moutsios-Rentzos **21**(23/09), 91 (2018)
37. Lee, B.K., Patall, E.A., Cawthon, S.W., Steingut, R.R.: The effect of drama-based pedagogy on PreK–16 outcomes: a meta-analysis of research from 1985 to 2012. Rev. Educ. Res. **85**(1), 3–49 (2015)
38. Ligthart, M.E.U., Neerincx, M.A., Hindriks, K.V.: Design patterns for an interactive storytelling robot to support children's engagement and agency. In: Proceedings of the 2020 ACM/IEEE International Conference on Human-Robot Interaction, pp. 409–418 (2020)

39. Loderer, K., Pekrun, R., Plass, J.L.: Emotional foundations of game-based learning (2020)
40. Mavroudis, N., Bournelli, P.: The role of drama in education in counteracting bullying in schools. Cogent Educ. **3**(1), 1233843 (2016)
41. Mazzone, E., Iivari, N., Tikkanen, R., Read, J.C., Beale, R.: Considering context, content, management, and engagement in design activities with children. In: Proceedings of the 9th International Conference on Interaction Design and Children, pp. 108–117 (2010)
42. Mishna, F., Scarcello, I., Pepler, D., Wiener, J.: Teachers' understanding of bullying. Can. J. Educ./Revue canadienne de l'éducation 718–738 (2005)
43. Muñoz, J.E., Dautenhahn, K.: Robo ludens: a game design taxonomy for multiplayer games using socially interactive robots. ACM Trans. Hum.-Robot Interact. **10**(4), 1–28 (2021)
44. Nocentini, A., Zambuto, V., Menesini, E.: Anti-bullying programs and Information and communication technologies (ICTs): a systematic review. Aggress. Violent. Behav. **23**, 52–60 (2015)
45. Norman, D.: The Design of Everyday Things: Revised and Expanded Edition. Basic Books (2013)
46. Nostadt, N., Abbink, D.A., Christ, O., Beckerle, P.: Embodiment, presence, and their intersections: teleoperation and beyond. ACM Trans. Hum.-Robot Interact. **9**(4), 1–19 (2020)
47. Olweus, D.: Bullying at school. In: Huesmann, L.R. (eds.) Aggressive Behavior. The Plenum Series in Social/Clinical Psychology. Springer, Boston (1994). https://doi.org/10.1007/978-1-4757-9116-7_5
48. Olweus, D.: Peer harassment: a critical analysis and some important issues. In: Juvonen, J., Graham, S. (eds.) Peer Harassment in School: The Plight of the Vulnerable and Victimized, pp. 4–18 (2001)
49. Omnicore: TikTok by the Numbers (2021): Stats, Demographics & Fun Facts (2021). www.omnicoreagency.com/tiktok-statistics/
50. Polanin, J.R., Espelage, D.L., Pigott, T.D.: A meta-analysis of school-based bullying prevention programs' effects on bystander intervention behavior. Sch. Psychol. Rev. **41**(1), 47–65 (2012)
51. Rantala, J., Manninen, M., den Berg, M.: Stepping into other people's shoes proves to be a difficult task for high school students: assessing historical empathy through simulation exercise. J. Curric. Stud. **48**(3), 323–345 (2016)
52. Rawlings, J.R., Stoddard, S.A.: A critical review of anti-bullying programs in North American elementary schools. J. Sch. Health **89**(9), 759–780 (2019). https://doi.org/10.1111/josh.12814
53. Ruberg, B.: Empathy and its alternatives: deconstructing the rhetoric of "empathy" in video games. Commun. Cult. Crit. **13**(1), 54–71 (2020)
54. Salmivalli, C.: Bullying and the peer group: a review. Aggress. Violent Behav. **15**(2), 112–120 (2010). https://doi.org/10.1016/j.avb.2009.08.007
55. Salmivalli, C., Kaukiainen, A., Voeten, M.: Anti-bullying intervention: implementation and outcome. Br. J. Educ. Psychol. **75**(3), 465–487 (2005)
56. Sanoubari, E., Johnson, A., Munoz, J.E., Houston, A., Dautenhahn, K.: Using robot-mediated applied drama to foster anti-bullying peer support. In: Robophilosophy (2022)
57. Sanoubari, E., Muñoz Cardona, J.E., Mahdi, H., Young, J.E., Houston, A., Dautenhahn, K.: Robots, bullies and stories: a remote co-design study with children. In: Interaction Design and Children, pp. 171–182 (2021)

58. Sanoubari, E., Young, J., Houston, A., Dautenhahn, K.: Can robots be bullied? A crowdsourced feasibility study for using social robots in anti-bullying interventions. In: 2021 30th IEEE International Conference on Robot & Human Interactive Communication (RO-MAN), pp. 931–938. IEEE (2021)
59. Schell, J.: The Art of Game Design: A Book of Lenses. CRC Press (2008)
60. Ttofi, M.M., Farrington, D.P.: Effectiveness of school-based programs to reduce bullying: a systematic and meta-analytic review. J. Exp. Criminol. 7(1), 27–56 (2011)
61. Twemlow, S.W., Sacco, F.C.: Why School Anti-bullying Programs Don't Work. Jason Aronson (2008)
62. Vaillancourt, T., Brittain, H., Krygsman, A., Farrell, A.H., Landon, S., Pepler, D.: School bullying before and during COVID-19: results from a population-based randomized design. Aggress. Behav. 47(5), 557–569 (2021)
63. Wiseman, A.M., Jones, J.S.: Examining depictions of bullying in children's picture-books: a content analysis from 1997 to 2017. J. Res. Child. Educ. 32(2), 190–201 (2018)
64. Wright, V.H., Burnham, J.J., Christopher, T.I., Heather, N.O.: Cyberbullying: using virtual scenarios to educate and raise awareness. J. Comput. Teach. Educ. 26(1), 35–42 (2009)
65. Zhonggen, Y.: A meta-analysis of use of serious games in education over a decade. Int. J. Comput. Games Technol. 2019 (2019)
66. Zwaan, J., Geraerts, E., Dignum, V., Jonker, C.M.: User validation of an empathic virtual buddy against cyberbullying. Stud. Health Technol. Inform. 181, 243–247 (2012)

Health Games

CogWorldTravel: Design of a Game-Based Cognitive Screening Instrument

Fernanda T. Oliveira[1,2]($\boxtimes$), Brandon W. Tong[1,3], Jaime A. Garcia[1,2], and Valerie C. Gay[2]

[1] University of Technology Sydney (UTS) Games Studio, Sydney, Australia
`Fernanda.TavaresVasconcelosOliveira@student.uts.edu.au`
[2] Faculty of Engineering and IT, UTS, Sydney, Australia
[3] Faculty of Health, UTS, Sydney, Australia

Abstract. Cognitive Screening Instruments are helpful in the early detection of cognitive changes and possible underlying dementia. These instruments test all major cognitive domains of an individual. Serious games have been investigated as an alternative approach for cognitive assessment because of their ability to motivate. Previous work mostly focused on finding out whether it is feasible to use a serious game for such purpose. We decided to investigate further how a serious game can be engaging and fun while prioritizing the cognitive assessment. In this paper, we describe the design, development, and evaluation of CogWorld-Travel, a serious game that has the potential to be used for cognitive screening as it measures at least one aspect of each cognitive domain. CogWorldTravel features six game tasks that involve recognition memory, attention, working memory, language, immediate memory span, processing speed, inhibition, recognition of emotions, visuoconstructional, perceptual-motor, and planning abilities. The serious game also accommodates age-related changes and considers the gameplay preferences of older adults.

Keywords: Serious Games · Games for health · Cognitive screening · Older adults · Dementia

1 Introduction

Older adults are at a greater risk for the onset of dementia, which is characterized by impaired cognition that represents a decline from a previously attained level of functioning [1]. Undiagnosed dementia has severe and expensive consequences for individuals, their families, and society [2]. Cognitive Screening Instruments (CSIs) are used to assist in the assessment of dementia [3]. Although these tools are not diagnostic, they are useful in the early detection of cognitive changes and possible underlying dementia. The detection of cognitive changes is the first step toward accurate diagnosis. Ideally, these instruments should test all major cognitive domains of an individual [4], namely complex attention, executive function, learning and memory, language, perceptual-motor, and social cognition [1].

H. Söbke et al. (Eds.): JCSG 2022, LNCS 13476, pp. 125–139, 2022.
https://doi.org/10.1007/978-3-031-15325-9_10

There are several well-researched CSIs currently used to detect dementia. However, these instruments do have limitations. A relevant barrier to the proper use of such instruments is the time required for administration in clinical settings. It is well known that the environment where the test is undertaken may affect performance [3]. Especially for pen-and-paper-based tests, results may vary across examiners [4]. In addition, most tests are dependent on language, and scores must be validated independently in each language as they may vary when tests are translated. Similarly, educational and cultural biases are evident in many instruments [3]. The development of CSIs that are less sensitive to language, education, and culture is still highly encouraged [5].

Serious games are regarded as games that entertain players while accomplishing another primary purpose. The rationale for using game technology for such serious purposes is its ability to motivate [6]. Serious games have been beneficial in delivering several personalized healthcare solutions for older people [7]. In the last years, considerable attention has been focused on investigating the use of serious games for cognitive screening [8]. Serious games have advantages in overcoming the limitations of traditional CSIs, particularly when compared to pen-and-paper-based tests. Game-based tests ease the administration process. As they can be self-administered, they can be used in clinical settings and remotely. Older adults can play the serious game at home while useful data is being collected and can be shared with a healthcare professional. As total and partial time-based measures for diverse tasks can be collected and scores can be calculated, recorded, and tracked automatically over time, it reduces the risk of biased administration.

Previous research in this field mostly focused on assessing the feasibility of using games for cognitive screening [8]. The common approaches involved collecting data through existing games or developing bespoke games that replicate the mechanics of cognitive tests. From existing games, Gielis et al. explored the Microsoft Solitaire Collection with an additional toolbox that captures digital biomarkers such as time spent thinking before making a move and error during gameplay that may be indicative of planning, executive functioning, or attention decline [9]. Intarasirisawat et al. developed their own version of Tetris, Fruit Ninja, and Candy Crush Saga to be able to collect in-game data through tap and swipe interaction patterns [10]. Siraly et al. analyzed time to complete the classical 'Find the pairs' memory game [11]. Bonnechere et al. investigated using a suite of eight brain training mini-games from the Peak mobile app [12]. Although these commercial or well-known games are fun and engaging, and studies found that a correlation between game performance and cognitive health exists, games that were not built for such purpose do not satisfy the requirements of CSIs, specifically the need to sample all cognitive domains. In addition, commercial games, in general, do not necessarily target older adults, and they have age-related changes that ideally must be addressed when designing for them.

On the other hand, other studies developed bespoke games for cognitive screening. Those bespoke games either simulate activities of daily living or try to replicate activities from traditional tests. Eraslan Boz et al. proposed a virtual supermarket [13], Vallejo et al. [14] and Manera et al. [15] developed virtual cooking tasks to evaluate participant performance in the simulated activities. Hagler et al. created the Scavenger Hunt, which is based on the pen-and-paper Trail Making Test that measures cognitive functioning

[16]. Tong *et al.* proposed The Whack-a-Mole, which is inspired by the classical Go/No-Go Discrimination Task that measures inhibition [17]. Valladares *et al.* presented the Panoramix suite that is based on multiple cognitive tests, including the California Verbal Test, the Pyramids, and Palm-trees test, the Corsi Cubes test, and the Pursuit Rotor Task test [18]. Although bespoke games offer the opportunity to explore different aspects of cognition and provide a measure of all cognitive domains, previous works did not exactly focus on this.

The use of commercial and bespoke games to assess cognitive functioning has demonstrated promising results; however, investigating design approaches to develop an ideal game-based CSI is still an open challenge. An ideal game-based CSI must comply with the criteria for such an instrument [4], satisfy age-related changes of older adults [19], and be engaging and fun for most older adults. In this context, we decided to investigate further how a serious game can be engaging and entertaining while prioritizing cognitive assessment. This paper describes the design, development, and evaluation of CogWorldTravel, a serious game for cognitive screening that measures at least one aspect of each major cognitive domain. The game features six game tasks that involve recognition memory, attention, working memory, language, immediate memory span, processing speed, inhibition, recognition of emotions, visuoconstructional, perceptual-motor and planning abilities.

The following section presents the methodology of this work. In Sect. 3, CogWorldTravel is unfolded. The evaluation of CogWorldTravel is described in Sect. 4. Discussions and conclusions can be found in Sect. 5 and Sect. 6, respectively.

2 Methodology

This section describes the methodology followed to design, develop, and evaluate Cog-WorldTravel. The aged cohort is very diverse, and there was no expectation of designing a 'one-size-fits-all' game. However, as traveling is an experience enjoyed by most people, we started by choosing this topic to revolve the game story around it.

We reviewed the literature, searching for design recommendations for older adults as they have a higher chance of presenting difficulties in hearing, vision, cognition, or mobility [19]. In addition, we reviewed classical CSIs currently used in clinical practices to understand the items contained in those tests and which cognitive aspects they measure. We also considered the features that an ideal CSI must include, as enunciated in the Report of the Committee on Research of the American Neuropsychiatric Association [4]. We reviewed the cognitive domains defined in the latest version of the Diagnostic and Statistical Manual of Mental Disorders (DSM-V), namely complex attention, executive function, learning and memory, language, perceptual-motor, and social cognition. We observed working definitions of each domain, examples of symptoms or observations regarding impairments in everyday activities, and examples of assessments.

After we conducted the literature review and understood the context of the problem, we defined the requirements that would drive the design of the game-based CSI for older adults to ensure the game accommodates age-related changes [20], includes all major cognitive domains [1], and can be administered remotely. The requirements were defined as follows:

The game-based CSI should:

1. avoid small font sizes.
2. use contrasting colors.
3. require simple inputs from the user during gameplay.
4. include slow-paced tasks with a clear objective explained through a tutorial.
5. measure one aspect of complex attention at a minimum.
6. measure one aspect of executive function at a minimum.
7. measure one aspect of learning and memory at a minimum.
8. measure one aspect of language at a minimum.
9. measure one aspect of perceptual-motor at a minimum.
10. measure one aspect of social cognition at a minimum.
11. not rely on literacy level.
12. not rely on language skills unless when assessing it.
13. be playable by older adults in a home environment without the supervision of a trained professional.
14. enable older adults to share their results with a healthcare professional.

The next stage consisted of designing a solution to meet the defined requirements as far as possible. Game tasks were brainstormed and discussed between the authors, and an initial design was agreed upon.

We developed a computer version of the serious game using Unity due to its versatility for developing game prototypes. The game is available at the following link: https://urf riendxd.itch.io/cogworldtravel. The data collected during gameplay are stored in a CSV file and can be shared with a healthcare professional. The Unity built-in recorder package supported the development of tutorials. The computer version of the game would allow us to ask participants to play the game remotely while having a Zoom session with them in case we needed to comply with social distancing restrictions due to COVID-19 throughout the study.

The evaluation of CogWorldTravel consisted of two phases. In the first phase, interviews with five experts in the assessment of dementia were conducted individually. Each mini-game was demonstrated, the rationale was explained, and they were asked whether they believed the mini-game had the potential to provide a measure of the cognitive aspects that it intended [21]. In the second phase, we interviewed six older adults aged 60+. They were asked to play the serious game. Then, we asked the following: (1) if they were able to understand the task from the tutorial, (2) if they had any issues playing the game, (3) if they enjoyed playing the game, and (4) how they would rate the game in terms of difficulty.

3   CogWorldTravel

CogWorldTravel is a serious game that features six game tasks for the assessment of all major cognitive domains. This section describes the structure of each game task, including game elements as defined by Fullerton *et al.* in [22]. Although anyone can play CogWorldTravel, the targeted players are older adults as they are the ones at a greater risk of developing dementia. As the name implies, travelling is the game's theme, and the game tasks are inserted in this context. All game tasks have their foundations in previous research and were refined during the iterative design process that involved stakeholders.

3.1 Familiar Faces

- Story: The player arrives at the airport and finds out that their luggage is gone. They will work closely with security to identify who has their luggage by mistake (see Fig. 1).
- Objective: The goal of the player is to select as many faces as they can without selecting the same face twice.
- Procedure: Sets of six to ten faces will be displayed at a time. The player uses the mouse to select one face. After the face is selected, the whole set disappears, and a new set is displayed, re-ordered, including faces already chosen by the player at any time and at least one face that has never been selected. The same process repeats until the player selects the same face for the second time.
- Rules: The players click on the faces to help security in identifying people, but they cannot click on the same person twice as it would be an awkward situation.
- Conflict: This is a cognitive challenge, and the player may be limited by their own ability to track the faces while performing the task. They need to resolve how to hold up to 50 different faces in memory to be able to go through as many as they can.
- Outcome: The game ends when the player selects someone for the second time, and the data collected during gameplay is the number of faces that were selected before losing the game. It is expected that the number of faces achieved is an indication of recognition memory, sustained attention, and working memory performance, as these are cognitive abilities required in this task and represent elements of the major cognitive domains of learning and memory, complex attention, and executive function, respectively. This game satisfies requirements 5, 6, and 7.
- Rationale: This task was inspired by the Warrington Recognition Memory Test for faces [23], which assesses deficits in recognition memory, which is an important expression of episodic memory. The decline of episodic memory is a hallmark of cognitive dysfunction associated with dementia. In the original test, which has been previously considered to have the ability to detect dementia [24, 25], 50 faces are presented to the participant, and later they are challenged with a pair of faces to identify which one they had seen before.

3.2 Padlock Combination

- Story: After the player retrieves the luggage, they realize they forgot the padlock combination to open it, and they will need to guess (see Fig. 1).
- Objective: The player should form as many words of three or four letters as they can with the given set of four letters from the padlock.
- Procedure: The padlock contains a set of four letters. Using the mouse, the player selects each letter to use it to form words. The player can unselect a letter by clicking again on it or clicking the clear button to delete all letters in one go. Once one word is formed, they click on the submit button. If the word is accepted, a green light appears. If the word exists but has already been submitted, yellow light is displayed. If the letters selected do not form an existing word, a red light is displayed. Each set of letters has a defined number of words that need to be formed. If the player completes it, a new one is given until the two-minute timer is over.

- Rules: The words formed by the player must be composed of three or fours letters and cannot include names. Each letter can only be used once for each word. The combination formed only can be submitted if it is an existing word. The same word cannot be submitted twice.
- Conflict: This task is timed, and the number of words that the player can generate is limited by the time provided to complete the task.
- Outcome: The game ends when the time ends, and the data collected during gameplay is the number of words that were successfully submitted. It is expected that the number of words achieved is an indication of language and working memory performance as these are cognitive abilities required in this task and represent elements of the major cognitive domains of language and executive function, respectively. This game satisfies requirements 6 and 8.
- Rationale: Although it is different due to the elimination of the human component in the administration of the game-based test, the task is inspired by the assessment of language skills of the Montreal Cognitive Assessment (MoCA) [26], where the participant is asked to say as many words as they can starting with a given letter, name low-familiarity animals, and repeat a sentence. In this task, the player uses an element of language to recall words that can be formed with the letters and needs to hold the words already submitted in memory.

3.3   The Metro

- Story: After all luggage-related issues are resolved, it is finally time to enjoy the trip. The player can visit tourist spots around the city using the metro system. A local expert will show those spots on the map (see Fig. 1).
- Objective: Memorize and repeat the longest sequence of highlighted stations as possible.
- Procedure: The player will see a metro map. The stations on the map will be highlighted. The player needs to repeat the sequence highlighted by using the mouse to click on the stations in the same order that they were shown. The game starts with a sequence of three stations. The player has two trials to attempt to repeat a three-stations-long sequence. If at least one sequence is correctly repeated, the next sequence displayed will be incremented by one station. The process repeats until the player cannot repeat any of the two trials of a given length.
- Rules: Two different sequences of the same number of stations will be displayed. One station is added to the number of stations highlighted if the player successfully repeats at least one of the sequences. The trial ends when the player selects the expected number of stations, even if it is not correct.
- Conflict: This is a cognitive challenge, and the player may be limited by their own immediate memory span ability.
- Outcome: The game ends when the player is not able to repeat at least one of the trials for a given length. The data collected during gameplay is the maximum length achieved and the total number of correct repetitions. It is expected that these data collected will provide an indication of immediate memory span, which is an element of the learning and memory domain. This game satisfies requirements 7.

– Rationale: This task was inspired by the Corsi Blocks Test, which requires memorization of relative positions in space in a temporal order. The test consists of nine square blocks positioned on a board [27]. The examiner taps the blocks starting with sequences of two cubes. The participant has to reproduce the sequence by tapping the blocks in the same order. The test has been considered the single most important nonverbal task in cognitive assessment [28].

3.4 Native Fauna

– Story: One of the places visited by the player is the beach. The player is instructed to take photos of the native wildlife at the beach (see Fig. 1).
– Objective: The player should take photos of flamingos that appear on the screen as quickly as possible and avoid photographing the coconuts.
– Procedure: The player goes around the screen with the mouse, which replicates the view from the lenses of a photographic camera. They should stay alert to the appearance of the flamingos on the screen. They must click on the flamingos as quickly as possible. Coconuts will also randomly appear as distractions, and the player must avoid taking photos of them.
– Rules: The player must click on the target (Flamingos) and avoid the distractions (coconuts). A green light is displayed when a target is hit, and red light is displayed when a distraction is hit.
– Conflict: Coconuts are included to test inhibition. The player must stop themselves from responding when coconuts are seen.
– Outcome: The player will be exposed to a defined number of targets and distractions, and the data collected during gameplay include reaction time, correct photos taken (target), wrong photos taken (distraction), and missed targets. It is expected that the data collected will provide a measure of processing speed, inhibition, and sustained attention, which are elements of complex attention and executive function. This game satisfies requirements 5 and 6.
– Rationale: The task replicates the same mechanics of the letter A item from the MoCA [26], where the participant listens to a list of letters and claps hands every time they listen to the letter A. One advantage of the game over the classical test is the ability to provide time-based measures, which enables the measurement of reaction time. Reaction time is acknowledged as an important parameter of cognitive efficiency [29]. The addition of the distraction element in the game also provides a measure of inhibition as it tests the ability to stop yourself from responding to a stimulus. This is measured in the go/no-go [30] cognitive test.

3.5 Messaging Home

– Story: The player has a little break from the trip to check in on their family back home. They talk to a family member through a messaging app (see Fig. 1).
– Objective: The goal of the player in this game task is to select the correct sticker that will support the conversation.

– Procedure: A text conversation between the player and their daughter is displayed. In the conversation, feelings are mentioned. The player is asked to choose a sticker to support the feeling mentioned in the conversation from a set of six faces expressing the basic emotions: happy, sad, angry, surprised, disgusted, and scared. All six emotions will be mentioned once, but the player is not aware of this beforehand.
– Rules: The player must choose one face at a time to support the feeling in the conversation. There are six faces and six trials. Once a face is selected, the conversation continues.
– Conflict: The correct face is shown among five other faces, and the player is limited by their ability to recognize emotions in faces when selecting it.
– Outcome: There is no losing criteria or time limit. The player can take their time to select the most appropriate face. The data collected during gameplay is the total number of correct faces of six trials. It is expected that it will provide a measure of recognition of emotions, which is one aspect of social cognition. This game satisfies requirement 10.
– Rationale: Social cognitive deficits are commonly seen in people with dementia [31], even though this domain is often overlooked in classical and game-based instruments. The game task is very similar to the Emotion Recognition Task [32], with the difference that the emotions are inserted in the context of the trip rather than simply showing a word.

3.6   Time to Pack

– Story: At the end of the trip, the player must pack their luggage before flying home (See Fig. 1).
– Objective: The player should place tetrominoes-shaped items inside suitcases and complete as many suitcases as they can.
– Procedure: The tetrominoes-shaped items will be displayed to the player alongside a suitcase. The player needs to organize the items inside the suitcase, and they may need to rotate the items. Items are rotated 90 degrees clockwise by selecting them and clicking the right mouse button, or pressing the space bar. Items must be dragged and dropped inside the suitcases. Once all items are placed inside the suitcase, it closes, and a new empty suitcase and new items are provided. This repeats until the two-minute timer is over.
– Rules: Players can drag and drop items inside and outside the suitcases. The player can change the position of the items as many times as they wish after placing them inside the suitcase. If the timer is over, the player cannot continue with the suitcase they were packing at that moment.
– Conflict: This is a cognitive challenge where items need to fit inside the suitcase perfectly. No spaces can be left. The game is limited by time.
– Outcome: The game ends when the time ends, and the data collected during gameplay is the number of suitcases completed in the given time. It is expected that it will provide a measure of visuoconstructional, perceptual-motor, and planning abilities, which are aspects of perceptual-motor and executive function. This game satisfies requirements 6 and 9.

– Rationale: This task was inspired by the Tetris puzzle game, which has been considered to involve rapid visual-spatial problem-solving and motor coordination skills [33].

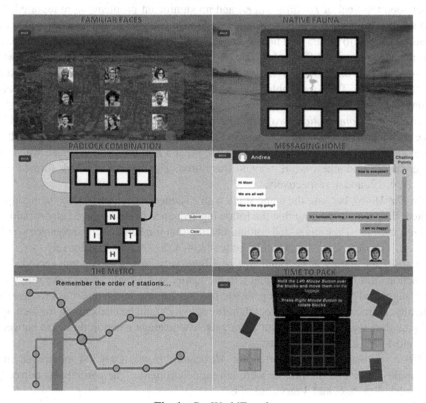

Fig. 1. CogWorldTravel.

4 The Evaluation of CogWorldTravel

In the first phase of the evaluation of CogWorldTravel, we interviewed five experts in the assessment of dementia. In general, the experts liked the concept of the game and assessed that *Familiar Faces* could provide a measure of recognition memory, attention, and working memory. *Padlock Combination* could provide a measure of executive function and a component of language. *The Metro* could provide a measure of immediate memory span, visual scanning, and visual awareness. *Native Fauna* could provide a measure of processing speed, sustained attention, and inhibition. *Messaging Home* could provide a measure of recognition of emotions. Finally, *Time to Pack* could measure perceptual-motor, attention, planning, and manipulation of visuospatial information. Further details on the evaluation of CogWorldTravel through the interviews with experts are described in [21].

In the second phase of the evaluation process, we tested the game with six participants, referred to as P1, P2, P3, P4, P5, and P6. The eligibility criteria considered during the recruitment included being 60 years old or older, speaking English fluently, and being able to consent. In total, four female and two male participants joined the study. Five understood the goal of *Familiar Faces,* and no significant problems were reported. P3 said she had an issue relating the game's story with the goal of the task but still knew what she needed to do. P5 said he was confused with the thumbs-up that appeared each time the player chose a different face. He said that it seems like you found the person who has your suitcase but actually, it means you are doing well in the game and not choosing the same person. They were able to select 25, 1, 27, 4, 6, and 21 faces, respectively, before making a mistake.

In *Padlock Combination*, two participants missed that the words could be formed by three or four letters. P3 said that because of the analogy with a padlock, she was expecting to see numbers instead of letters. P4 suggested that a hint could be provided when the player cannot find a new word to avoid frustration. The number of words formed was 12, 6, 5, 6, 12, and 4, respectively.

In *The Metro*, because the game starts with a sequence of three stations being highlighted, they were expecting that the following sequence to be displayed also would be of three stations. They suggested communicating that the length of the sequence would increase. The maximum length achieved was 3, 4, 4, 5, 3, and 4, respectively.

Two of the participants found *Native Fauna* very fast. The coconut included as distractions did not make a difference in the game, as the participants have rarely hit it. P5 suggested that the distraction should be more similar to the target to increase the difficulty. P4 mentioned that the length of the activity could be challenging for their age group as they were expected to hit 50 targets. The average reaction time was between 1.60 and 1.90 s for all participants.

No major issues were reported for *Messaging Home.* Only P4 mentioned that she would prefer that the images were not monochromatic. The participants correctly selected 4, 3, 5, 6, 6, and 4 faces out of 6.

Time to Pack was expected to be the most challenging game due to the need to rotate the blocks. Indeed, P1 and P5 reported issues handling the mouse and rotating the items. The other participants did not have any problems. They completed 1, 1, 3, 3, 2, and 2 suitcases.

5   Discussion

CogWorldTravel is a serious game that has the potential to measure the cognitive performance of older adults while entertaining them both in clinical settings and remotely. The assessment of cognitive performance is particularly important for the early detection of dementia, which is beneficial for individuals, their families, and society. We expect that the introduction of game elements can alleviate the anxiety of taking a test, motivate users, and improve the user experience.

The design process was particularly challenging because of the interdisciplinary nature of this research. We had to come up with game tasks that at the same time engage and entertain, accommodate the special needs of older adults, and involve different cognitive aspects. To accomplish all of that, we defined a set of requirements and chose to proceed with a bespoke game to satisfy them as far as possible. The relationship between the requirements, the design, and the verification method is presented in Table 1.

Table 1. Requirements, design, and verification.

Requirement ID	How the requirement is met	How the requirement is verified
1	Choice of font size	Test with older adults
2	Choice of colors	Test with older adults
3	Tasks can be completed with mouse clicks	Test with older adults
4	Choice of game tasks	Test with older adults
5	Included in familiar faces and Native fauna	Analysis by experts
6	Included in familiar faces, Padlock combination, Native fauna, and Time to pack	Analysis by experts
7	Included in familiar faces and The metro	Analysis by experts
8	Included in padlock combination	Analysis by experts
9	Included in time to pack	Analysis by experts
10	Included in messaging home	Analysis by experts
11	Choice of game tasks	Analysis by experts
12	Choice of game tasks	Analysis by experts
13	Tool delivered as a serious game	Test with older adults
14	Total and partial scores are automatically recorded	Test with older adults

In order to target the aged cohort, we defined requirements 1 to 4 and took them into consideration when designing the game. We considered that players might have low familiarity with computers and designed game tasks that do not require advanced computer skills. Most tasks can be completed only by clicking with the mouse, except for the *Time to Pack* task, where clicking with both mouse buttons and drag and drop are required. We expected players to concentrate on completing the task rather than on the user interaction. In addition, we have carefully chosen contrasting colors, avoided small font sizes, and involved older adults to ensure most average older adults would not have problems playing the game.

Requirements 5 to 10 were included to ensure the serious game would satisfy the requirements of a CSI. CogWorldTravel measures at least one aspect of the six major cognitive domains of an individual. From the complex attention domain, sustained attention and processing speed are included. From the executive function domain, planning, working memory, overriding habits, and inhibition are included. From the learning and memory domain, immediate memory span and recent memory are included. From the language domain, expressive language is included, and receptive language is required throughout the game. From the perceptual-motor domain, visuoconstructional and perceptual-motor are included. Finally, recognition of emotions is included to represent social cognition skills. Experts in the assessment of dementia were involved to verify if the game had the potential to measure the cognitive element that it intended to measure.

Satisfying requirements 11 and 12 and designing tasks that were not reliant on literacy and language required considerable thought. We designed the tasks to be valid when translating to other languages. Except for the instructions on how to play each game task and the conversation surrounding the stated emotion in *Messaging Home*, the tasks are independent of language. We verified this by analysis with the involvement of stakeholders. We wanted the language to be involved only in the occasion of measuring this specific skill. The language-related task still needs to be validated when translating to other languages. Likewise, we attempt to design game tasks that people with any level of education could perform in a reasonably fair manner. Recognition of faces, recognition of emotions, assembly of items, memorizing highlighted stations in a metro map, and taking photos of an animal as quickly as possible are activities that do not seem to be highly influenced by education or even culture.

Other specific aspects of the game tasks required some consideration. In *Familiar Faces*, we expected that similarity among the displayed faces could affect the performance of the player. The difficulty of the task would increase if the faces included had similar age, gender, and ethnicity. In *Padlock Combination*, we were specifically concerned that people could be stuck if the words to be formed were not commonly used words. To avoid that, we decided that the person would not need to form all possible words before moving to the next set of letters. In addition, we noticed the difficulty of the task was associated with the arrangement of the set of letters. It is much easier to visualize and find words if the letters are organized in the shape of a cross when compared to if the letters were in a linear arrangement. In *The Metro*, the speed at which the stations are highlighted affects the difficulty of the task. If it is very slow, people will have to hold it in working memory for longer before starting. If it is very fast, they have a reduced chance to encode it in memory before the next one appears. In *Native Fauna*, we decided that the number of flamingos should be the same amount of A's in the letter A task of the MoCA if we wanted those tasks to be comparable. In *Messaging Home*, we decided that the name of the emotion needed to be clearly stated rather than allowing people to determine how they would feel about the described situation because the feelings of people may vary when facing the same situation.

We developed the tutorials for the mini-games using the Unity built-in recorder package. Before the start of each mini-game, a video and a set of instructions were shown to the player. From the interviews with the participants, we observed that video-based tutorials are confusing for the aged cohort. All participants could not differentiate the video from the actual game.

Finally, this serious game was implemented as a computer version due to COVID-19 restrictions and the possibility of testing via Zoom meeting; however, a tablet version could still facilitate further as touching the screen is more intuitive than using the mouse. Either way, both versions would allow remote administration and satisfy requirements 13 and 14.

6 Conclusion and Future Work

This paper describes the design, development, and evaluation of a serious game for cognitive screening. This new game is an example of how to involve different aspects of cognition in game tasks. CogWorldTravel focused on sampling at least one aspect of each major cognitive domain to comply with the requirement of an ideal cognitive screening instrument. In addition, our careful design ensures that the game is appropriate to be played by older adults. Age-related changes were carefully considered to provide a smooth experience to the aged cohort. The tasks included in the game are slow-paced and have simple objectives. The inputs required from the player are straightforward, which makes the game suitable for people with low familiarity with computers.

The game sample one aspect of each cognitive domain; however, not every element of each cognitive domain is included. There are many opportunities to improve Cog-WorldTravel. Games offer many options to test different aspects of cognition. The first improvement to this game will be the inclusion of a task to measure delayed recall, as it is an important parameter that healthcare professionals analyse during a clinical assessment. Another way of enhancing this serious game will be the development of a task to measure cognitive flexibility, which is another important aspect of the executive function. The assessment of different aspects of each cognitive domain is helpful for clinicians in differentiating diagnosis. Therefore, the development of serious games to measure as many cognitive aspects as possible is encouraged.

Acknowledgment. This research is supported by an Australian Government Research Training Program Scholarship and the 2021 Social Impact Grant from the University of Technology Sydney (UTS). Ethics approval UTS HREC REF NO. ETH21-6304.

References

1. American Psychiatric, A.: Diagnostic and Statistical Manual of Mental Disorders (DSM-5®). American Psychiatric Publishing, Washington (2013)
2. Rasmussen, J., Langerman, H.: Alzheimer's disease - why we need early diagnosis. Degenerative Neurol. Neuromuscul. Dis. **9**, 123–130 (2019)
3. Larner, A.J.: Cognitive Screening Instruments: A Practical Approach. Larner, A.J. (ed.) Springer, London (2013)
4. Malloy, P., et al.: Cognitive screening instruments in neuropsychiatry: a report of the committee on research of the American neuropsychiatric association. J. Neuropsychiatry Clin. Neurosci. **9**, 189–197 (1997)
5. Molnar, F.J., et al.: One size does not fit all: choosing practical cognitive screening tools for your practice. J. Am. Geriatr. Soc. **68**(10), 2207–2213 (2020)

6. Johnson, D., et al.: Gamification for health and wellbeing: a systematic review of the literature. Internet Interv. **6**, 89–106 (2016)

7. Martinho, D., Carneiro, J., Corchado, J.M., Marreiros, G.: A systematic review of gamification techniques applied to elderly care. Artif. Intell. Rev. **53**(7), 4863–4901 (2020). https://doi.org/10.1007/s10462-020-09809-6

8. Valladares-Rodríguez, S., et al.: Trends on the application of serious games to neuropsychological evaluation: a scoping review. J. Biomed. Inform. **64**, 296–319 (2016)

9. Gielis, K., et al.: Collecting digital biomarkers on cognitive health through computer vision and gameplay: an image processing toolkit for card games. In: 2019 IEEE International Conference on Healthcare Informatics (ICHI), IEEE (2019)

10. Intarasirisawat, J., et al.: Exploring the touch and motion features in game-based cognitive assessments. Proc. ACM Interact. Mob. Wearable Ubiquitous Technol. **3**(3), 1–25 (2019)

11. Sirály, E., et al.: Monitoring the early signs of cognitive decline in elderly by computer games: an MRI study. PLOS ONE **10**(2), e0117918 (2015)

12. Bonnechère, B., et al.: Evaluation of cognitive functions of aged patients using video games. ACM, pp. 21–24 (2016)

13. Eraslan Boz, H., et al.: A new tool to assess amnestic mild cognitive impairment in Turkish older adults: virtual supermarket (VSM). Neuropsychol. Dev. Cogn. B Aging Neuropsychol. Cogn. **27**(5), 639–653 (2020)

14. Vallejo, V., et al.: Evaluation of a new serious game based multitasking assessment tool for cognition and activities of daily living: comparison with a real cooking task. Comput. Hum. Behav. **70**, 500–506 (2017)

15. Manera, V., et al.: "Kitchen and cooking", a serious game for mild cognitive impairment and Alzheimer's disease: a pilot study. Front. Aging Neurosci. **7**, 24 (2015)

16. Hagler, S., Jimison, H., Pavel, M.: Assessing executive function using a computer game: computational modeling of cognitive processes. Biomed. Health Inf. IEEE J. **18**, 1442–1452 (2014)

17. Tong, T., Chignell, M., DeGuzman, C.A.: Using a serious game to measure executive functioning: response inhibition ability. Appl. Neuropsychol. Adult **28**(6), 673–684 (2019)

18. Valladares-Rodriguez, S., et al.: Design process and preliminary psychometric study of a video game to detect cognitive impairment in senior adults. PeerJ **5**, e3508–e3508 (2017)

19. Gamberini, L., et al.: Cognition, technology and games for the elderly: an introduction to ELDERGAMES project. PsychNology J. **4**(3), 285–308 (2006)

20. Machado, M.D.C., Ferreira, R.L.R., Ishitani, L.: Heuristics and recommendations for the design of mobile serious games for older adults. (Research article). Int. J. Comput. Games Technol. **2018**, 1–15 (2018)

21. Tavares Vasconcelos Oliveira, F., Gay, V., Garcia Marin, J.: Evaluation of CogWorldTravel: a serious game for cognitive screening. In: 10th International Conference on Serious Games and Applications for Health, SeGAH 2022, Sydney, Australia (2022)

22. Fullerton, T., Swain, C., Hoffman, S.: Game Design Workshop: A Playcentric Approach to Creating Innovative Games. CRC Press, London (2008)

23. Warrington, E.K.: Recognition memory test: Manual. Nfer-Nelson (1984)

24. Soukup, V.M., Bimbela, A. and Schiess, M.C.: Recognition memory for faces: reliability and validity of the Warrington recognition memory test (RMT) in a neurological sample. J. Clin. Psychol. Med. Settings **6**(3), 287–293 (1999)

25. Diesfeldt, H.F.A.: Recognition memory for words and faces in primary degenerative dementia of the Alzheimer type and normal old age. J. Clin. Exp. Neuropsychol. **12**(6), 931–945 (1990)

26. Nasreddine, Z.S., et al.: The montreal cognitive assessment, MoCA: a brief screening tool for mild cognitive impairment. J. Am. Geriatr. Soc. **53**(4), 695–699 (2005)

27. Corsi, P.M.: Human memory and the medial temporal region of the brain (1972)

28. Berch, D.B., et al.: The corsi block-tapping task: methodological and theoretical considerations. Brain Cogn.**38**(3), 317–338 (1998)

29. Collins, L.F., Long, C.J.: Visual reaction time and its relationship to neuropsychological test performance. Arch. Clin. Neuropsychol. **11**(7), 613–623 (1996)

30. Yechiam, E., et al., A formal cognitive model of the go/no-go discrimination task: evaluation and implications. Psychol. Assess. **18**(3), 239 (2006)

31. McCade, D., Savage, G., Naismith, S.L.: Review of emotion recognition in mild cognitive impairment. Dement. Geriatr. Cogn. Disord. **32**(4), 257–266 (2011)

32. Montagne, B., et al.: The emotion recognition task: a paradigm to measure the perception of facial emotional expressions at different intensities. Percept Mot Skills **104**(2), 589–598 (2007)

33. Haier, R.J., et al.: MRI assessment of cortical thickness and functional activity changes in adolescent girls following three months of practice on a visual-spatial task. BMC. Res. Notes **2**(1), 174 (2009)

A Serious Game for a Serious Situation: Encouraging Healthy Behaviors for Children with ASD During COVID-19 Pandemic

Menna Elshahawy[1]([✉])(iD), Said Mostafa[1](iD), and Nada Sharaf[2](iD)

[1] Department of Computer Science, Faculty of Media Engineering and Technology,
German University in Cairo, Cairo, Egypt
menna.elshahawy@guc.edu.eg, said.elhamamsy@student.guc.edu.eg
[2] Faculty of Informatics and Computer Science,
The German International University Egypt, Cairo, Egypt
nada.hamed@giu-uni.de

Abstract. During the past two years, several announcements that are possibly perceived as scary were made about the COVID-19 pandemic and the safety regulations people should follow. Those announcements affected everyone, especially children with Autism Spectrum Disorder since they find difficulties coping with the changes caused by the pandemic. Helping them to adapt during those extraordinary circumstances is even more demanding for their families and caregivers. Hence, as a solution, we designed, developed, and evaluated a serious game that promotes healthy behaviors that are most important during the pandemic for them. The game design follows the guidelines in literature for designing a User Interface suitable for children with ASD. Our preliminary experimental study shows that the presented game is engaging for children with ASD.

Keywords: Serious games · Autism Spectrum Disorder · Healthcare · Special education · Coronavirus

1 Introduction

Autism spectrum disorder (ASD) is a range of neurodevelopmental disorders that affect one's ability to interpret and process what they see, hear, or sense. [12]. That affects their social behavior, interactions, relationships, and coping with change. ASD is one of the most prevalent disorders, with statistics showing that 1 in 54 children is on the spectrum in the United States, and prevalence increases between 10% and 17% every year [3]. The prevalence of ASD among children with developmental disorders in Egypt was reported to be 33.6% [16]. Technology-Based interventions for children with ASD have proven to be more effective than traditional methods in teaching them different skills if applied

H. Söbke et al. (Eds.): JCSG 2022, LNCS 13476, pp. 140–154, 2022.
https://doi.org/10.1007/978-3-031-15325-9_11

in the early stages of their development [9,19]. Technology was reported to be amongst the most effective methods for teaching skills and changing behaviours in a safe and fun way.

Numerous studies have addressed the usage of serious games as interventions for teaching individuals with ASD several essential skills. The skills introduced in previous studies include; the concept of money [11], how to cross the street [1], and basic programming skills [7,8]. Moreover, researchers utilized games as an attempt to change behaviors such as maintaining eye contact during a conversation [6] and exercising regularly [10]. The evaluation of those studies demonstrates that serious games motivate children with ASD to learn skills and change behaviors in an engaging and safe environment. Furthermore, transferring this to real-life situations effectively when used for a proper time.

The World Health Organization (WHO) declared the coronavirus (COVID-19) outbreak a global pandemic on March 11, 2020 [26]. COVID-19 has impacted everyone negatively. Individuals with ASD are among the most affected population. They have difficulties tolerating uncertainty and coping with unexpected changes [18]. As a result, families with children with ASD may be at risk for anxiety and mental disorders during quarantine. Researchers expect that people might not return to activities they made before the pandemic and that they will continue following the same safety regulations [18]. Technology should be used to help children with ASD cope with new changes in routines and learn new behaviors to protect themselves.

2   Previous Work

Multiple studies reported that Serious Games (SGs) encourage the development of communication, learning, and social behavior in individuals with ASD. On the other hand, traditional therapeutic and evaluation approaches were not as constructive [23]. This is because SGs create personalized interactive environments aimed to improve the learning outcome for them.

Most of the SGs designed and developed for individuals with ASD concentrate on therapy, education (learning and training), and social communication skills improvement [23]. Various methods of SGs were introduced and used to help children with ASD. Several games used the concept of "Immersive Serious Games" which includes using Augmented Reality (AR), Virtual Reality (VR), and Mixed Reality (MR) in the learning game to provide a realistic and relatable environment for the players. That can minimize the concerns related to learning transfer and support the generalization of children with autism education [13].

Serious Games Design for children with ASD

Researchers have shown ten ingredients that can make a great game in general. Employing some of these ingredients can enhance serious games developed for children with ASD [9]. Table 1 portrays the mentioned ten ingredients. Each of those ingredients improves the effectiveness and engagement of serious games.

Table 1. "Ten ingredients of great games [9]"

Num.	Ingredients of great games
1	Self representation with avatars
2	Three-dimensional environments
3	Narrative context
4	Feedback
5	Reputations, ranks and levels
6	Marketplace and Economy
7	Competition under rules that are explicit and enforce
8	Teams
9	Parallel communication systems
10	Time pressure

Additionally, the study in [9] shows that it is beneficial to indicate rules that are explicit and easy to understand for children with ASD. It also shows that most of the technology-based interventions examined used only one game rule at a time. This method eliminates the additional distractions and thus simplifies the SG for children with ASD. It is also highly reasonable to use 3D context within games for children with ASD since children with ASD tend to react positively to visual input [17,24]. Moreover, it is crucial to include a rewarding system in the games to assist children with autism figure out if they are doing their tasks the correct way. Keeping this reward unified across the game helps the children stay focused and maximizes their learning gains [20].

The process of designing an SG for children with ASD should incorporate the instructor or the caregiver responsible for the children [5]. That helps gather helpful information and insights on the performance of each player. It also ensures that children are comfortable while using any platform. MEDIUS [5] is a serious game that accomplished that by adding a database accessible to the instructors. Instructors can preview data about users' favorite color, font, scores, attempts, and concentration ratios. Concentration was measured by adding face tracking and then calculating the focus time and distraction time ratios. Consequently, help instructors make better decisions and help with future interventions.

Healthcare Serious Games for children with ASD

Several SGs were invented to teach children healthy behavior during the pandemic, such as "Can you save the world?". The game helps children understand the importance of social distancing during the coronavirus pandemic. The game helps children understand the importance of social distancing during the coronavirus pandemic. During the game, players are supposed to save lives by keeping away from others in busy areas. The goal of the game is to save as many lives as possible. Even though several games for healthcare target children, a few of them target children with ASD who require extra guidelines for the interfaces designed.

As mentioned earlier, children with ASD experience changing routines as a major and a tough challenge. Hence, the need for adaptation during the COVID-19 pandemic may have caused significant problems for families and caregivers with children on the spectrum [2]. During the past two years, experts forced new behaviors to protect people from getting infected, and our routines changed severely. Those changes include disinfecting our hands, not touching our mouths and nose, and regularly wearing masks [14]. Thus, researchers should exert an effort to ease those challenges and assist caregivers in protecting children with ASD.

Due to those facts, researchers and developers should deliver solutions to help them cope. Research suggests that gamifying positive social behavior can influence individuals' actions in the real world [2]. The use of serious games introduces an easily accessible and fun intervention for children with autism and might help them adapt and cope with the changes made by the coronavirus, which is an effective way to encounter the sudden changes and avoid stress and anxiety caused by it [13]. Some of the positive social behaviors to introduce in serious games are:1) Using masks and sanitizers 2) Maintaining social distance 3) Taking care of hygiene. The use of SGs helps individuals with autism spend more fun time at home. Hence, helping with the challenge of altering their routine and staying home during the pandemic, and at the same time, the use of serious games helps them learn positive social behavior.

3 Game Design

The presented SG aims to teach children with ASD the essential healthcare, hygiene tips, and behaviors to keep them safe during the COVID-19 pandemic. Literature was first reviewed to extract the guidelines for interfaces designed for children with ASD. The outcome of this stage was a list of the essential UI guidelines mentioned in studies [13,20,25]. Those guidelines include, for instance, eliminating the distractions within the screen, having a minimal number of choices, animating images, and adding voice-over commentary.The SG constitutes of the following stages:

1. **Customization:** the player gets to set up their game (Name - Gender - Language). The player personalizes the game visuals by choosing the font and the background color. The player can change any of the options throughout the game.
2. **Tutorial:** At the beginning of the game, the player gets an animated tutorial with audio commentary and subtitles explaining the COVID-19 situation in a friendly way. The player then gets tested on the simple tasks used in the Game stage as microgames (Social Distancing - Advice - Giving items like [masks - hand sanitizers]).

3. **Game:** The player gets introduced to a 3D map and a 3D character. The player should control the 3D humanoid character to walk around the map. The objective of the game is to help as many people around the map as they can using the previously mentioned tasks. While helping people, the player needs to protect themselves by using the correct healthy behaviors when they meet people.

Customization. Providing the ability to choose different aspects such as the difficulty level and preferred language has positive impacts when teaching children with ASD [25]. Thus, in the first stage of the game, the user tailors the interface to match their needs. The player enters information (Name - Age - Gender) and customizes preferences (Font - Favorite color). Before getting to know the user's favorite color, the default background color is clear white. The font text of the buttons is grey and has black shadows. The dialogue text is white and is backed with a grey background panel to apply contrast to the white background as depicted in the Fig. 1.

The usage of minimal colors and animations was to avoid confusion and distraction. As researchers have proven that children with ASD love to explore the environment and player controls [22]. Thus, one 3D character is present in the game to help players feel engaged. The character's emotions also change every time the player clicks next. Controls that are not required to finish the levels were disabled.

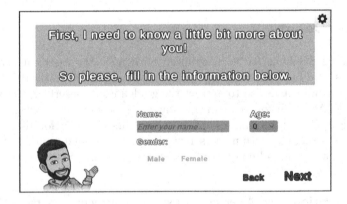

Fig. 1. Information entering screen

Tutorial. The player gets an animated tutorial with Arabic voice-over commentary and on-screen subtitles. The player then goes through multiple tests to evaluate if they learned from the video. This is a preparation stage for the actual game. After passing the tests, the player is automatically directed to the main game.

The player meets the characters who will guide them throughout the game. The game presents the player with the characters using a voice-over commentary. The player can turn the subtitles and the voice-over on or off. To effectively explain the COVID-19 situation in a child-friendly way, the virus is portrayed by two evil-looking characters with funny Arabic names (Mashmoosh and Do'rom). The game portryas the guides with two characters who list the instructions and guide the players throughout the game (Dr. Nahla and Nurse Basma). The characters are shown in Fig. 2.

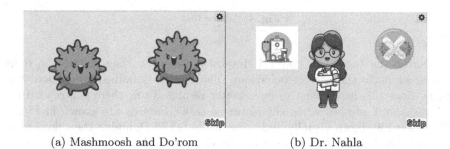

(a) Mashmoosh and Do'rom   (b) Dr. Nahla

Fig. 2. Introducing characters to player

(a) Washing Hands   (b) Keeping Distance

Fig. 3. Tutorial instructions

The second component is the testing part. We test the players to check if they have learned the controllers they will use throughout the game. This happens using three main tests. Each test corresponds to one of the missions presented within the game. Those tests are as follows:

1. Giving advice to someone who is confused about the correct action during the pandemic, as shown in Fig. 4.
2. Giving items to people in need (Mask - Hand Sanitizer), as depicted in Fig. 5.
3. Helping people keep distance to achieve social distancing. This is shown in Fig. 6.

(a) Test   (b) Test Passed

Fig. 4. Advice test

During the tests, the player is rewarded whenever they choose the right answer or make the correct behaviour. The reward is unified throughout the game, since this has proven to have better results. Thus, there is a reward for sub-tasks and another when completing a task. Rewards are shown in Fig. 7. The reward is shown visually and acoustically by: 1) Dimming the color of the screen in the background. 2) Showing the character celebrating with confetti in the background. 3) Playing the reward sound.

Game Stage: After finishing the tutorial and passing the tests successfully, the player is ready to start the game. The player can move their character freely along the map. The map contains interactable 3D buildings that allow them to enter the home layout, store layout, or start a mission. Missions are the same as what was previously presented during the tutorial stage and use the same objectives mentioned.

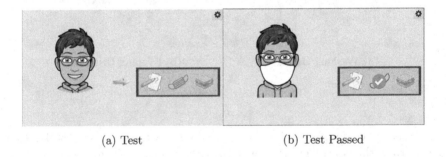

(a) Test   (b) Test Passed

Fig. 5. Items test

(a) Test   (b) Test passed

Fig. 6. Social distancing test

The player also gets introduced to their health bar which decreases as they meet people through missions. Figure 8 shows the 3D environment and the components it consists of. The components are: 1) 3D character 2) Character status 3) Interactable 3D buildings 4) Inventory 5) Health bar 6) Background 7) Ground.

3D Character: The character based on the gender chosen in stage one is generated in this stage. The presence of a character that matches the gender of the player was reported by researchers to help children with ASD identify themselves throughout the game [21]. Each character has three animations (Idle - walking - running).

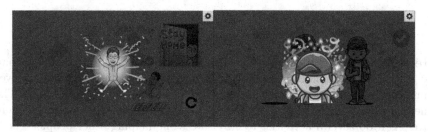

(a) Reward for sub-tasks   (b) Reward when completing a task

Fig. 7. Rewarding mechanism

Character Status: For both characters, 2D stickers were created to represent the status of the player. As shown in Fig. 9. The player status could be one of the following: 1) Having a mask on (Also shows the number of masks left). 2) Having no mask on. 3) Having a sanitizer. 4) Being able to use their sanitizer (Health is not full and sanitizer is with player).

Fig. 8. Game overview

Fig. 9. Characters' status

Interactable 3D Buildings: The player can move freely around the map and interact with buildings by getting close to their radius. Once the player approaches a building, a panel appears that is unique for each building. The panel shows the content of the building. Figure 10 shows the Home UI where players can do several activities to stay safe while helping other people. Those activities include wearing a mask, using a hand sanitizer, washing hands for 20 s. The player can also go to the store, found on map, where they can buy items they need to fulfill the missions' requirements.

Interacting with **Missions** is shown in Fig. 11. The figure shows the mission where the players can help people with three objectives that were in the tutorial stage with the risk of getting contaminated and losing some health due to contact with people. The health they lose depends on whether they are wearing a mask. Passing a mission turns the red indicator to green and allows the players to access the next one.

Fig. 10. Home interactable

Fig. 11. Mission UI

Inventory: Players can access an inventory, shown in Fig. 12, where they can view and modify their owned items. Inventory have three item slots that can carry either a mask or a hand sanitizer. Inventory items can be deleted and replaced. Items can only be used during missions, and can be refilled from the store.

Health Bar: The health bar indicates the player's current health and shows it visually on the screen with colors that change with the change of the current health's value using the color gradient shown in Fig. 13.

Background: The background color for the map as well as the UI elements' background are both set to the previously chosen favorite color and can be changed through settings. This is depicted in Fig. 14.

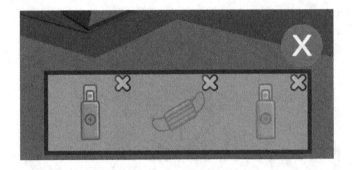

Fig. 12. Inventory UI

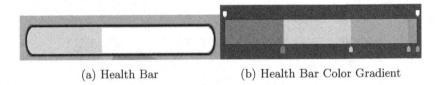

(a) Health Bar   (b) Health Bar Color Gradient

Fig. 13. Health bar

(a) Background color before change   (b) Background color after change

Fig. 14. Color customization

4   Implementation

Unity 3d game engine was used to develop the game due to the wide variety of libraries and assets it provides. Unity uses C# scripts which follow the principles of object-oriented programming. This made the development considerably easier for developers who were already familiar with the programming language.

Images were gathered from Bitmoji, FreePik, and Adobe Stock. Images were edited using Adobe Photoshop. They were then added to Unity, where the animations were designed using both LeanTween and Unity Animator Tool. The animated tutorial was created using the Unity Timeline Tool and Unity Animator Tool. The main characters' 3D models and animations were downloaded from Mixamo. Other 3D figures and objects were collected from the unity asset store. The voice-over commentary was recorded, trimmed, and imported to unity.

Sound effects were downloaded from various websites and were then manipulated to fit the game.

Firebase real-time database was used to store data for each player. The instructors can access the database to review game sessions and progress of each player. The database stores every item, preference, and player's progress to allow the player to continue where they left off.

5 Study Design

Our preliminary study aims to test the effectiveness of gamifying healthcare for children with ASD. Thus, for the game to achieve its purpose, the game was tested using multiple quantitative tests that will be mentioned shortly. Experts from **"El Yosr Community"** were interviewed. **"El Yosr"** is a local center whose mission is to provide adequate services for children with several developmental disorders including ASD. Experts requested some minor changes that were added later in the design phase. Children with ASD were recruited based on experts' recommendations of who might gain the most from the game.

Six participants were recruited. They all have autism. Their ages vary, but this is normal when testing with individuals with autism, since they have different mental ages. The demographic data about the participants is shown in Table 2.

Each participant was asked to play the game for 10 to 15 min. To ensure that the participants are comfortable during the experiment, they were allowed to ask for the help of their instructor whenever needed. At the end of the session, the instructor is asked to fill out the following surveys for each participant:

1. *System Usability Scale (SUS):* to ensure the system is easy to use, the system usability scale was used. SUS is a standardized test that consists of 10 items that investigate the usability of a platform [4].
2. *Engagement Test:* to ensure the game is engaging for children with ASD, the engagement test was used. It is a questionnaire, inherited from [15], that evaluates the user's overall engagement through nine points. Each point should be answered on five Likert scale responses.

Table 2. Participants for the study

ID	Age	Gender	Computer Skills
P1	12	Male	Moderate
P2	15	Female	Moderate
P3	21	Male	High
P4	17	Male	Moderate
P5	12	Male	Low
P6	10	Male	Moderate

6   Results and Discussion

Quantitative Data

1. *System Usability Scale (SUS):* All of the participants rated the systems with an average value greater than 68. The results show that the usability score for the serious game (M = 83.33, SD = 9.09) is considered reasonable for a usable system, since the threshold is reported to be 68.
2. *Engagement Test:* The engagement test results shows that all the participants in this experiment found the system fun, engaging, and interesting (M = 3.65, SD = 0.11). Participants were motivated to keep helping more people and they were curios to find out more stories of people in need of their help. Some players needed more energy to focus on the task at hand than others, but players with good experience with computer games were totally engaged during the whole session.

Qualitative Data

During the experiments notes were taken on the players' behaviours during the game session, and after the game session the instructors were interviewed to deduce the following points:

- Players showed a lot of interest to the fact that they can personalize the game and choose their own favorite color. They kept playing around with colors.
- Players enjoyed the drag and drop behaviour more than the mouse as they felt the effect of their actions on the screen visually and acoustically.
- Players felt a lot more motivated when they passed any task and got rewarded.
- When players understood the goal and the requirements, they got motivated to try more levels.
- Most of the players were actively listening to the voice-over commentary and watching the animated tutorial.
- Players tried to touch the screen multiple times during the session, since they were used to playing games on touch screens.

7   Conclusion and Future Work

The COVID-19 pandemic has created a major challenge for individuals with ASD and their families. That happened due to sudden changes in our routines and behaviors. Serious games have proven to be useful as interventions for individuals with autism in different aspects. Thus, a serious game was designed and developed to promote healthy behaviors and provide a fun way for players to stay home and learn those behaviors.

An experiment was conducted to test the usability and engagement levels of the game. The results show that participants were engaged in the game and motivated to play it. As the game session went on, they noticed the patterns and behaviors of the in-game characters (Not wearing masks and staying too close to other characters deduct health points). They were motivated to keep helping more people, and they were content to see the influence of their actions, which was possible through visual rewards and acoustic feedback. The SUS test results showed that the game is usable and suitable for the target group. The focus group included various age groups. The more experienced individuals with computer games achieved better results in a shorter amount of time. Although the game has proven to be engaging, the study is still in its preliminary stage. Therefore, there is still no evidence of whether acquired skills will be transferred to real life.

We plan on implementing a more comprehensive experiment to test the transfer of acquired behaviors to real-life situations. First of all, a considerably higher number of participants is needed. Second, a comparison between traditional teaching methods and the serious game should be conducted. Last but not least, we plan on extending the game itself to include more usual healthcare tips and guidelines in a gamified manner.

References

1. Alharbi, A., Aloufi, S., Assar, R., Meccawy, M.: Virtual reality street-crossing training for children with autism in Arabic language. In: 2020 International Conference on Innovation and Intelligence for Informatics, Computing and Technologies (3ICT), pp. 1–6. IEEE (2020)
2. Amorim, R., Catarino, S., Miragaia, P., Ferreras, C., Viana, V., Guardiano, M.: The impact of COVID-19 on children with autism spectrum disorder. Impacto de la COVID-19 en niños con trastorno del espectro autista. Revista de neurologia, **71**(8), 285–291 (2020). https://doi.org/10.33588/rn.7108.2020381
3. Baio, J., et al.: Prevalence of autism spectrum disorder among children aged 8 years-autism and developmental disabilities monitoring network, 11 sites, United States, 2014. MMWR Surveill. Summ. **67**(6), 1 (2018)
4. Brooke, J.: SUS: a "quick and dirty" usability. In: Usability Evaluation in Industry, vol. 189, no. 3 (1996)
5. Daouadji Amina, K., Fatima, B.: Medius: a serious game for autistic children based on decision system. Simul. Gaming **49**(4), 423–440 (2018)
6. Elgarf, M., Abdennadher, S., Elshahawy, M.: I-interact: a virtual reality serious game for eye contact improvement for children with social impairment. In: Alcañiz, M., Göbel, S., Ma, M., Fradinho Oliveira, M., Baalsrud Hauge, J., Marsh, T. (eds.) JCSG 2017. LNCS, vol. 10622, pp. 146–157. Springer, Cham (2017). https://doi.org/10.1007/978-3-319-70111-0_14
7. Elshahawy, M., Aboelnaga, K., Sharaf, N.: CodaRoutine: a serious game for introducing sequential programming concepts to children with autism. In: 2020 IEEE Global Engineering Education Conference (EDUCON), pp. 1862–1867. IEEE (2020)
8. Elshahawy, M., Bakhaty, M., Sharaf, N.: Developing computational thinking for children with autism using a serious game. In: 2020 24th International Conference Information Visualisation (IV), pp. 761–766. IEEE (2020)
9. Ern, A.M.: The use of gamification and serious games within interventions for children with autism spectrum disorder. B.S. thesis, University of Twente (2014)

10. Finkelstein, S., Nickel, A., Lipps, Z., Barnes, T., Wartell, Z., Suma, E.A.: Astro-jumper: motivating exercise with an immersive virtual reality exergame. Presence Teleoperators Virtual Environ. **20**(1), 78–92 (2011)
11. Hassan, A.Z., et al.: Developing the concept of money by interactive computer games for autistic children. In: 2011 IEEE International Symposium on Multimedia, pp. 559–564. IEEE (2011)
12. Mubashir, S., Farrugia, M., Coretti, L., Pessia, M., D'Adamo, M.C.: Autism spectrum disorder (2020)
13. Mubin, S.A., Poh, M.W.A., Rohizan, R., Abidin, A.Z.Z., Wei, W.C.: Gamification design framework to support autism children interaction skills: a systematic. Int. J. Cur. Res. Rev. **12**(22), 120 (2020)
14. Narzisi, A.: Handle the autism spectrum condition during coronavirus (Covid-19) stay at home period: ten tips for helping parents and caregivers of young children (2020)
15. Pearce, J.M., Ainley, M., Howard, S.: The ebb and flow of online learning. Comput. Hum. Behav. **21**(5), 745–771 (2005)
16. Seif Eldin, A., et al.: Use of M-CHAT for a multinational screening of young children with autism in the Arab countries. Int. Rev. Psychiatry **20**(3), 281–289 (2008)
17. Shipley-Benamou, R., Lutzker, J.R., Taubman, M.: Teaching daily living skills to children with autism through instructional video modeling. J. Posit. Behav. Interv. **4**(3), 166–177 (2002)
18. Spain, D., Mason, D., Capp, S.J., Stoppelbein, L., White, S.W., Happe, F.: "This may be a really good opportunity to make the world a more autism friendly place": professionals' perspectives on the effects of Covid-19 on autistic individuals. Res. Autism Spectr. Disord. **83** (2021)
19. Speaks, A.: Autism and health: a special report by autism speaks 2018–09 (2017). Retrieved 19 Dec 2018
20. Tang, J.S., Falkmer, M., Chen, N., Bölte, S., Girdler, S.: Designing a serious game for youth with ASD: perspectives from end-users and professionals. J. Autism Dev. Disord. **49**(3), 978–995 (2019)
21. Tomé, R.M., Pereira, J.M., Oliveira, M.: Using serious games for cognitive disabilities. In: Ma, M., Oliveira, M.F., Baalsrud Hauge, J. (eds.) SGDA 2014. LNCS, vol. 8778, pp. 34–47. Springer, Cham (2014). https://doi.org/10.1007/978-3-319-11623-5_4
22. Tsikinas, S., Xinogalos, S.: Studying the effects of computer serious games on people with intellectual disabilities or autism spectrum disorder: a systematic literature review. J. Comput. Assist. Learn. **35**(1), 61–73 (2019)
23. Vallefuoco, E., Bravaccio, C., Pepino, A.: Serious games in autism spectrum disorder-an example of personalised design. In: Special Session on Serious Games on Computer Science Learning, vol. 2, pp. 567–572. SciTePress (April 2017)
24. Whalen, C., Liden, L., Ingersoll, B., Dallaire, E., Liden, S.: Behavioral improvements associated with computer-assisted instruction for children with developmental disabilities. J. Speech Lang. Pathol. Appl. Behav. Anal. **1**(1), 11 (2006)
25. Whyte, E.M., Smyth, J.M., Scherf, K.S.: Designing serious game interventions for individuals with autism. J. Autism Dev. Disord. **45**(12), 3820–3831 (2015)
26. World Health Organization: Coronavirus disease 2019 (covid-19) situation report-51 (2020)

Game Design for Covertly Combating Covid-19 Vaccination Hesitancy

Sonia-Ruxandra Suciu[1], Helmut Hlavacs[1]([✉]), and Charly Harbord[2]

[1] Entertainment Computing Research Group, University of Vienna, Vienna, Austria
helmut.hlavacs@univie.ac.at
[2] School of Design and Informatics, Games and Arts Research, Abertay University, Dundee, Scotland

Abstract. Digital games have over the past few years have become increasingly important, particularly during Covid-19 lockdowns, not just as a way to spend free time but also in many more serious fields. One such area is healthcare, where applied games are increasingly utilized to educate individuals and encourage compliance with health measures, such as vaccination. This paper analyses several techniques for developing persuasive games that help change people's attitudes and therefore their behaviours, in this case focussed on Covid-19 vaccination. These techniques are based on a covert approach to persuasion to avoid triggering individuals' reactance and hence reaching a wider audience. Evaluation of the designed game shows promising results in terms of the impact of emotional engagement on attitudes toward vaccine uptake.

1 Introduction

With the constant advances in technology and its easy accessibility to a growing number of people, entertainment technologies have also gained popularity. Digital games play an essential aspect of this and are characterised by their ability to create an immersive experience for the user [1]. Their evolution lies not only in the complexity of their development, but above all in their potential to have a social impact. This potential has led to a steady growth in non-entertainment games [2] such as serious or applied games which are "used for purposes other than mere entertainment" [3]. They take on a different dimension through the serious purpose they are meant to serve, while maintaining their entertaining side by creating a captivating experience for the user [3]. Serious games are used in various domains such as education, healthcare, training and public policy [4], so their purpose is to provide knowledge, train or raise awareness [5]. This, combined with the fact that people can gain knowledge and understanding through experiencing them [5], digital games into a powerful tool not only for learning but also for addressing current issues concerning the population. Such an issue is the ongoing Covid-19 pandemic and the reluctance that some people had about getting vaccinated. The fact that the focus of digital games has shifted from pure entertainment to dealing with real issues opens up an additional way to reach

H. Söbke et al. (Eds.): JCSG 2022, LNCS 13476, pp. 155–165, 2022.
https://doi.org/10.1007/978-3-031-15325-9_12

individuals. Therefore, digital games can be used as a platform to address public health issues such as vaccination hesitancy [6] and therefore be utilised as a tool to inform the target audience of the importance of vaccination through more implicit methods. One way for these persuasive games to reach their audience in a meaningful way and transform their attitudes and thus their behaviour is to rely on a covert strategy, which is explored in this paper. In general, people tend to resist change, especially they feel forced to do so. Moreover, they may even adopt behaviours that are contrary to the ones that were desired. For this reason, such games make use of proven techniques to persuade players without them noticing this attempt. The game this work is based on uses covert techniques as presented in the 'Embedded Design' model [7], combined with the transformative benefits of storytelling and the way it can reach people affectively.

2   Change Resistant Attitudes

A key element to consider when trying to persuade someone to do something is the counter-effects it might cause. It is therefore important to examine the attitudes that may develop in individuals when they encounter an attempt of persuasion. As soon as a person feels persuaded to do something, they can develop a negative attitude towards it, thus being less inclined to act accordingly. **Persuasion** is especially important in regard to health-related issues [9], and trying to convince people to get vaccinated is an example of that.

An **attitude**, as defined by the Cambridge Dictionary, is "a feeling or opinion about something or someone, or a way of behaving that is caused by this". Hence, a person's attitude is composed of their beliefs, feelings and actions taken towards the object of their interest [10]. As mentioned here [11], attitudes towards the vaccine are crucial to the decision to get vaccinated or not, so preventing the user from cultivating any negative attitudes is a high priority. A lack of persuasive messages or intents will likely prevent that.

When considering attitudes, perception is also a factor worth mentioning. **Perception** describes the way someone interprets a stimulus based on previous experiences [10]. It does not always reflect the reality, but can be subjective. This can lead individuals to only accept information that is in accordance with their existing beliefs or attitudes and disregard that which is not.

Reactance can manifest as a result of either internal or external threats, the latter being triggered by social attempts to influence [8]. Once reactance is experienced, the affected individual becomes motivated to act against the desired way [9] and thus becomes even more motivated not to take the vaccine.

3   Attitudes Towards Vaccination

Vaccination Vaccination has always been a controversial subject, even though it has proven to be a highly successful public health measure. Vaccines not only provide protection for the vaccinated person, but by slowing down transmission of a virus or disease, they also help to achieve herd immunity [12]. The attitudes towards it can be seen as ranging from acceptance of all vaccines to outright rejection [13]. Within the boundaries of these extremes lies another category, that of hesitancy. Since ending the ongoing Covid-19 pandemic is highly dependent on a "large-scale uptake of vaccines" [14], any unwillingness or hesitancy among individuals poses a real hindrance in reaching this goal.

Vaccine hesitancy refers to delaying the acceptance of a vaccine or the refusal to accept it, even though it is available [13]. The way this manifests in an individual is reflected by him either refusing some vaccines and accepting others, or by accepting them suspiciously due to social pressure. Hesitancy can also be defined as a "motivational state of being conflicted about or opposed to getting vaccinated" [15]. Another factor that can help reduce hesitancy and also influence actual behaviour is anticipated regret. In our case, this is something that is addressed by the narrative.

Reactance, as explained in the previous section, refers to a state that people experience when they sense a threat to their freedom, motivating them to act against that threat. In this case, being externally pressured into getting vaccinated can reduce an individual's perception of control [11]. A study mentioned here [15] has shown that merely being provided with evidence is not enough to convince people to change their beliefs but that this in fact can have the opposite effect motivating them to reinforce their opposing views. Considering the above, it is clear that reactance has a direct impact on vaccination hesitancy, as higher reactance leads to less willingness to get vaccinated. For this reason, the game was designed in a way which doesn't overtly try to encourage vaccination, but uses established covert techniques, which are presented below. In this way, users are prevented from feeling reactant, giving them the opportunity to change their minds without feeling pressured to do so from the outside.

Digital games, which fall into the category of serious games, can be an effective tool to educate people on the topic of healthcare and more importantly on vaccination. With this in mind, an increasing amount of educational games, which still maintain interactive and fun elements, has been developed for this sector. As part of these tools, gamification is crucial in getting users involved and engaged and hence contributes to them learning and changing their behaviours. The approach adopted in this paper is not intended for spreading knowledge, but rather to change the perception of people towards the importance of vaccination against Covid-19. As many people who have not yet been vaccinated are sceptical, hiding the true aim of the game is a key factor in reaching these individuals, without them getting reactant.

4 Related Work

We have seen that the reaction of people to any attempt to persuade them is not necessarily the desired one, but rather one of reactance. This leads to them becoming defensive and less open and receptive to the message being conveyed. Therefore, well-defined strategies have been developed to solve various problems related to persuading individuals, without this persuasive intention being obvious to them.

The 'Embedded Design' model is based on hiding the game's persuasive objective among the created content and the gameplay, as it has been shown to be more effective not to have the main persuasive message in focus in order to achieve real impact. In this regard, three strategies have been developed, namely intermixing, obfuscating and distancing [7].

Intermixing refers to balancing the ratio between content that is related to the subject and content that is unrelated. By adding content that is playful and unrelated to the topic, the attempt to persuade is less obvious, so the message is perceived as less threatening and therefore more approachable [7]. In this way, the player is less likely to perceive the game as an external force trying to change their attitude, so there's a smaller chance of their reactance getting triggered. The game designed for this paper focuses on relating relatively usual events, but also adds messages related to the topic from time to time, without focusing too much attention on them.

Obfuscation is achieved through the use of framing devices or game genres as a means to divert the user's attention from the true purpose of the game [7]. If the player is focused on something else, there's a slimmer chance of them perceiving any intent of persuasion. One way to achieve this is by placing the game in a genre that is not known for having the objective to change the player's attitude, a genre that allows them to open-mindedly emerge into a new space [7].

Distancing aims to keep the user and their beliefs further away from the characters and persuasive content presented in the game. In other words, it aims to create a gap between real life and the game, enabling the player to become detached from their identity and less resistant to change [7]. By allowing themselves to be transported into another world, users are likely to enjoy the experience more, as well as leave more room to be persuaded by the central message. The storytelling components described in the next section can contribute to achieving this strategy.

Realism supports the two concepts mentioned above and is described as the perception of the narrative being as close to the real world and as genuine as possible [23]. By having this perception, the likelihood that the player will be transported into the story and identify with the characters grows. Realism is achieved by keeping the events close to the current reality for which the game was developed, but also maintaining a certain distance so that the player can safely experience the events as they unfold.

Covert persuasion techniques such as those mentioned above and in combination with others have been successfully used in other applications to change people's attitudes on various issues. The use of covert strategies in such an application is described in the paper entitled "Designing Game-Based Interventions for Subverting Normative Attitudes" [25]. The paper focuses on modifying an existing game, originally intended for a queer-friendly audience, through the use of covert persuasion strategies, such as the ones contained in the 'Embedded Design' model. The aim was to change people's prejudices and attitudes to stereotypes.

5   Design and Idea

Based on the 'Embedded Design' model and making use of storytelling as a means to apply the techniques contained in this model, a game was designed with the purpose of persuading those people not vaccinated against the Covid-19 virus to get vaccinated. As this subject is likely to give rise to resistant attitudes such as reactance among these individuals, it was important to disguise the persuasive intention of the game so that it could have the desired transformative effect.

The game on which this paper is based is a text-messaging game, which can be played in the browser. The story presented in the game unfolds as a dialogue between the main character and other supporting characters and follows the struggles of the protagonist while he waits to see if his grandfather, who is in critical condition due to Covid, will survive. The main character first appears as an NPC, but then gets to be controlled by the player. How the player interacts with the created environment is via a decision-based mechanic whereby it is believed that the choices for the avatar behaviour and reactions in various situations impacts the narrative and therefore outcome of the game. The player is free to choose whichever option they want, that option supposedly affecting the story-line going further, as is the case for most applications of this kind. Usually such games have different endings, the choices made by the person playing being crucial in determining the outcome of the story. For the persuasive purpose of this application though, that being to convince people into getting vaccinated, no multiple endings are featured. This way, regardless of the choices the player makes at any given time, the story leads to the same conclusion, namely, that the characters were wrong about the vaccine and have reconsidered getting it. So, even if the player feels in control, as is desired, the outcome is the same.

The game is designed for unvaccinated people, who should be persuaded into getting vaccinated. These are individuals who found themselves unconvinced by regular campaigns informing them on why the vaccine is necessary and might have their own fixed opinion on the subject. Such individuals are also likely to experience reactance, which makes the type of covert approach used here a better option compared to directly telling them what to do. Furthermore, the audience the game is addressed to is rather comprised of simple people, so the language used was kept to a regular conversational level. The ones most likely to be positively affected by the game, so, to be influenced by it, are those able to identify with the main character (Narrative Theory - Identification). But, subject to change can also be those identifying with other secondary characters and mostly individuals who are more family-oriented, or have people they care for in their lives.

Identification of the player with a character substantially assists the persuasive attempt of the game. Having found themselves in similar situations or having experienced similar emotions, people can both learn from the characters or become more open to change. Either young people or people any age who are concerned for their loved ones and can relate to the protagonist's struggles can easily identify with him. Additionally, other individuals could directly be affected by identifying with the grandfather or indirectly, by knowing someone resembling the protagonist. It is possible for the players to find themselves worrying for someone who will be at risk of contracting the virus, or to think about the struggle they would put others through if it happens to them. This way, players can be reached at an emotional level and thus brought into reconsidering their attitude on the vaccine topic.

The game is built on the "story within a story" structure. The player first meets an NPC, who introduces himself and invites the player into his life, asking for his help to uncover a mystery. Meanwhile, the NPC also lets him know that his contribution is needed. Afterwards, as the inner story begins to unfold, the NPC becomes a playable character, controlled by the player. The player is now in charge of helping the protagonist expose the truth. After the actual story ends, the player meets with the NPC again, who thanks the player for helping him. This kind of approach has the advantage of creating an additional level of abstraction, therefore allowing the user to experience the events from a safe distance. By adding another layer to the story, the player's defence systems can decrease, enabling his transportation into the story. The choices regarding the structure of the story enforce both the distancing strategy in the 'Embedded Design' model and transportation.

The story follows Mark, a young man, who is going through a rough time because a person he loves, his grandfather, is struggling after contracting the coronavirus. At the beginning of the inner story, everything seems to be in balance, as Mark navigates through daily life as normally as possible, given the circumstances. He is invited to meet with his friends and while doing so he has a quick conversation with someone who recently recovered from Covid. This conversation is cut short when Mark receives a phone call from his mother, informing him that something happened to his grandfather. This is the event that disrupts the prior balance and also creates suspense, as the player, although he can assume what happened, doesn't yet know for certain. The player finds out what happened after Mark gets home to his mother. The plot now follows the protagonist's inner conflict, while trying to navigate through this situation, being unable to do anything to restore the balance. After more time has passed, with the two helplessly waiting, the grandfather is now better. The conflict was finally resolved and the story ends with a dialogue between Mark and his grandfather where they both realise that they were mistaken in their attitudes and beliefs regarding the whole situation and the vaccine. They have come to the conclusion, that for their well-being and for avoiding such an event in the future, maybe with a worse outcome, they should get the vaccine.

The game's user interface has been kept quite simple, so as not to draw the player's attention away from the main story. The interface resembles that of a text messaging game (cf. Fig. 1(b)), in order to keep the focus on the characters and their conversations. There are buttons at the bottom of the screen for the user to interact with the game. New text bubbles appear as the user taps on the 'Tap to Continue' button. This approach was chosen because being in charge of the amount of time spent on reading a message gives more control to the player, whereas, the opposite approach where messages automatically appear after some time, could reinforce the idea that decision are trying to be made for him. As the dialogue moves along, new text bubbles appear on the screen, starting to automatically scroll horizontally, leaving enough space for the images depicting the unfolding events to be seen throughout each chapter. The images (cf. Fig. 1) were done as simple drawings, in the style of cartoons, so they would not take the focus away from the story, but rather emphasize it and help awaken the player's emotions.

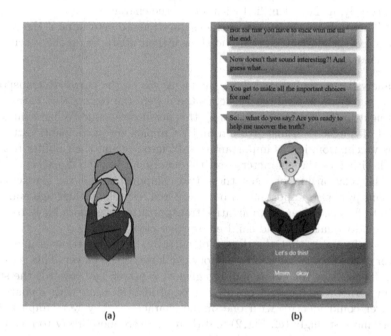

Fig. 1. Graphical design.

6   Evaluation and Discussion

As an evaluation method for the designed text messaging game, a questionnaire was created and given to different participants to fill out after they had played the game. The study was conducted with ten participants ranging in age from 19 to 52 years, with the average age being around 28 years; half of the participants were male and the other half were female. The individuals were both employed and unemployed or students. The average playing time was about seven minutes and the questionnaire took about two to three minutes to complete. The questionnaire was written in such a way that, as much as possible, did not disclose the persuasive purpose of the game, in order to avoid triggering any reactant attitudes. Both quantitative and qualitative data were collected on the participants. Quantitative response options ranged from 1 (Complete Disagreement with the statement) to 6 (Complete agreement with the statement), with this scale leaving no room for a neutral response The structure of the questionnaire was divided into three parts, with each part being structured as follows:

- Part One - Personal Information (contains questions about the subject, perhaps the most relevant being relationship with his family)
- Part Two - Narrative Transportation (this part aimed at establishing whether the individual was transported into the narrative, captivated by it, and more importantly, if they identified with any of the characters)
- Part Three - Final Thoughts (includes questions to determine if the participant's reactance was triggered and show if their attitudes on the vaccination have changed at all)

In analysing the submitted data, the focus was on the narrative transportation and perceived level of reactance, as these were the factors that carried the most weight in the premise of designing this persuasive game. When examining the level of narrative transportation and its impact on participants' attitudes towards vaccination, it was important to take into account their ability to identify with either of the characters and the emotional impact the story had on them. The relationship between these two components and the participants' background was also important to be considered, especially their age and relationship to family. In general, narrative transportation was more likely to occur for those individuals who had children or other close family.

The study shows that the degree of narrative transportation is indeed an indicator of the persuasive effect the story can have on the player. This is particularly influenced by the emotional engagement a person had towards the story, which in turn was influenced by the degree of identification with a character. If a player could identify with one of the characters, they were impacted by the story more strongly (cf. Fig. 2) and therefore were more likely to reconsider taking the vaccine (cf. Fig. 3). Identification with a character was enhanced if the person in question either had children or other close relatives. This probably made it easier for those players to imagine themselves in a similar situation, get transported into it and get emotionally involved. This in turn softened their attitudes towards the Covid-19 vaccine and made them more open to it. Low identification and low emotional engagement, on the other hand, indicated that there was little to no change in users' attitudes towards the vaccine uptake.

The generally positive response to the story overall, and to the attitudes towards vaccination in particular, may also be related to the covert persuasion approach that was implemented. Most participants stated that they did not feel that the game was forcing them to do anything (cf. Fig. 4). This speaks to the fact that the game's attempt to persuade remained hidden. Furthermore, most of those players' responses to the question of whether they would reconsider their decision regarding the Covid-19 vaccine were on the positive side of the spectrum, while those who responded negatively were those who were not emotionally affected by the story. This shows that the approach did not trigger any negative attitudes among users, let alone reactance.

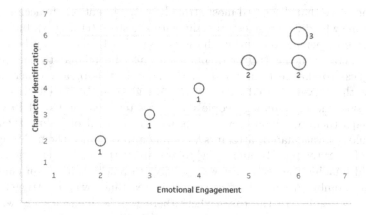

Fig. 2. Emotional engagement.

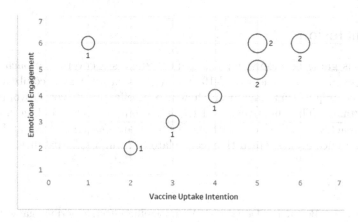

Fig. 3. Impact of emotional engagement on vaccine attitude.

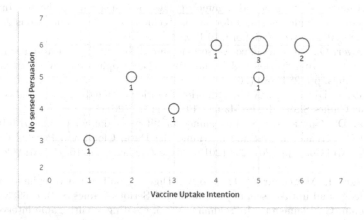

Fig. 4. Impact of sensed persuasion on vaccination attitude.

The one case that disagreed most strongly to the intention of vaccine uptake was someone who did engage emotionally with the story (cf. Fig. 3), but noticed some degree of persuasion during the game (cf. Fig. 4). This may be a result of their reactance being triggered, but could also be related to the person's unwillingness to change their mind on the issue in this or any other way. In summary, the survey showed that covert strategies can be an effective means of persuasion and of changing people's attitudes towards the Covid-19 vaccine and perhaps their behaviour towards its uptake. Instead of telling them why they should get vaccinated, attempts were made to convince them through the benefits of storytelling. By managing to transport them in a situation where they could imagine themselves, it was possible to reach them on an emotional level. This, combined with the fact that their reactance was not triggered, led to promising results. In the cases where there was no identification with the character or an attempt at persuasion was noticed, the results were worse, as expected.

7 Conclusion

The serious game developed for this paper explores a covert approach to persuading people to get the Covid-19 vaccine, making use of a combination of existing techniques that have been shown to be effective in not provoking people's reactance. The effectiveness of the game, apart from avoiding triggering people's reactance, relied on reaching them on an emotional level and letting them experience events which they can relate to from a safe distance.

References

1. Bellotti, F., Berta, R., De Gloria, A.: Designing effective serious games: opportunities and challenges for research. Int. J. Emerg. Technol. Learn. 5(SI3), 22–35 (2010)
2. Janarthanan, V.: Serious video games: games for education and health. In: Ninth International Conference on Information Technology - New Generations 2012, pp. 875–878 (2012). https://doi.org/10.1109/ITNG.2012.79
3. De Troyer, O.: Towards effective serious games. In: 2017 9th International Conference on Virtual Worlds and Games for Serious Applications, VS-Games 2017 - Proceedings, pp. 284–289 (2017)
4. Alvarez, J., Djaouti, D.: An introduction to serious game definitions and concepts. Serious Games Simul. Risks Manag. 11(1), 11–15 (2011)
5. Gupta, D., Gupta, K.: Serious games in different domains. In: 2019 International Conference on Machine Learning, Big Data, Cloud and Parallel Computing (COMITCon), pp. 201–204 (2019). https://doi.org/10.1109/COMITCon.2019.8862437
6. Montagni, I., Mabchour, I., Tzourio, C.: Digital gamification to enhance vaccine knowledge and uptake: scoping review. JMIR Serious Games 8(2), e16983 (2020)
7. Kaufman, G., Flanagan, M., Seidman, M.: 5. creating stealth game interventions for attitude and behavior change: an 'Embedded Design' model. In: Persuasive Gaming in Context, pp. 73–90. Amsterdam University Press (2021)

8. Steindl, C., Jonas, E., Sittenthaler, S., Traut-Mattausch, E., Greenberg, J.: Understanding psychological reactance. Zeitschrift für Psychologie (2015)
9. Miller, C.H., Massey, Z.B., Ma, H.: Psychological reactance and persuasive message design. In: The Handbook of Applied Communication Research, pp. 457–483 (2020)
10. Pickens, J.: Attitudes and perceptions. In: Organizational Behavior in Health Care, vol. 4, no. 7, pp. 43–766 (2005)
11. Drazkowski, D., Trepanowski, R.: Reactance and perceived disease severity as determinants of COVID-19 vaccination intention: an application of the theory of planned behavior. Psychol. Health Med. (2021)
12. Dubé, E., Laberge, C., Guay, M., Bramadat, P., Roy, R., Bettinger, J.A.: Vaccine hesitancy: an overview. Hum. Vaccines Immunotherapeutics 9(8), 1763–1773 (2013)
13. MacDonald, N.E.: Vaccine hesitancy: definition, scope and determinants. Vaccine 33(34), 4161–4164 (2015)
14. Sprengholz, P., Felgendreff, L., Boehm, R., Betsch, C.: Vaccination policy reactance: predictors, consequences, and countermeasures. J. Health Psychol. 27(6), 1394–1407
15. Brewer, N.T., Chapman, G.B., Rothman, A.J., Leask, J., Kempe, A.: Increasing vaccination: putting psychological science into action. Psychol. Sci. Public Interest 18(3), 149–207 (2017)
16. Lu, F., Sun, Y.: COVID-19 vaccine hesitancy: the effects of combining direct and indirect online opinion cues on psychological reactance to health campaigns. Comput. Hum. Behav. 127, 107057 (2022)
17. Sprengholz, P., Betsch, C., Böhm, R.: Reactance revisited: consequences of mandatory and scarce vaccination in the case of COVID-19. Appl. Psychol. Health Well-Being 13, 986–995 (2021)
18. Ohannessian, R., Yaghobian, S., Verger, P., Vanhems, P.: A systematic review of serious video games used for vaccination. Vaccine 34(38), 4478–4483 (2016)
19. Mitchell, G., Leonard, L., Carter, G., Santin, O., Brown Wilson, C.: Evaluation of a 'serious game' on nursing student knowledge and uptake of influenza vaccination. PLoS ONE 16(1), e0245389 (2021)
20. Kampa, A., Haake, S., Burelli, P.: Storytelling in serious games. In: Dörner, R., Göbel, S., Kickmeier-Rust, M., Masuch, M., Zweig, K. (eds.) Entertainment Computing and Serious Games. LNCS, vol. 9970, pp. 521–539. Springer, Cham (2016). https://doi.org/10.1007/978-3-319-46152-6_19
21. McKee, R., Fryer, B.: Storytelling that moves people. Harv. Bus. Rev. 81(6), 51–55 (2003)
22. Simmons, A.: The Story Factor, Basic Books, revised edn., 4 April 2006. ISBN-13 978-0465078073
23. Lee, H., Fawcett, J., DeMarco, R.: Storytelling/narrative theory to address health communication with minority populations. Appl. Nurs. Res. 30, 58–60 (2016)
24. Lugmayr, A., Suhonen, J., Sutinen, E.: Serious storytelling-serious digital storytelling. In: International SERIES on Information Systems and Management in Creative eMedia (CreMedia), (2014/1), pp. 29–33 (2015)
25. Polzer, M., Hlavacs, H.: Designing game-based interventions for subverting normative attitudes. In: Munekata, N., Kunita, I., Hoshino, J. (eds.) ICEC 2017. LNCS, vol. 10507, pp. 113–124. Springer, Cham (2017). https://doi.org/10.1007/978-3-319-66715-7_12

Games Application

Communication Skills in Construction Projects and Promoting Them Through Multiplayer Online Games

Ezra Jansen and Heinrich Söbke(✉) (iD)

Bauhaus-Institute for Infrastructure Solutions (b.is), Bauhaus-Universität Weimar, Goetheplatz 7/8, 99423 Weimar, Germany
ezra.jansen@live.nl, heinrich.soebke@uni-weimar.de

Abstract. Construction projects are complex processes that demand high communication skills of all involved stakeholders. Multiplayer Online Games (MOG) are considered to be training environments for meta skills, including communication skills. This study aims to analyze whether communication skills required for construction projects could be trained in MOGs. For this purpose, based on literature research, initially half-hour interviews with construction project experts (N = 9) were conducted aiming at elaborating the problems of communication in construction projects and thus deriving learning goals regarding communication skills. As a result, five typical challenges affecting communication in construction projects were identified from literature and eight learning goals were derived from the analysis of the interviews. The learning goals were examined in focus group discussions with players of the MOG EVE Online (N = 14) to determine whether these learning goals regarding communication skills are also in demand in the MOG and trained accordingly. As a result, each of the learning goals could be trained at least basically through EVE Online. However, as a prerequisite of successful training, players must actively participate and communicate in the MOG. Accordingly, EVE Online might be used as a training environment for communication in construction projects especially for MOG-affine stakeholders in construction projects.

Keywords: EVE Online · MMOG · Serious game · Meta skill · Interdisciplinary skill · 21st Century skill

1 Introduction

Construction projects, i.e., projects that aim at constructing buildings, at times can be very complex. Contributing to the complexity are technical factors such as conflicting standards, organizational factors such as lack of experience of the parties involved, and organizational factors such as the competitive environment [1]. As complexity increases, the odds for success of construction projects are reduced [2]. However, it is also known that as complexity increases, the role of effective communication becomes more important to project success [3]. Effective communication is defined in the context of this study

H. Söbke et al. (Eds.): JCSG 2022, LNCS 13476, pp. 169–181, 2022.
https://doi.org/10.1007/978-3-031-15325-9_13

as purposeful communication regarding the projects' goals, using methods and media, such as those described by Ellis (2017) [4]. Effective communication within construction projects is considered critical to the projects' failure or successful completion [5]. Thus, Emmitt and Gorse [6], argue that effective communication within a construction project is extremely significant to its success. Communication in construction projects has several aspects. Hence, Taleb et al. (2017) [5] suggest a communication project management plan, for which planning inputs, stakeholders and their needs, for example, are systematically collected and implemented into a plan. Different cultures of stakeholders involved in construction projects are another aspect [7], which also influences communication [8]. Likewise, digital tools to support communication need to be mentioned [9].

However, the ability to communicate effectively is usually taken for granted in the construction industry, as the interviews conducted for this study indicate. Although digitization can contribute to an objectification of communication, as Building Information Modeling demonstrates [10], effective communication in construction projects depends to a large extent on stakeholders participating in construction projects. In addition, construction projects have specific characteristics compared to other projects [5], which might hamper communication in many respects.

Communication skills belong to the meta skills. [11]. As with meta skills in general, the training of communication skills in formal education, such as higher education, is usually given little attention [12]. Meta skills - despite their great importance for professional success [13–15] - are therefore mostly acquired during professional practice. In formal education, such as higher education, on the other hand, the training of communication skills usually takes place only implicitly in student projects. These study projects usually have a subject-specific background and mostly require individual set-up and supervision by teachers. Hence study projects tend to be effort-prone for teachers.

Furthermore, serious games have been developed specifically for fostering communication skills. Already 20 years ago *Virtual Leader* was developed, a serious game for the development of leadership skills, for which communication skills are of great importance [16]. Vaassen and Daelemans describe a serious game designed to train communication in business contexts [17]. The serious game *Communicate!* promotes communication skills in physician-patient conversations [18]. In nurse education, the serious game *Comunica-Enf* practices communication with patients [19]. Another group of serious games is used for autistic patients to train social communication [20, 21]. Strien et al. describe a serious game to train the skills needed to manage general practice, which likewise include communication skills [22]. In addition, Bodnar and Clark demonstrated that a game-based pedagogy had a beneficial effect on the spoken and written communication of engineering students [23]. While specific serious games can be tailored to detailed learning objectives, they often also have drawbacks such as high (development) cost and lower game enjoyment [24]. Therefore, multiplayer online games (MOG) are discussed in the following.

Multiplayer online games (MOG) in particular are attributed with the characteristic of training meta skills in game players [25–27] and thus also communication skills in particular [28]. Thus, MOGs might be considered as a generic training environment for communication skills. However, until today there is little guidance on meaningful usage of MOGs for training of communication skills, especially in the context of construction projects. At this point the study begins, aiming at examining in how far communication skills relevant in construction projects may be gained by using MOGs.

The article is organized in five sections. Following the introduction in the second section the methodology of the study consisting of the three steps is presented – a) the literature review to characterize communication in construction projects b) the expert interviews to derive learning objectives and c) the focus group interviews to evaluate the learning objectives in terms of their attainability through a specific MOG. The results of each step are described in the third section. Finally, the results are discussed and a followed by a conclusion in sections four and five.

2 Methodology

Methodologically, this study is based on qualitative methods to reconcile the needs of training communication skills in construction projects and the respective opportunities offered by MOGs. A literature review was conducted to identify challenges of communication in construction projects. As a result, five specific challenges of communication in construction projects were discussed. The challenges were then presented for discussion in a second step in semi-structured interviews about communication in construction projects with nine construction industry experts, each half an hour in length, and substantiated with the experts' practical experiences. The experts were acquired from the personal construction industry network of the study lead and, as a prerequisite, had to have practical experience in management of construction projects. Table 1 shows the demographics of the 5 female and 4 male experts, who had an average of 14.0 years of professional experience. The interviews were subsequently transcribed, and a qualitative analysis was conducted according to Schmidt (2004) [29]. As a result, eight learning objectives most frequently mentioned in the interviews were derived.

The next step was then to conduct focus group interviews with 14 participants of a higher education course that teaches meta skills [12] using the MOG EVE Online [30]. The focus group interview took place at the end of the course. At that point of time all participants had equally 15 weeks of game experience with EVE Online. None of the participants had played EVE Online before the course started. The age of the participants was 24.1 years on average (SD = 3.97, min = 20, max = 34). Six participants studied construction management and four each studied civil engineering and environmental engineering. Four participants were enrolled in a master's program, ten in a bachelor's program. The eight learning objectives were brought up for discussion in the focus group interview in terms of the extent to which they could be achieved through playing EVE Online. The results of the focus group interview were again subject to a qualitative analysis.

Even if the boundary is not always complied with, in the context of this study communication is considered in particular as interpersonal communication, e.g., the transfer of information in meetings and conversations. There is less emphasis on technical (e.g., plans and user guides) digitized (e.g., e-mails) or written (e.g., letters) communication, instead primarily interpersonal communication is examined. Digital and analog communication media are not the focus of this study, although they cannot be completely excluded since the MOG used is also a digital communication medium.

Table 1. Demographics of experts interviewed; column "Years" refers to years of professional experience

#	Gender	Years	Education, Professional experience, Working environment and/or Tasks
1	Female	34	Engineer, worked in architectural companies for 16 years, worked as construction manager for 16 years. Currently project developer and asset manager
2	Female	4	Civil engineer, prospective managing director of a medium-sized company in road construction and earthworks
3	Female	4	Civil engineer, project manager in asset management
4	Male	20	Construction manager and project manager in a construction company for turn-key projects
5	Female	20	Architect, church building manager, supervising the renovation of existing buildings, mainly heritage buildings such as churches or parsonages
6	Male	12	Civil engineer, construction department of a water supplier, planning and realization of construction projects
7	Female	12	Architect. Project management in an architectural company
8	Male	16	Heating technician, working on large and small construction sites
9	Male	4	Civil engineer, family-run property development company and engineering office, project development in the field of residential construction

3 Results

In the following, the results of the study are systematically presented according to the steps performed within the study framework.

3.1 Challenges of Communication in Construction Projects

During construction projects, many of the challenges that arise are a result of the temporary and interdisciplinary nature of project teams. Boddy & Paton (2004) [31] categorized the challenges. They argue that challenges originate in the subjective interpretations of a project itself and in the cultural, structural, political, and professional interests of its stakeholders. Dainty et al. (2006) [32] cite as particular challenges of communication in construction projects also the temporary project structure with stakeholders previously largely unfamiliar with one another, and further aspects that hamper communication such as technical language, a to some degree self-interested project culture, and an environment that is often not conducive to communication due to noise and mess. Gorse & Emmitt (2007), on the other hand, could not confirm the adversarial environment, but they characterized construction meetings as more task-focused than socio-emotionally focused [33]. Furthermore, the construction site is also addressed as a specific feature of communication in construction projects and corresponding communication techniques are described [4].

In summary, as a result of the literature review, the following challenges to effective communication were identified and supported with items to clarify in the subsequent interviews.

Structural Challenge. Effective communication in construction projects depends on a sound and resilient project structure. This premise is analyzed through various aspects of project structure.

Information Challenge. Effective communication in construction projects depends on whether project stakeholders have the information required. Information problems define the aspects that occur when messages are send in conversations.

Semantic Challenge. Effective communication in construction projects relies on an equal understanding of a coded message among all project stakeholders. Message decoding, or understanding the information in the message, is important and may involve stakes.

Cultural Challenge. To ensure effective communication in construction projects, cultural differences among project stakeholders must be considered. In terms of both organizational culture and cross-cultural differences, difference aside different languages must be understood and accounted for.

Socio-Emotional Challenge. For effective communication in construction projects, it is important to know the socio-emotional concerns and how to deal with them.

3.2 Learning Objektives

In the interviews the extent to which the challenges could be met in trainings were discussed. In doing so, the analysis derived learning objectives that were guided by Bloom's learning objectives taxonomy [34] and expressed in the noun-verb form [35] (Table 2).

In the following the learning objectives are explained in more detail.

Learning Objective 1: Project Structuring. For better communication, a structured project is important. There should be a structure in the team as well as in the project. A structure allows communication to be conducted more effectively. A project can be structured by working through questions that should be answered in the project team.

Learning Objective 2: Knowledge Gap Analysis. Knowledge gaps may include both technical understanding and experience. Possible solutions on how to generate this knowledge are, for example, to analyze the work practices of experienced colleagues and then apply them oneself.

Learning Objective 3: Information Handling. Due to the large amount of information in construction projects, information is shortened during forwarding and thus may lose comprehensibility. The shortened forwarding of information without limiting the comprehensibility must be trained.

Table 2. Challenges of communication in construction projects and learning objectives assigned

#	Learning objektive (Challenge)	Description of the learning objective
1	Project structuring (Structural challenge)	Learners are able to structure a project by clarifying necessary questions at the beginning, creating a foundation for further communication
2	Knowledge gap analysis (Information challenge)	Learners are able to recognize their knowledge gaps and identify possible solutions to eliminate the knowledge gaps
3	Information handling (Information challenge)	Learners are able to transfer information in the project without loss of semantics
4	Listening (Semantic challenge)	Learners are able to understand complex matters by listening to project stakeholders and expressing them in the form of language or actions
5	Inquiries (Semantic challenge)	Learners are able to understand information by asking specific questions, creating a basis for effective communication
6	Trust building (Cultural challenge)	Learners are able to build trust with stakeholders in the project, thereby encouraging open communication to address issues
7	Constructive communication (Socio-emotional challenge)	Learners are able to control negative emotions and separate them from the substantive
8	Social empathy (Socio-emotional challenge)	Learners are able to deal with different personalities and adapt their communication to the personality if necessary

Learning Objective 4: Listening. Complex matters are often prevalent in construction projects. Understanding is frequently gained by listening and communicating further on the basis of the understanding gained. Therefore, listening is extremely important for better communication in construction projects.

Learning Objective 5: Inquiries. The topic of asking questions was brought up again and again in many interviews. Because many stakeholders work together in the project and all have different understandings and knowledge, asking questions can help improve communication and achieve results.

Learning Objective 6: Trust Building. Trust in construction projects was mentioned more frequently in the interviews. Trust causes communication and also cooperation to function more effectively and better. The ability to build trust is a meta skill.

Learning Objective 7: Constructive Communication. Negative emotions were often mentioned as an obstacle to effective communication. Therefore, it is important to control negative emotions and to focus on the technical project work.

Learning Objective 8: Social Empathy. Construction projects are characterized by many stakeholders having differing personalities. This holds potential for conflicts that might be solved with the help of communication. Knowing which personalities there are and how to communicate is therefore important for the success of projects.

Other learning objectives include retrospective analysis of a construction project to determine how each objective was met and what approaches exist to further improve communication.

3.3   Potential Support of the Learning Objectives in EVE Online

For each learning objective, the question was asked in the focus group discussion whether the learning objective could be achieved in EVE Online. If it is achievable, participants were asked to explain where in the game the learning objective was achieved and if it could not be achieved, why this was not possible. The recording of the discussion in a collaborative online whiteboard [36] allows insight into the discussion. The evaluation is based on a qualitative analysis and gives an overview of the participants' thoughts on the discussion.

Learning Objective 1: Project Structuring. In the discussion on the topic of project structuring, some examples of projects that have been carried out in EVE Online were listed. One of the projects mentioned was the production of goods. In this project, project-relevant questions were clarified at the beginning, such as: What product do we want to produce? Can the product be sold profitably? What materials are needed? Where can the materials be procured and at what prices? How long will production take? The perception that the players gain the ability to structure projects by asking appropriate questions when carrying out a project like this was subject of discussion. This example is just one of numerous projects that can be conducted in EVE Online. It was pointed out that in EVE Online as a sandbox MOG, almost any activity can be expanded into a collaborative project between multiple players to be structured through communication. During the discussion, a major advantage of projects in EVE Online compared to building projects was also outlined. The failure of projects in EVE Online due to poor structuring has little impact on real life. This means that the next project may be started easily, in which the lessons learned may be applied.

Learning Objective 2: Knowledge Gap Analysis. In the discussion on this learning objective, it was pointed out that EVE Online is a complex game, whose familiarization requires considerable effort and an organized approach, during which simultaneous communication with others must be maintained. Thus, communication is trained as well. It was also noted that learning EVE Online is a longer process, during which previous knowledge is repeatedly built upon for identifying gaps in knowledge that need to be overcome. Knowledge gaps are analyzed not only through interpersonal communication, but also by tapping into knowledge sources, such as the EVE University Wiki [37]. Therefore, identifying knowledge gaps is a skill that is strongly encouraged in EVE Online because the game is not self-explanatory in many regards. A relevant part of the knowledge gaps is analyzed through communication.

Learning Objective 3: Information Handling. The learning objective information handling was discussed contrary. It was expressed that for meaningful activities in EVE Online, there is a lot of information provided in EVE Online and outside of EVE Online, e.g., in forums. Processes of collaborative information collection were mentioned. For example, groups created spreadsheets that were used for group decision making. The observation that media are sought out for sharing and consolidating information is indicative of players in EVE Online who have developed the ability of handling information. On the other hand, however, it was also explained that there is information in EVE Online that cannot be easily shared through media, such as gameplay attitude. Such information is considered important to challenge and train communication. The need to share information and thus the ability to handle information in a beneficial way - avoiding losses of meaning and content - is supported by EVE Online.

Learning Objective 4: Listening. There have been frequent reports of communication in group activities in EVE Online. Communication, however, forms the basis for listening. In the discussion of the extent to which listening is encouraged in EVE Online, both positive and negative aspects were mentioned. Confirmatively, it was stated the cooperation leads to each player having different knowledge in EVE Online and being able to pass this on in exchange. Here, it was pointed out that the ability to listen was intensively promoted, since the players are interested in the other groups and want to understand the facts to increase their game knowledge. On the other hand, it was pointed out that it is often easier to understand the facts from other sources than to get them explained by other players. The knowledge of other sources, such as the EVE University Wiki [37], was characterized as mostly more comprehensive. Furthermore, it was negatively noted that listening to complex facts might decrease the fun of playing the game. For example, playing fun increases, when an activity is to be carried out in a group and complex facts have to be explained first. Overall, it was determined that the ability to listen is unconsciously promoted, which means that this learning goal is basically promoted by EVE Online.

Learning Objective 5: Inquiries. One undisputed result of the discussion was that the complexity of the game requires players to ask specific questions, whether in personal conversations or in forums. An important aspect is the anonymity in the game: it was reported that having an avatar name makes it less strenuous to ask questions or to address other players. The possibility to ask questions in the chat rooms of the game, for example, was also perceived as positive by the majority. Specifically, it was stated that the fear of asking questions is lost in the EVE Community Chat. However, the complexity of the game was described as an obstacle to achieving the learning goal, as not all questions could be answered and formulating a question presents difficulties. On the other hand, the perceived difficulties of formulating a question may also be interpretable as learning opportunities. The hypothesis that EVE Online is a conducive environment for training the formulation of purposeful questions and the associated increase in understanding was also agreed to in the discussion by naming further examples (including the targeting of experienced players).

Learning Objective 6: Trust Building. About building trust in the game, different opinions were expressed in the discussion. On the one hand, it was mentioned that trust was already there from the beginning, since every player had the same intentions and attitudes. Other discussants stated that trust was built during the game. Activities were mentioned through which trust was built, for example, in combat situations, in the assignment of tasks, or else in receiving authorization over the resources of the coopera- tion. On the other hand, some players stated that they did not have to build trust because the tasks performed did not require trust. It was also noted that the risks of breaking trust - for example, stealing the cooperation's resources - would have lower consequences in the game than similar violations of trust in reality. Lower consequences also lead to faster trust establishment, so trust in the game seems less comparable to trust in reality. Accordingly, EVE Online is credited with the requirement to build trust. However, the comparability is not given due to less importance of trust abuse.

Learning Objective 7: Constructive Communication. In the discussion, a reference to the real professional life was pointed out: Negative emotions arise both in the game and in reality, when the result of an action does not correspond to the positive expectations. It was likewise elaborated that a higher emotional attachment is created as longer the game is played and therefore negative emotions may occur in case of a loss. Moreover, it was found that the repetition of losses leads to an improvement in the ability to deal with negative emotions. On the other hand, there were also contradictory arguments. For example, there were game endings in which no negative emotions had occurred so far due to the nature of the game and thus the learning objective was not met. Also, the comparison to reality was often drawn and it was stated that dealing with emotions was more difficult in reality than in the game. Both arguments may be an indication that the game is not taken as seriously as the professional life, either because the game merely serves to relax or the engagement with the game was not completely intrinsically motivated due to its embedding in a higher education course. In conclusion, to promote constructive communication, a high level of engagement in the game with attachment to the game seems to be necessary. Even with constructive emotion-free communication, the experiences in the game seem to be less authentic for some of the players than in the real professional life of a construction project. The learning objective is considered partially achievable.

Learning Objective 8: Social Empathy. In the discussion on the eighth learning objective, the participants stated that a basic requirement of EVE Online is communica- tion with other players. This requirement fundamentally promotes dealing with different characters. However, it was also pointed out that in many other situations in daily life, people communicate with other people and therefore implicitly learn to deal with dif- fering personalities. As an advantage of EVE Online in this regard, however, was seen the sheer number of people who can be encountered in EVE Online. This results in a greater potential in terms of quantity, so that empathy is clearly promoted. The fact that communication in EVE Online usually takes place without video transmission was seen as detrimental to achieving the learning objective. This means that facial expressions are missing as an important communication channel, which may limit the feeling of empathy. The willingness to communicate was also mentioned as a prerequisite for the training of empathy. The learning objective is considered achievable partially.

4 Discussion

According to the statements of the participants in discussion, the identified learning objectives for promoting communication skills in construction projects seem to be achievable partly very well or at least rudimentarily through involvement in the MOG EVE Online. There are also some limitations to be mentioned. First, the small sample sizes prevent the results found from being representative. Further, the elaborated challenges and the resulting learning objectives may not be exhaustive but may still need additions. Moreover, a comparison of the learning effectiveness against serious games existing would also have been of interest. Although the participants of the focus group interviews had been made familiar with specific serious games for training communication skills during the higher education course, this topic had not been explicitly addressed in the focus groups interviews. Furthermore, the use of MOGs as training environments is more likely to be seen as a win to learners with an affinity for games. When playing the game is prescribed and becomes work, a key advantage of playing - the increase in motivation - is lost [38], and the engagement required for learning success is reduced. Therefore, a MOG to promote communication skills is only an option for a sub-cohort and should be supplemented with a training opportunity for the remaining cohort. However, even with the sole offer only for the sub-cohort showing an affinity for games, there would already be an improvement compared to the current state, in which the training of communication skills is not systematically anchored in formal education. In the present study, qualitative methods were used to develop indications of the actual usability of MOGs for training communication skills in construction projects. For actual use, didactic scenarios still need to be developed first, and the implementation then needs to be evaluated in practice. For the didactic design, it might be also helpful to know, which activities in EVE Online in particular lead to the training of communication skills and should be focused accordingly on tasks of the didactic scenarios. Furthermore, the approach presented hereto is presumably not limited to construction projects but may be applied to many other subject areas. Also, for other subject areas, the training of meta skills is not very well anchored in study curricula, thus there is a need of specific training. Didactic scenarios need be designed specifically for the subject area and the meta skills to be trained.

5 Conclusion

As complex processes, construction projects place high demands on the communication skills of all stakeholders. There are only vestigial formal learning scenarios in which communication skills are trained specifically for stakeholders involved in construction projects. Multiplayer online games (MOGs) are known to foster meta skills, which include communication skills, through game activities. Accordingly, the approach of training communication skills for construction projects using MOGs was conceptually validated in this study. To this end, the specific characteristics of communication in construction projects were first elaborated through literature review, and then appropriate learning objectives were devised with the help of interviews with construction project experts. These learning goals were then analyzed in focus group discussions conducted with students having played the MOG EVE Online in a higher education course to determine the extent to which the learning objective might be promoted through activities in EVE Online. For most learning goals, promotion through activities in EVE Online was found. Based on these findings, an upcoming task is the design of didactic scenarios for implementing the approach suggested in practice with the aim of conducting evaluations. Furthermore, quantitative measures in the MOG indicating the learning outcomes need to be identified. The transfer of the results to further learning objectives and subject areas should also be investigated. Also relevant is the identification of additional MOGs that support the training of meta skills. Overall, the study has outlined an option of fostering success-critical communication skills, whose regular training is currently marginalized in formal education, among game-affine stakeholders in construction projects. Hence, the results might contribute to improving the success rate of construction projects.

Acknowledgements. The authors gratefully acknowledge the financial support provided by the German Federal Ministry of Education and Research (BMBF) through grant FKZ 033W011B provided for the "TWIST++" project. Any opinions, findings, conclusions, or recommendations expressed in this paper are those of the authors and do not necessarily reflect the views of the institution mentioned above.

References

1. Qazi, A., Quigley, J., Dickson, A., Kirytopoulos, K.: Project complexity and risk management (ProCRiM): towards modelling project complexity driven risk paths in construction projects. Int. J. Proj. Manag. **34**, 1183–1198 (2016). https://doi.org/10.1016/j.ijproman.2016.05.008
2. Luo, L., He, Q., Xie, J., Yang, D., Wu, G.: Investigating the relationship between project complexity and success in complex construction projects. J. Manag. Eng. **33**, 04016036 (2017). https://doi.org/10.1061/(asce)me.1943-5479.0000471
3. Kennedy, D.M., McComb, S.A., Vozdolska, R.R.: An investigation of project complexity's influence on team communication using monte carlo simulation. J. Eng. Technol. Manag. JET-M. **28**, 109–127 (2011). https://doi.org/10.1016/j.jengtecman.2011.03.001
4. Ellis, R.: Constructive Communication: Skills for the Building Industry. Routledge, Milton Park (2017)
5. Taleb, H., Ismail, S., Wahab, M.H., Mardiah, W.N., Rani, W.M., Amat, R.C.: An Overview of project communication management in construction industry projects. J. Manag. Econ. Ind. Organ. 1–9 (2017). https://doi.org/10.31039/jomeino.2017.1.1.1
6. Emmitt, S., Gorse, C.: Communication in Construction Teams. Routledge, London (2006). https://doi.org/10.4324/9780203018798
7. Ochieng, E.G., Price, A.D.F., Ruan, X., Egbu, C.O., Moore, D.: The effect of cross-cultural uncertainty and complexity within multicultural construction teams. Eng. Constr. Archit. Manag. **20**, 307–324 (2013). https://doi.org/10.1108/09699981311324023
8. Ochieng, E.G., Price, A.D.F.: Managing cross-cultural communication in multicultural construction project teams: the case of Kenya and UK. Int. J. Proj. Manag. **28**, 449–460 (2010). https://doi.org/10.1016/j.ijproman.2009.08.001
9. Wikforss, Ö., Löfgren, A.: Rethinking communication in construction. J. Inf. Technol. Constr. **12**, 337–346 (2007)
10. Shen, W., Shen, Q., Sun, Q.: Building Information modeling-based user activity simulation and evaluation method for improving designer-user communications. Autom. Constr. **21**, 148–160 (2012). https://doi.org/10.1016/j.autcon.2011.05.022

11. Sipayung, H.D., Sani, R.A., Bunawan, W.: Collaborative inquiry for 4C skills. **200**, 440–445 (2018). https://doi.org/10.2991/aisteel-18.2018.95
12. Pagel, M., Söbke, H., Bröker, T.: Using multiplayer online games for teaching soft skills in higher education. In: Fletcher, B., Ma, M., Göbel, S., Baalsrud Hauge, J., Marsh, T. (eds.) JCSG 2021. LNCS, vol. 12945, pp. 276–290. Springer, Cham (2021). https://doi.org/10.1007/978-3-030-88272-3_20
13. Pereira, O.P.: Soft skills: from university to the work environment. Analysis of a survey of graduates in Portugal. Reg. Sect. Econ. Stud. **13**, 105–118 (2013)
14. Stevens, M., Norman, R.: Industry expectations of soft skills in IT graduates a regional survey. ACM Int. Conf. Proc. Ser. 01–05-Feb (2016). https://doi.org/10.1145/2843043.2843068
15. Wilkie, D.: Employers say students aren't learning soft skills in college. https://www.shrm.org/resourcesandtools/hr-topics/employee-relations/pages/employers-say-students-arent-learning-soft-skills-in-college.aspx
16. Aldrich, C.: Learning Online with Games, Simulations, and Virtual Worlds: Strategies for Online Instruction. Wiley, Hoboken (2009)
17. Vaassen, F., Daelemans, W.: Emotion classification in a serious game for training communication skills. In: Proceedings of the 20th Meeting of Computational Linguistics in the Netherland, CLIN 2010, pp. 155–168 (2010)
18. Jeuring, J., et al.: Communicate! — A serious game for communication skills —. In: Conole, G., Klobučar, T., Rensing, C., Konert, J., Lavoué, É. (eds.) EC-TEL 2015. LNCS, vol. 9307, pp. 513–517. Springer, Cham (2015). https://doi.org/10.1007/978-3-319-24258-3_49
19. Hara, C.Y.N., Goes, F. dos S.N., Camargo, R.A.A., Fonseca, L.M.M., Aredes, N.D.A.: Design and evaluation of a 3D serious game for communication learning in nursing education. Nurse Educ. Today. **100**, 1–7 (2021). https://doi.org/10.1016/j.nedt.2021.104846
20. Bernardini, S., Porayska-Pomsta, K., Smith, T.J.: ECHOES: an intelligent serious game for fostering social communication in children with autism. Inf. Sci. (Ny) **264**, 41–60 (2014). https://doi.org/10.1016/j.ins.2013.10.027
21. Zakari, H.M., Ma, M., Simmons, D.: A review of serious games for children with autism spectrum disorders (ASD). In: Ma, M., Oliveira, M.F., Baalsrud Hauge, J. (eds.) SGDA 2014. LNCS, vol. 8778, pp. 93–106. Springer, Cham (2014). https://doi.org/10.1007/978-3-319-11623-5_9
22. Strien, J., Batenburg, R., Dalpiaz, F.: A serious game for teaching general practice management. In: Proceedings of DiGRA FDG First International Joint Conference (DiGRA/FDG 2016), pp. 1–16 (2016)
23. Bodnar, C.A., Clark, R.M.: Can game-based learning enhance engineering communication skills? IEEE Trans. Prof. Commun. **60**, 24–41 (2017). https://doi.org/10.1109/TPC.2016.2632838
24. Söbke, H., Bröker, T., Kornadt, O.: Using the master copy - adding educational content to commercial video games. In: de Carvalho, C.V., Escudeiro, P. (eds.) Proceedings of the 7th European Conference on Games-Based Learning, vol. 2. pp. 521–530. Academic Conferences and Publishing International Limited, Reading (2013)
25. Qian, M., Clark, K.R.: Game-based learning and 21st century skills: a review of recent research. Comput. Human Behav. **63**, 50–58 (2016). https://doi.org/10.1016/j.chb.2016.05.023
26. Sourmelis, T., Ioannou, A., Zaphiris, P.: Massively multiplayer online role playing games (MMORPGs) and the 21st century skills: a comprehensive research review from 2010 to 2016. Comput. Human Behav. **67**, 41–48 (2017). https://doi.org/10.1016/j.chb.2016.10.020
27. Gee, J.P.: Affinity spaces : online and out of school. Phi Betta Kappan. **99**(6), 8–13 (2018)
28. Söbke, H., Bröker, T.: A Browser-based advergame as communication catalyst: types of communication in video games. J. Commun. Soc. **27**, 75–94 (2015). https://doi.org/10.17231/comsoc.27(2015).2090

29. Schmidt, C.: The analysis of semi-structured interviews. In: Flick, U., von Kardorff, E., Steinke, I. (eds.) A Companion to Qualitative Research, pp. 253–258. SAGE Publications, London (2004)
30. CCP: EVE online. http://www.eveonline.com/
31. Boddy, D., Paton, R.: Responding to competing narratives: lessons for project managers. Int. J. Proj. Manag. **22**, 225–233 (2004). https://doi.org/10.1016/j.ijproman.2003.07.001
32. Dainty, A., Moore, D., Murray, M.: Communication in Construction: Theory and Practice. Routledge, London (2006). https://doi.org/10.4324/9780203358641
33. Gorse, C.A., Emmitt, S.: Communication behaviour during management and design team meetings: a comparison of group interaction. Constr. Manag. Econ. **25**, 1197–1213 (2007). https://doi.org/10.1080/01446190701567413
34. Anderson, L.W., et al.: A Taxonomy for Learning, Teaching, and Assessing: A Revision of Bloom's Taxonomy of Educational Objectives, Abridged Edition. Allyn & Bacon (2000). https://doi.org/10.1207/s15430421tip4104_2
35. Merrill, M.D.: Instructional Design Theory. Educational Technology Publications, Englewood Cliffs (1994)
36. Miro: Miro https://miro.com/
37. EVE University Wiki. https://wiki.eveuniversity.org/Main_Page
38. Rockwell, G.M., Kee, K.: Game Studies - the leisure of serious games: a dialogue. Game Stud. - Int. J. Comput. game Res. **11**(2) (2011)

Ecosystem Simulator

A Learning Game About Genetic Algorithms

Qianqi Huang, Heinrich Söbke$^{(\boxtimes)}$ (ID), and Tom Lahmer (ID)

Bauhaus-Universität Weimar, Marienstraße 15, 99423 Weimar, Germany
{heinrich.soebke,tom.lahmer}@uni-weimar.de

Abstract. Genetic algorithms (GA) are a subclass of machine learning methods that allow an automated determination of optimal points. Learning games seem to be very well suited for teaching GA principles, although learning games are still not state of the art. Accordingly, this article presents the development and evaluation of the learning game *Ecosystem Simulator* for teaching GA principles. The development cycle is described here, which includes the selection of a game theme, the identification of the learning content, the definition of the game mechanics to two subsequent iterations consisting each of development and evaluation. The evaluation of the second development iteration's prototype reveals attaining high scores both for learning motivation and intrinsic motivation along with a significant increase in knowledge. Thus, a learning game has been developed, which, in view of its rather young development timeline, seems to offer an appealing gaming experience combined with decent learning outcomes. All in all–as a motivating learning game–the *Ecosystem Simulator* enriches GA teaching.

Keywords: Serious game · Machine learning · Higher education · Game development · Development cycle

1 Introduction

Genetic Algorithms. Genetic Algorithms (GA)–first introduced by John Holland in the 1970s [1]–describe a search heuristic, which reflects the process of natural selection. GA are stochastic search algorithms, which are often used in machine learning applications for finding optimal solutions and which are widely applied in science, engineering, and business [2]. Katoch et al. (2021) [3] give an overview of GA and present the common types of GA operations *Selection*, *Crossover* and *Mutation* with their advantages and disadvantages. As an example of the diverse application areas of GA, Lee (2018) [4] considers the discipline of operations management and identifies the categories of process and product design, operations planning, and operations improvement. Furthermore, Drachal & Pawłowski (2021) [5] examine GA applications for predicting prices of commodities. Similarly, GA have been applied for a bankruptcy prediction modeling [6]. Moreover, GA have been successfully implemented in the optimization of wireless sensor networks (WSNs) regarding node placement, network coverage, clustering, data aggregation, and routing [7]. Further, GA have been applied in software testing [8, 9] for generating test data covering the most critical paths in the software and thus reducing

H. Söbke et al. (Eds.): JCSG 2022, LNCS 13476, pp. 182–197, 2022.
https://doi.org/10.1007/978-3-031-15325-9_14

the testing effort. Riechmann (2001) [10] investigates the connection of GA to evolutionary game theory by extracting rules using threshold values marking companies as being at risk. In conclusion, GAs have been widely applied in a variety of search and optimization problems due to their broad applicability, ease of use, and global perspectives. These affordances provide significant meaning to include GA in contemporary curricula, especially in engineering-oriented curricula.

Game-Based Learning. As media evolve, so do the requirements of learners for learning processes and the media used in those learning processes. The increasing popularity of digital games is also driving the adoption of digital games in learning processes [11]. When games are leveraged in learning processes, the learning processes are referred to as Game-based Learning (GBL) [12]; games themselves, which are applied for further purposes beyond entertainment, such as learning, are called Serious Games (SGs) [13]. SGs with the further purpose of learning, thus featuring GBL, are also called *learning games*. GBL approaches have been proved to be able to promote a student-centered environment, which provides more interesting, motivating, and engaging learning experiences [12, 14, 15]. Learning targets in GBL scenarios often focus on elementary knowledge, conceptual thinking, and social science [16–20]. Less often, computer science-related learning objectives, such as programming, algorithms and computational thinking skills, are featured in GBL scenarios [21–24]. Learning games with regard to GA are mentioned in literature rather sporadically [25].

Hence, the article describes the development and the evaluation of a learning game conveying knowledge about GAs. The remainder of this article is structured as follows: In the next section, the methodology is outlined. The section thereafter presents the results, which are divided into theme finding, first prototype evaluation and second prototype evaluation. Section 4 discusses the results and possible limitations. The final Sect. 5 contains the conclusions.

2 Methodology

The development of learning games requires the coordination of different disciplines. Harteveld et al. [26] suggest balancing pedagogy, game design, and reality into a functioning whole—a task requiring a structured approach. Accordingly, the work guided by Winn's [27] expanded Design, Play, Experience (DPE) framework, which differentiates in layers and aspects in matrix form. In particular, this article describes three specific phases of learning game development: The first phase is the conceptualization, in which especially theme selection (corresponding to the *Storytelling* layer) and target group selection (corresponding to the *Learning* layer) are described. The second phase is the development, which yields two prototypes and reflects the *Design* aspect. The evaluations of the two prototypes follow at the end of the *Experience* aspect, which were thirdly evaluated in both cases and thus form the basis for further development stages in the *Design* aspect.

2.1 Study Outline

This section outlines the methodologies applied in the three phases.

Phase 1: Theme Selection and Target Group Characterization. Two proposals were developed for the selection of a theme, which were offered for selection via an online questionnaire. A snowball sampling was used to acquire a total of 102 participants via social network profiles of the study lead.

Phase 2: Development of the Game Prototypes. The development of the game prototypes is generally an iterative process. Unity v2019.4.3f1 [28], was used as the development environment. Most of the 3D models, particle effects, and sound effects are downloaded from Unity Asset Store [29] and Zapsplat [30]. Some of the artwork has been done from scratch using Adobe Photoshop [31]. Several iterations were performed, with the evaluation results being used in the development of the prototype for the next iteration. Methodologically, walkthroughs were conducted from iteration to iteration with experts in learning games.

Phase 3: Evaluation. Two prototypes were each subjected to a formal evaluation. The evaluation of the first prototype was conducted by a game test with 9 participants recruited from the pool of current and former research assistants of the institution independently of their possible participation in the questionnaire of phase 1. In the second evaluation, after an initial questionnaire including a pre-test, the 20 subjects were invited to play the prototype for a run of about 10 min and then to answer a final questionnaire including a post-test. Again, participants were recruited via social network profiles of the study lead announcing testing a serious game about GA. Also, no participants were specifically targeted or excluded regarding participation in the surveys of earlier phases.

2.2 Learning Outcomes

Essential for learning game development is the determination of intended learning outcomes. In detail, the players are expected to understand and be able to apply the following fundamental GA learning outcomes:

1) Chromosomes represent the **genes** of the individual, usually taking the form of bit strings and each locus in the chromosome has two possible alleles: 0 and 1. If the allele is 1, it dominates the other allele at the same locus and the gene feature presented by this locus is dominant, otherwise it is recessive.
2) The **fitness function** determines how fit (the ability of an individual to compete with other individuals) an individual is. It gives a fitness score to every individual. The probability that an individual will be selected for reproduction is merely based on its fitness score.
3) **Parent selection** ideally is to select the fittest individuals and let them pass their genes to the next generation. Normally, to avoid local maxima, two pairs of individuals (parents) are selected based on their fitness scores. Individuals with high fitness scores have more chances to be selected for reproduction.
4) **Crossover** is the most significant phase in a genetic algorithm. For each pair of parents to be mated, a crossover point is chosen at random from within the genes. Although other crossover strategies exist [3], the only strategy induced is "one-point crossover" at different positions of the gene selectable by the player.

5) **Mutation** is the final step of gene processing. After new offspring are formed, some of their genes may be subjected to a mutation with a low random probability. This implies that some of the bits in the bit string are flipped.

In general, there are four major steps of GA to be mirrored in the game, namely in this order **Parent Selection, Crossover, Mutation**, and **Breed**.

The second prototype is freely available for play [32]. The results of the three phases are described in the following.

3   Results

3.1   Theme

Two theme proposals were prepared, which were presented in the questionnaire and offered for selection. Both theme proposals were based on the principle of evolutionary development of parameter-controlled behavior of a game character group, which then had to measure its performance against an algorithm-controlled character group. One was a *Battlefield* theme using human-like characters. On the other, an *Ecosystem* theme was proposed using animal-like characters. 55% of the respondents chose the Ecosystem theme. The close decision might demonstrate the inhomogeneity of the target group regarding their gaming preferences.

For better characterization of the target group, the questionnaire included a few more questions. Accordingly, the participants were also asked whether they had already played digital games. 8% denied having played digital games. When asked about daily game consumption, 49% of respondents indicated that they used computer games for less than 1 h per day. 30% play 1 to 3 h per day, 12% up to 5 h. When requested about the game platforms predominantly used, 37% answered mobile games, 30% PC games, and 9% console games. 16% play on all platforms, 8% on none. Asked about attitudes towards whether games can support learning, 15% answered in the negative, 50% saw a requirement for appropriate game design, and 35% saw rather limited support in some games. Overall, the results show that the target group is reachable with digital games, but that the target group still has doubts about potential learning outcomes.

3.2   First Prototype

For the creation of the first prototype several specifications are essential, which are described in the following. In particular, the learning outcomes have to be defined, a semantic class model of the characters contained in the game has to be developed, and the game rules, which drive the game dynamics, have to be defined.

Semantic Class Model. Taking the learning objectives as a starting point, the characters of the game were defined by means of a semantic class model. Central characters for modeling a food chain for simulating an ecosystem are Wolf, Rabbit and Grass. In the following, the class Rabbit is introduced. The class Rabbit consists of four (class) components, each of which is expressed as a class (Fig. 1).

- **RabbitGene** contains gene information of rabbits, and the method to translate genes into specific features of the rabbit's behavior or the rabbit's attributes.
- **RabbitFOV** contains the attributes controlling the field of view of the rabbit, and the methods for searching closest foods, predators, and obstacles.
- **RabbitProperties** contains the attributes of the rabbit's properties controlling the status of rabbit, such as health point, alive or not, hunger point and speed. It also contains methods for updating the status of the rabbit.
- **RabbitMotion** controls the rabbit's behavior based on the attributes from RabbitFOV and the current status provided in the class RabbitProperties.

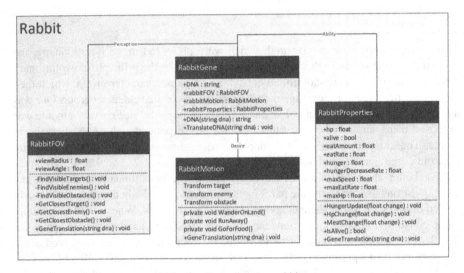

Fig. 1. Class diagram: rabbit

The genes essential for the game are mapped to a chromosome comprised of five genes. The five genes each influence the rabbit's behavior, appearance, and attributes. The value for each gene is either 0 or 1 with the respective meanings of no gene possession (recessive gene) and gene possession (dominant gene).

- **Vision**: this gene provides the ability of doubling the view angle and the view distance of the rabbit. Furthermore, the gene is adverse to the health of the rabbit: the maximum health points of the rabbit will be half of the health points of a normal rabbit.
- **Gut**: this gene prompts the rabbit to be more focused on food acquisition, which means the prior desire of the rabbit is switched from searching for the predator to searching for food.
- **Giant**: the rabbit with this gene grows into a giant individual having doubled in size, maximum hunger, and maximum health compared to the normal rabbit. However, in turn, the speed and eat speed are halved compared to the normal rabbit.
- **Agile**: the rabbit with this gene enters an excited state with four times move speed, eat speed, and hunger decrease compared to the normal rabbit.

- **Cure**: this gene provides self-cure ability by transferring hunger points to health points if the rabbit gets wounded and its current health points are lower than the maximum value.

The attribution of each gene is independent, which means that if a rabbit possesses all the five genes, it gains all the effects from these genes. By means of this principle, overlapping effects could occur, for example if the rabbit possesses the Giant and Agile gene, there will be a compensation for the rabbit's speed due to the Giant gene causing reduction of speed, while the Agile gene causes increase of speed. Thus, this simulation, mirrors natural selection and GAs without considering effects of dependent genes.

The Wolf is modeled as an NPC (Fig. 2), i.e. the player cannot influence controlling parameters, but the parameters are used statically to balance the game play during prototype development.

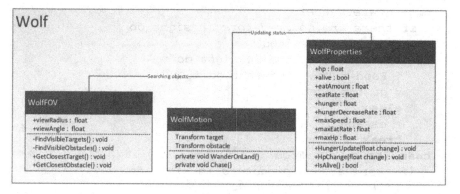

Fig. 2. Class diagram: wolf

Game Play. The game consists of multiple rounds of the interactive Parent Selection (Fig. 3), Crossover (Fig. 4), Mutation (Fig. 5), and Breed (Fig. 6) cycle ("mating season"), between each of which the food chain is simulated based on the actual genes (Fig. 8). In food chain simulation, rabbits and wolves are controlled solely by algorithms based on the actual set of genes (NPCs). The result of a food chain simulation is on the one hand whether the animals have survived, and if so, in which nutritional state they are. At the start of every mating season, there will be a maximum amount of four rabbits alive selected by the system for parent selection. For manipulating the gene combination of offspring, the players are required to select two rabbits among the chosen four as the parents for mating. The criteria for Parent Selection are based on the fitness value of each rabbit. The fitness value is calculated by a fitness function, which has been defined in a heuristic manner. To increase the suspense in the game, the environmental conditions are suddenly changed by randomly occurring scenarios. Besides the normal scenario that starts the game, there are the *Wolf Scenario* (for 40 to 60 s 2 or 3 wolves appear and hunt the rabbits), the *Thunder Scenario* (for 40 to 60 s random lightening are generated that damage all animals in the surrounding area), and the *Snowy Scenario* (besides the visualization of snow, for 40 to 60 s the number of grass tufts is reduced to 5, creating a food shortage for the rabbits). In each scenario, the fitness function is different from the others because a specific gene might deal a positive impact in one scenario but a negative one in another. In this way, the meaning of the fitness function might emerge to the players. Playing the role of prey in the food chain, there are three major behavior patterns designed for the Rabbit, which are implemented using the State Machine technique [33]. The algorithm's pseudocode is as follows:

```
Food found;
Predator found;
States {Wander, Escape, GoForFood}
state = Wander;
Switch (state) {
  case State.Wander:
    if there are no predators in sight do
      searching for food;
      if there are food in sight do
        Food = the closest food found;
        go for food;
      else
        escape from predators;
      break;
  case State.GoForFood:
    if there are no predators in sight do
      if Food still exist do
        go for Food;
        if distance to Food is inside the eat range do
          eat Food;
        else
          searching for food;
      else
        escape from predators;
      break;
  case State.Escape:


    if there are predators in sight do
      Predator = the closest predator found;
      if Predator is still insight do
        escape from Predator towards the opposite
        direction of the direction pointing to Predator;
      else
        searching for food;
      break;
  end
```

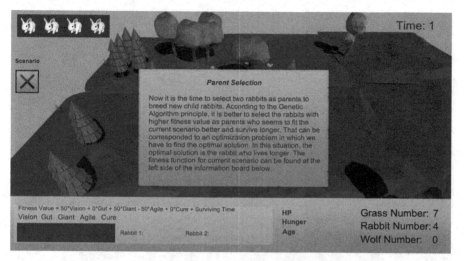

Fig. 3. Ecosystem simulator: explanation parent selection (Screenshot)

Playtest. The playtest for the first prototype involved a class of engineering students. Methodically, the playtest was accompanied in a one-on-one set-ting by the study lead, who also gave a short introduction, according to Fullerton (2008) [34]. Afterwards, participants were asked to play through a play cycle of approximately 10 min while vocalizing their thoughts (think-out-loud). The playtest was concluded with a semi-structured interview on the topics of game play, game mechanics, usability and learning. The observations during the playtest could be summarized as follows:

- The prototype is functional: Players are able to interact with the game unsupported by the study lead.
- The prototype is (partially) complete: Most players understand the winning condition of the game after introduction by the study lead. Only one player has trouble understanding the winning condition. There are no loopholes and dead ends in the game play.
- The prototype is not balanced: Most players are able to understand the characteristic of each gene and dynamically generate strategies to complete the game. However, there is a dominant species, the wolf, breaking the balance.

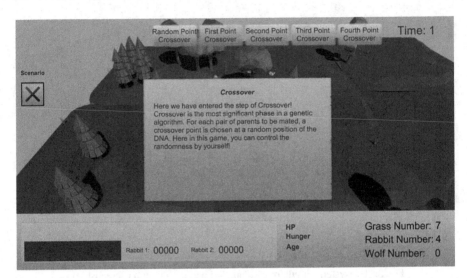

Fig. 4. Ecosystem simulator: explanation crossover (Screenshot)

Furthermore, the results of the semi-structured interviews were categorized (Table 1). Several software errors were indicated by all participants (#2, #3) and unclear visualizations were pointed out (#1, #4). Overall, the interviews confirmed the observations. In particular, a tutorial was missed, and the previous introduction was perceived as insufficient. Accordingly, the game's ability to convey knowledge still needed to be improved.

Table 1. Topics of interviews of first playtest (N = 9, ordered by Category and Frequency)

#	Category	Topic	Freq.
1	Gameplay	Display information of selectable rabbits unclear	9
2		Game end panel display bug	9
3		Mutation visualizer bug	9
4		Visualization of introduction on gene characteristics confusing	9
5		Motivation and interest decrease due to lack of rewards and player stats	4
6		Screen with technical terms unclear	3
7		Dominant object (wolf) causes imbalance	2
8	Learning	GA learning obstacles, lack of tutorial guide	7
9		Memorization of parent rabbits DNA impossible	5
10	Other	Adaption of different screen resolution	3
11		Desire better camera controlling	2
12		Better UI design required	2

3.3 Second Prototype

Based on the evaluation of the first prototype, a second prototype was developed, which included an extended player guidance through a tutorial as well as detailed explanations of the individual game steps. This second prototype was then subjected to further evaluation. Participants were recruited from GA-interested students in online forums for students at the institution. The evaluation of the prototype [32], took place online unattended using a pre-post-test design. In addition to pre- and post-tests, further standardized measurements were included in the two questionnaires. Due to the online unattended implementation of the study without any rewards for the participants, the number of participants slightly dropped from study step to study step. A total of 18 participants answered the pre-game questionnaire and 13 participants answered the post-game questionnaire in a valid manner, after for both questionnaires two answers had been excluded due to recognizable unsuitable answers (incorrect answer for a randomly inserted item "Please select '2' on this scale"). In the following, the results regarding the two standardized questionnaires used as well as the learning outcomes are summarized.

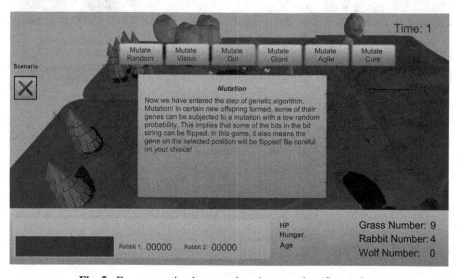

Fig. 5. Ecosystem simulator: explanation mutation (Screenshot)

Learning Motivation. Motivation in learning scenarios influences the success of learning significantly. The *Questionnaire of Current Motivation in Learning Situations (QCM)* [35] in its short form having 12 items [36] in four subscales was used to measure this motivation (Fig. 7). The scores show a good probability of success (4.5), interest in the game (4.4), and challenge (4.7) provided by the game. Anxiety in the lower half of the scale (3.4) is also important since higher values are seen as hampering learning. However, the scores achieved in unsupervised individual play are not at all competitive with those of a learning activity in groups [37] in which SimCity is facilitated–and which is consequently motivationally enhanced [38]. The comparatively strong drop of the subscale interest (4.4 vs. 5.3) is striking and could not have been predicted, since the participants were recruited on the basis of their interest in GA. Overall, however, the values of the QCM - also in view of the prototype stage - are to be considered positive and indicative of the game character.

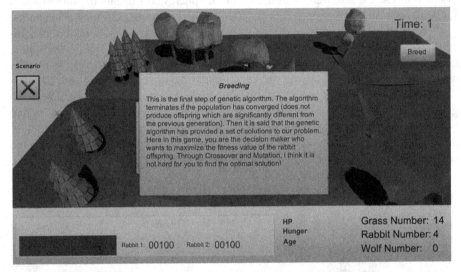

Fig. 6. Ecosystem simulator: explanation breeding (Screenshot)

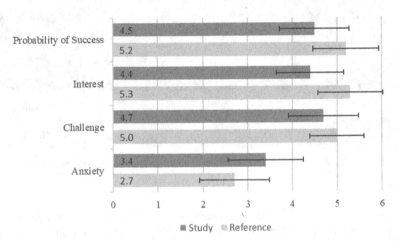

Fig. 7. QCM subscales: values of the study (N = 18, 7-point Likert scale), references adapted from a facilitated SimCity learning activity [37]

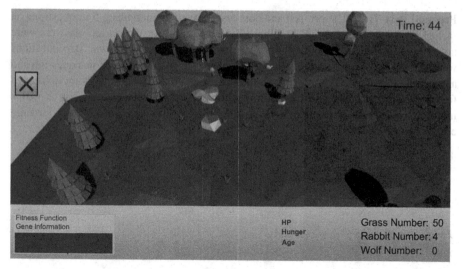

Fig. 8. Food chain simulation GA cycles (Screenshot)

Intrinsic Motivation. A game derives from triggering intrinsic motivation and being played for the sake of playing the game. Intrinsic motivation was captured during the post-game questionnaire using the *Measure of Intrinsic Motivation* (MIM) by Isen & Reeve [39], which consists of 8 items on a 7-point Likert scale. The MIM items were textually adapted to the game, i.e., the pronoun "it" was replaced by "the game." The score was 4.6 (N = 13), which is in the upper half of the scale. In comparison, for a likewise interactive app for rotating objects the scores 4.2 (static) and 4.7 (dynamic) were measured [40]. From this result, the conclusion is to be drawn that the Ecosystem Simulator is capable of arising intrinsic motivation.

Table 2. Pre- and post-test: questions (Correct answers are <u>underlined</u>)

Type	Question
Single-Choice	Genetic Algorithms are generally considered to solve what kind of problem? Evolutionary problem, Systematic problem, Numerical problem, <u>Optimization problem</u>
Multiple choice	Which practical problem can be solved by Genetic Algorithms? (<u>Searching the shortest path between two locations</u>, <u>Ordering a series of numbers</u>, <u>Searching the maximum value of a function</u>, Separating an area into average pieces)
Multiple choice	What are the main steps for Genetic Algorithms? (<u>Parent Selection</u>, Extension, <u>Crossover</u>, <u>Mutation</u>, Recursion, <u>Breeding</u>)
Open	If you know the steps of Genetic Algorithms, please write down the steps in the correct order

Pre- and Post-Test. The pre-test and post-test were conducted using four questions on factual knowledge regarding GA (Table 2). In the pre-test, the correct answers were not revealed, so no learning could occur from the pre-test on its own. Two questions were multiple choice questions, and one question each was a single-choice question and an open-text question. A total of 11 points could be scored, with one point de-ducted for each incorrect answer in the multiple choice questions. On average, partic-ipants improved 46% on the pre-test to 87% on the post-test (Table 3). Thus, a clear learning effect is observed overall.

Table 3. Results of the pre-test and the post-test

	N	Mean	SD	Correct
Pre	18	5.1	3.10	46%
Post	13	9.5	2.22	87%

4 Discussion

The development of the Ecosystem Simulator into a playable, online available learning game, which is able to impart knowledge, may be a solid base for teaching the basics of GAs. Nevertheless, there are limitations to be mentioned and open questions to be pointed out. For example, there may be a bias due to the attrition of participants in the post-game questionnaire, since presumably the most diligent and motivated participants dutifully participated in the second questionnaire.

In the initial questionnaire, there was a balanced choice between two theme candi-dates. To increase motivational effects of the game, it might be worth evaluating to what extent the both themes might be used at little cost as a kind of theme skin for the algo-rithms that have now been implemented. In this way, learners could select their preferred theme at the beginning of the learning activity and, on average, increased motivation might be achieved.

The fitness function used to evaluate the genome was first determined in a heuristic approach. At the same time, a natural fitness function results from the gameplay, i.e. depending on the genes, the rabbits have different survival times or different health states at the end of the game. Fitness functions reflecting the actual survival times of the rabbits were determined using a simulation analysis. The results of this simulation analysis still need to be incorporated into the fitness functions that are actually implemented.

5 Conclusions

This article outlines the development of the learning game *Ecosystem Simulator* for teaching the fundamentals of the machine learning sub-discipline Genetic Algorithms (GA). The complete development cycle was carried out, from the selection of a theme, the identification of the learning content, the definition of the game mechanics, to two development iterations with subsequent evaluations. The result is a learning game, which is available online and, which–in view of its comparatively short development history– already offers an encouraging gaming experience with good learning outcomes. Upcoming work includes the implementation of additional game mechanics, such as numerical player stats, to further increase the motivation generated by the game, as well as testing the game in real-world learning settings to approve appropriate didactic scenarios. Overall, the Ecosystem Simulator enriches GA teaching with a motivating learning game.

Acknowledgements. The authors gratefully acknowledge the financial support provided by the German Federal Ministry of Education and Research (BMBF) through grant FKZ 033W011B provided for the "TWIST++" project. Any opinions, findings, conclusions, or recommendations expressed in this paper are those of the authors and do not necessarily reflect the views of the institution mentioned above.

References

1. Holland, J.H.: Adaptation in Natural and Artificial Systems: An Introductory Analysis with Applications to Biology, Control, and Artificial Intelligence. The MIT Press, Cambridge (1992)
2. Mitchell, M.: An Introduction to Genetic Algorithms. The MIT Press, Cambridge (1999)
3. Katoch, S., Chauhan, S.S., Kumar, V.: A review on genetic algorithm: past, present, and future. Multimedia Tools Appl. **80**(5), 8091–8126 (2020). https://doi.org/10.1007/s11042-020-101 39-6
4. Lee, C.K.H.: A review of applications of genetic algorithms in operations management. Eng. Appl. Artif. Intell. **76**, 1–12 (2018)
5. Drachal, K., Pawłowski, M.: A review of the applications of genetic algorithms to forecasting prices of commodities. Economies **9**, 6 (2021)
6. Shin, K.S., Lee, Y.J.: A genetic algorithm application in bankruptcy prediction modeling. Expert Syst. Appl. **23**, 321–328 (2002)
7. Norouzi, A., Zaim, A.H.: Genetic algorithm application in optimization of wireless sensor networks. Sci. World J. **2014**, 286575 (2014)
8. Srivastava, P.R., Kim, T.: Application of genetic algorithm in software testing. Int. J. Softw. Eng. Appl. **3**, 87–96 (2009)
9. Xu, B., Xie, X., Shi, L., Nie, C.: Application of genetic algorithms in software testing. In: Advances in Machine Learning Applications in Software Engineering, pp. 287–317. IGI Global (2007)
10. Riechmann, T.: Genetic algorithm learning and evolutionary games. J. Econ. Dyn. Control. **25**, 1019–1037 (2001)
11. Squire, K.R.: Video Games and Learning: Teaching and Participatory Culture in the Digital Age. Teachers College Press, New York (2011)
12. Anastasiadis, T., Lampropoulos, G., Siakas, K.: Digital game-based learning and serious games in education. Int. J. Adv. Sci. Res. Eng. **4**, 139–144 (2018)
13. Michael, D.R., Chen, S.L.: Serious Games: Games That Educate, Train, and Inform. Course Technology, Mason (2005)
14. Yue, W.S., Zin, N.A.M., Jaafar, A.: Digital game-based learning (DGBL) model and development methodology for teaching history. WSEAS Trans. Comput. **8**, 322–333 (2009)

15. Coleman, T.E., Money, A.G.: Student-centred digital game–based learning: a conceptual framework and survey of the state of the art. High. Educ. **79**(3), 415–457 (2019). https://doi.org/10.1007/s10734-019-00417-0

16. Al-Azawi, R., Al-Faliti, F., Al-Blushi, M.: Educational gamification vs. game based learning: comparative study. Int. J. Innov. Manag. Technol. **7**, 131–136 (2016)

17. White, K., McCoy, L.P.: Effects of game-based learning on attitude and achievement in elementary mathematics. Netw. Online J. Teach. Res. **21**, 1–17 (2019)

18. Rose, S.P., Habgood, M.P.J., Jay, T.: Designing a programming game to improve children's procedural abstraction skills in scratch. J. Educ. Comput. Res. **58**, 1372–1411 (2020)

19. Hussein, M.H., Ow, S.H., Cheong, L.S., Thong, M.-K., Ebrahim, N.A.: Effects of digital game-based learning on elementary science learning: a systematic review. IEEE Access **7**, 62465–62478 (2019)

20. Cheng, C.H., Su, C.H.: A Game-based learning system for improving student's learning effectiveness in system analysis course. Procedia Soc. Behav. Sci. **31**, 669–675 (2012)

21. Kazimoglu, C., Kiernan, M., Bacon, L., Mackinnon, L.: A serious game for developing computational thinking and learning introductory computer programming. Procedia Soc. Behav. Sci. **47**, 1991–1999 (2012)

22. Gentile, M., et al.: The role of disposition to critical thinking in digital game-based learning. Int. J. Serious Games. **6**, 51–63 (2019)

23. Frankovic, I., Hoic-Bozic, N., Prskalo, L.N.: Serious games for learning programming concepts. In: Conference Proceedings. The Future of Education, p. 354. libreriauniversitaria. it Edizioni (2018)

24. Ouahbi, I., Kaddari, F., Darhmaoui, H., Elachqar, A., Lahmine, S.: Learning basic programming concepts by creating games with scratch programming environment. Procedia Soc. Behav. Sci. **191**, 1479–1482 (2015)

25. Cirkovic, I.: EvoEnvi: a collaborative serious game played on an interactive table for teaching evolution using genetic algorithms (2018). https://studenttheses.uu.nl/handle/20.500.12932/30527

26. Harteveld, C., Guimarães, R., Mayer, I., Bidarra, R.: Balancing pedagogy, game and reality components within a unique serious game for training levee inspection. In: Hui, K.-C., et al. (eds.) Edutainment 2007. LNCS, vol. 4469, pp. 128–139. Springer, Heidelberg (2007). https://doi.org/10.1007/978-3-540-73011-8_15

27. Winn, B.M.: The design, play, and experience framework. In: Handbook of Research on Effective Electronic Gaming in Education, vol. 5497 (2011)

28. Unity Technologies: Unity - Game Engine. https://unity3d.com/

29. Unity Technologies: Unity Asset Store - Discover Top-Rated Game Assets. https://assetstore.unity.com

30. Zapsplat: Free Sound Effects. www.zapsplat.com

31. Adobe Inc.: Adobe Photoshop. https://www.adobe.com/de/photoshop.

32. Huang, Q.: Ecosystem Simulator. https://gamejamq.itch.io/ecosystem

33. Schneider, F.B.: Implementing fault-tolerant services using the state machine approach: a tutorial. ACM Comput. Surv. **22**, 299–319 (1990)

34. Fullerton, T.: Game Design Workshop: A Playcentric Approach to Creating Innovative Games. Morgan Kaufmann, Burlington (2008)

35. Rheinberg, F., Vollmeyer, R., Burns, B.D.: QCM: a questionnaire to assess current motivation in learning situations. Diagnostica **47**, 57–66 (2001)

36. Freund, P.A., Kuhn, J.T., Holling, H.: Measuring current achievement motivation with the QCM: short form development and investigation of measurement invariance. Pers. Individ. Dif. **51**, 629–634 (2011)

37. Söbke, H., Arnold, U., Montag, M.: Intrinsic motivation in serious gaming a case study. In: Marfisi-Schottman, I., Bellotti, F., Hamon, L., Klemke, R. (eds.) GALA 2020. LNCS, vol. 12517, pp. 362–371. Springer, Cham (2020). https://doi.org/10.1007/978-3-030-63464-3_34

38. Baalsrud Hauge, J., et al.: Current competencies of game facilitators and their potential optimization in higher education: multimethod study. JMIR Serious Games 9, e25481 (2021)

39. Isen, A.M., Reeve, J.: The influence of positive affect on intrinsic and extrinsic motivation: facilitating enjoyment of play, responsible work behavior, and self-control. Motiv. Emot. 29, 297–325 (2005)

40. Zander, S., Montag, M., Wetzel, S., Bertel, S.: A gender issue? - How touch-based interactions with dynamic spatial objects support performance and motivation of secondary school students. Comput. Educ. 143, 103677 (2020)

Catch Me If you Can: An Educational Serious Game to Teach Grammatical English Rules

Reham Ayman[1]([✉]), Reem Ayman[1], and Nada Sharaf[2]

[1] Department of Computer Science, Faculty of Media Engineering and Technology, German University in Cairo, Cairo, Egypt
reham.ayman@guc.edu.eg, reem.saad@student.guc.edu.eg
[2] Faculty of Informatics and Computer Science, The German International University Egypt, Cairo, Egypt
nada.hamed@giu-uni.de

Abstract. English is a necessary language in different disciplines nowadays. It is used worldwide as the primary communication language [10]. Most parents care about teaching children the English language as a foreign language. They believe that it gives them a better opportunity of having a good job [8]. Thus, the work presented in this paper aims to teach English language concepts to (L2) learners of different ages. To achieve that, an escape room game was implemented. The game teaches two concepts in the English language, the effect of the vowel "E" on pronouncing the preceding vowel, and the mass nouns. To evaluate the platform, two groups of participants were recruited, school students and university students. The ages were between 11 to 14 and 18 to 24 respectively. An independent sample t-test was applied to the learning gain and engagement. The results proved that the game can be used to teach the different age ranges where all parties feel engaged and immersed in the game with no significant p-value. According to flow and usability results, only minor modifications need to be applied according to the age range.

Keywords: Serious games · Education · Language · Phonetics · Grammar

1 Introduction

Serious games have steadily become more and more incorporated into our formal and non-formal educational systems due to the fact that they are far more efficient and effective than traditional education [11]. Traditional education methodologies still primarily focus on constrained learning methods such as verbal and logical [7]. According to studies, children are extremely engaged while playing games; [15] their brains achieve a high degree of attention and immersion, resulting in the highest educational gain while keeping them amused and ready to grow and return for more.

H. Söbke et al. (Eds.): JCSG 2022, LNCS 13476, pp. 198–209, 2022.
https://doi.org/10.1007/978-3-031-15325-9_15

As a result, the work presented in the paper utilizes serious games with the educational field through an Escape Room game to enhance the interactivity with the game and to get better results for the educational part than normal educational methods. The choice of this game is based on targeting different ages of (L2) learners. Thus, keeping all users interested, eager to learn, and entertained.

After their native tongue, English is the most essential language that children learn from primary school [20, 23]. Teaching kids grammatical rules, on the other hand, is a difficult endeavor [9]. Thus, the aim of this work is to develop a serious game to work as an efficient educational tool that can teach different age ranges (not only children) grammatical and phonetics English rules to (L2) learners. The game targets the mass nouns as a grammatical rule and the effect of the vowel "E" at the end of the word on pronouncing the preceding vowel [6].

2 Related Work

Serious games are games that aim not only for entertainment and enjoyment but also aim to deliver a purpose as its main aim. Thus, embedding this purpose into a game to make it more engaging and interactive. Serious games targets various fields including marketing, health care, education [17]. Compared to traditional educational methods, educational games proved to improve the learning gain due to be more engaging and enjoying [2, 4, 5, 12, 24, 25].

The work introduced in [1] aims to contribute to the development of the professional qualifications of future foreign language teachers. The experiment was performed over the period of 11 weeks (8 weeks of gaming and 3 weeks of reading activities). Data were collected before and after these 11 weeks using questionnaires for the participants to measure the technical features of the game, linguistic content, and the effectiveness of reproductive writing and reading activities. A game diary was used as another data collection tool. Students were given the task to document their gaming experiences, difficulties, and problems, the daily/weekly playing time as well as newly learned words and structures, country-specific information, in-game language exercises, and dictionary use. Over the period of 11 weeks, students played the game as it was added to their school curriculum. The results showed a significant change in their vocabulary levels before and after the 11-week course. This indicates that using game activities were useful for the participants.

In addition, the work presented in [19] aimed to present a novel clustering-based profiling method for analyzing serious games learners. GraphoLearn was used as the game for this testing experiment and the results divided the learners into profiles. Learning reading skills requires connections between the spoken and written language which GraphoLearn offers. Data were gathered from 1632 players who were 6.5 to 8.75 years. The player's actions during the game were logged into a database (Player's inputs and time spent with each task). There were profiles after analyzing the findings as follows: one *high performing*, three *high performing*, and two *high performing* profiles with the different sound-letter pair errors. The players in the two weakest profiles showed the best progression while playing the game, which suggests that the combination of GraphoLearn and school-provided reading instruction helps children who have difficulties in reading acquisition. This supported the first hypothesis which states that there are different profiles that can be interpreted, based on the variability in the reading skills of the readers. The results also proved that most of the errors were related to confusing phonetically and visually similar letters taking into account the confusions exceeding 10%.

The study presented [21] required Swedish-speaking beginners of learning English to write down as many English words as they could think of that began with given letters. It was concluded that the words that were immediately accessible to the learners were, in general, words that had been repeated regularly in class or introduced recently in the class textbook. Any variability in their vocabulary-production patterns, on the other hand, could largely be explained by the individual interests of the learners, especially rock music, but also computers and computer adventure games. The experiment used computer games and learner interests as a starting point. The experiment aimed to study the effects of children's interaction with computers on their learning of foreign vocabulary. A game called Pirate Cove was introduced to two Swedish children aged 9 and 11. The experiment consisted of three phases where the learners were exposed to the game for three-quarters of an hour with one-month intervals between each phase and the one after it. In the first and second phases, the learners used the game while in the third one they were given a list of 50 English words and were asked to translate it. From this experiment, it was concluded that with the aid of Pirate Cove, the learners learned the major part of the vocabulary used in the game.

3   Methodology

"Catch Me If you Can" aims to develop an educational game that suits different ages. "Catch Me If you Can" teaches phonetics concepts in addition to mass nouns in the English language to (L2) learners. It mainly focuses on the effect of the vowel "E" on pronouncing the preceding vowel. As in cut and cute, the vowel "E" at the end of the word cute lengthens the pronunciation of the vowel "U". Mass nouns is a grammatical concept where some words are treated as only plural, only singular, or using a continuous quantifier (*much, some*) [6].

To achieve that, two groups of sentences are displayed after a specific puzzle is solved. On answering 5 or more sentences correctly, the player receives a hint to help him throughout the game. When choosing an answer, a feedback sound is played indicating if the chosen answer is correct or not. On starting the game, 10 sentences appear to the player one by one, and he has to answer if these sentences are contextually correct or not. First, the phonetic problem is introduced at the start of the first room, to help the player with the hint (if he received any), if needed. For example, in Fig. 1a the sentence is contextually incorrect where the word "bar" should be "bare". Then after solving the first puzzle, the second batch of sentences is displayed in sequence. As in Fig. 1b, the word "advice" is a mass noun, and to be treated as a plural the word "some" is added to the sentence.

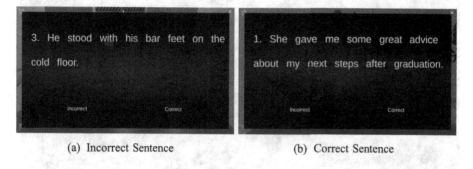

(a) Incorrect Sentence   (b) Correct Sentence

Fig. 1. Sentences examples

3.1   Game Structure

A first-person escape room game was implemented to achieve the desired aim. It is a single-player game where the player controls the navigation via keyboard and mouse to walk in the rooms and interact with the objects. At the beginning of the game, the player has to go through a tutorial level to learn how to interact with the objects in the rooms.

Room 1. The first room is a 2-level puzzle where the player has to open 2 consecutive doors. To open the first door the player has to find a key that is hidden underneath a pillow. On clicking on the pillow it moves and the key is revealed. The player collects the key by clicking on it, then it gets stored in the bag as in Fig. 2. This key opens a chest that contains 4 playing cards as in Fig. 3c which build up the code to open the door. However, the cards should be ordered according to the shapes drawn on the wall. After figuring out the key and opening the door, another door appears at the end of the hall. To open this door, the player has to change the clock pointer to match the spoon and the fork on the plate which are placed beside the bed in the room as shown in Figs. 3a, and 3b. After rotating the clock pointers, the clock moves where the player finds a key behind it. This key opens a locker that has an ID card inside that unlocks the door.

Room 2. The aforementioned door leads to the second room which has 2 puzzles to unlock the escape door. The first puzzle is an audio mixer that the player has to adjust to a specific level illustrated in Fig. 4b, in order to get a missing chess piece. This adjustment can be deduced from the pendulum placed next to the cheeseboard shown in Fig. 4a. On adding this chess piece to the chessboard,

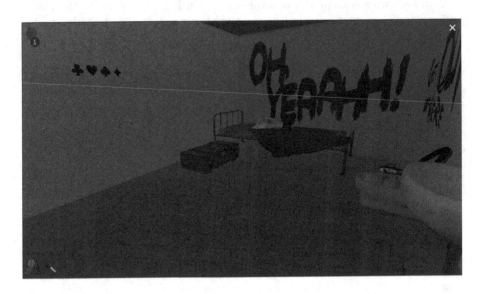

Fig. 2. Room 1

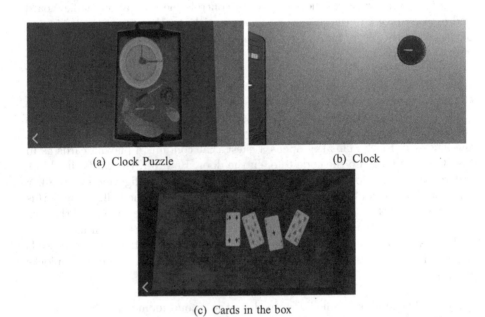

(a) Clock Puzzle   (b) Clock

(c) Cards in the box

Fig. 3. Room 1 puzzles

a drawer is opened which contains colored papers. These papers have the same colors as the numbers on the wall which unlocks the escaping door. The player has to rearrange the number according to the colored papers' order before entering the numbers into the door keypad as in Fig. 5. Finally, when the door opens, a congratulation message is displayed to greet the player for escaping and finishing the game.

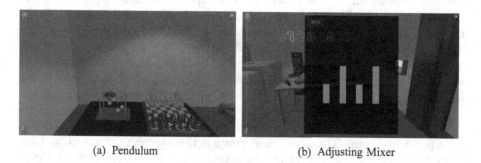

(a) Pendulum   (b) Adjusting Mixer

Fig. 4. Mixer puzzle

Fig. 5. Unlock the escape door

4   Experimental Design

This research experiments if the proposed game can be used to teach children as well as adults. This was achieved by implementing the Escape Room game which teaches some English grammar and phonetics. The game was tested by measuring how much the participants enjoyed playing and learned [14]. The targeted groups are school students between the age of 11 and 13 and university students between the age of 18 and 24. The experiment aims to prove or reject the null hypothesis. The null hypothesis states that there is no difference between the effect of using the game on different age groups. The first hypothesis (H1): There is no difference in the learning gain between the two groups. The second hypothesis (H2): There is no difference in the engagement level between the school students and the university students. The third hypothesis (H3): There is no difference in the usability of the game between the control group and the experiment group.

The model used is a between-group design that has a control group and an experiment group. The experiment group is the university students, and the control group is the school students. Each participant in each group was selected randomly. The participants had to fill out a total of 5 online forms, 2 quizzes, and 3 questionnaires. The experiment flow went as follows: pre-quiz, playing the game, post-quiz, engagement tests, and finally a system usability test.

5   Procedure

A sample of 26 participants experimented with the game where 13 participants were from the control group (school students) and the other was from the experiment group (university students). The duration of the experiment lasted 20 to 30 min including the tests and the questionnaires. The learning gain, engagement level, flow, and system usability of the different age groups were measured to examine the different behavior between the control group and the experiment group.

5.1   Learning Gain

Learning gain is a measure of how much knowledge is gained from a particular activity. The participants were tested before the activity to measure their current knowledge then they conducted the same test to measure how much they learned from doing the activity [16]. In this work, the participants conducted a pre-quiz to examine their knowledge of the English grammar and phonetics introduced in the game. The quiz consists of 14 multiple choice questions whereas 7 questions are about the mass nouns where each question has one of the answers a plural verb and a singular verb, and the other 7 are about the phonetic concept where each question has one of the answers a word without "E" (fin) and with "E" (fine) at the end of the word. After playing the game, each participant answered an identical copy of the pre-quiz. To measure the learning gain of a participant, each correct answer receives a point, then the total grade of the pre-quiz is subtracted from the total grade of the post-quiz.

5.2   Engagement Level

Immersion, attention, involvement, interest, enjoyment, identification, effort, and arousal are the main factors of game engagement. Engagement is the sense of "being there" and immersed in the game [13,26]. A self-reported questionnaire was used to measure the engagement of the participants from the different groups. Each participant answered the questionnaire after completing the game. It is a 9-items 5-Likert Scale questionnaire proposed by [22].

5.3   Usability

The usability of the game can be defined as system usability. Thus, to measure the game usability, the system usability scale (SUS) questionnaire was used. It is a 10 questions 5-Likert scale standardized questionnaire [3]. It examines how understandable the game is, and how likely the participant would play it again. Additionally, it checks if the participants needed any guidance or needed to learn external aspects before playing the game.

5.4   Flow

According to [18], flow is the balance between the skill and the challenge of the user while doing an activity. The best-case scenario is when there is a linear relation between the two factors. However, high skill level and low challenge level lead to boredom while anxiousness is the result of low skill and high challenge. After playing the game, the participants answer two flow questionnaires where each questionnaire corresponds to one of the rooms (levels) of the game and consists of 2 5-Likert scale questions: "How did the participant find this level challenge?" and "Is the skill of the participant appropriate for this level?" [22].

6   Results

An independent sample t-test was used to examine if there is a significant difference between the learning gain, engagement and system usability scale of the two groups.

6.1   Learning Gain

The results shows that the learning gain revealed by the experiment group (M = 1.54, SD = 1.127) is not significant from the control group (M = 1.69, SD = 1.377) ($t(13) = 0.312$, $p > 0.05$). This doesn't reject the hypothesis that stated that there is no difference in the learning gain between the two groups.

6.2   Engagement Level

The results shows that the engagement experienced by the experiment group (M = 3.48, SD = 0.412) is not significant from the control group (M = 3.5, SD = 0.333) (t(13) = 0.407, p > 0.05). This doesn't reject the hypothesis that stated that there is no difference in the engagement level between the school students and the university students.

6.3   Usability

The results showed that the system usability achieved by the experiment group (M = 85, SD = 12.97) is not significant from the control group (M = 64, SD = 14.3) (t(13) = 0.441, p < 0.05). This rejects the hypothesis that stated that there is no difference in the usability of the game between the control group and the experiment group. The scores interpret a difference between the groups. The school students group scored 64 which corresponds to a grade of C, however the university students scored 85 which maps to a grade of A [3].

6.4   Flow

The graphs in Figs. 6 and 7 are derived by the equation [22].

$$0.25 \times (Skill - Challenge) \tag{1}$$

These graphs illustrate how far is the flow of each level from the zero flow (best case). In the first Fig. 6 the flow from distance in the first room is 0.1 which indicates that the participants felt a little bit more skillful, however, in the second room they found it more challenging with a value of flow from distance equals 0.06. In addition, according to the Fig. 7, the university students found the game less challenging than the school students. They scored a flow from distance of 0.3 for the first room, and 0.14 for the second room. The participants felt skillful and had a little challenge in the first room, then the challenge increased in the second room.

7   Discussion

According to the previous results, the game can be used to teach different age groups, however some modifications should be done according to the targeted age group. For young age children, the game should be more illustrated, easy to use, and controlled. Additionally, the challenge of the first room should be increased in case of using the game with young age students. The second room shouldn't be modified because the far from distance value is too small which can be neglected. However, according to the results obtained from the university students, the older the students, the more challenging the game should become.

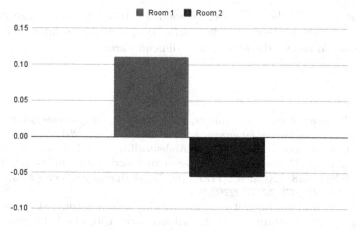

Fig. 6. Flow from distance of school group

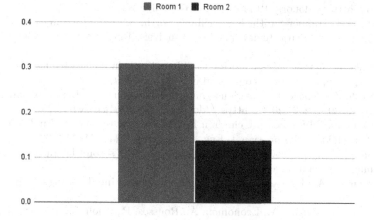

Fig. 7. Flow from distance of university group

8   Conclusion and Future Work

Building a serious game that teaches and engages different age ranges is not an easy task. The main aim of this work is to implement an educational game that teaches different age groups some English grammar and phonetics. Thus, an escape room game was developed to teach noun words and the effect of the letter "E" at the end of the word on pronouncing the preceding vowel. The game was evaluated with different age ranges (11–13) and (13–24). The results showed that there is no significance in the learning gain, and engagement. Thus, the game proved to be suitable to teach different age ranges. However, the usability score shows that the game usage should be easier the younger the user is. Additionally, according to the flow results, increasing the game challenge would be more engaging in the case of high school students and older.

For future work, the game can be modified to adapt to the age range by asking the user about the age at the start of the game. According to the answer, the game would choose the appropriate difficulty level.

References

1. Alyaz, Y., Spaniel-Weise, D., Gürsoy, E.: A study on using serious games in teaching German as a foreign language. J. Educ. Learn. **6**, 250–264 (2017)
2. Ayman, R., Sharaf, N., Ahmed, G., Abdennadher, S.: MiniColon; teaching kids computational thinking using an interactive serious game. In: Göbel, S., et al. (eds.) JCSG 2018. LNCS, vol. 11243, pp. 79–90. Springer, Cham (2018). https://doi.org/10.1007/978-3-030-02762-9_9
3. Bangor, A., Kortum, P., Miller, J.: Determining what individual SUS scores mean: adding an adjective rating scale. J. Usability Stud. **4**(3), 114–123 (2009)
4. Chee, Y.S.: Embodiment, embeddedness, and experience: game-based learning and the construction of identity. Res. Pract. Technol. Enhanc. Learn. **02**(01), 3–30 (2007). https://doi.org/10.1142/S1793206807000282
5. Clark, D.B., Tanner-Smith, E.E., Killingsworth, S.S.: Digital games, design, and learning: a systematic review and meta-analysis. Rev. Educ. Res. **86**(1), 79–122 (2016)
6. Colunga, E., Gasser, M.: Attention to different cues in noun learning: the effect of English vs. Spanish mass/count syntax. Citeseer (2001)
7. Darwesh, A.: Concepts of serious game in education. Int. J. Eng. Comput. Sci. **4**(12), 15229–15232 (2016). https://doi.org/10.18535/Ijecs/v4i12.25
8. Djiwandono, P.I.: Teach my children English: why parents want English teaching for their children. Indonesian J. Eng. Lang. Teach. **1**(1), 64–72 (2005)
9. Hoffman, V.: A program for teaching inquiry in the second language to children learning English as a second language (2021)
10. Ilyosovna, N.A.: The importance of English language. Int. J. Orange Technol. **2**(1), 22–24 (2020)
11. Kokkalia, G., Drigas, A., Economou, A., Roussos, P., Choli, S.: The use of serious games in preschool education. Int. J. Emerg. Technol. Learn. **12**(11), 15–27 (2017)
12. Liu, Z., Moon, J., Kim, B., Dai, C.-P.: Integrating adaptivity in educational games: a combined bibliometric analysis and meta-analysis review. Educ. Tech. Res. Dev. **68**(4), 1931–1959 (2020). https://doi.org/10.1007/s11423-020-09791-4
13. Martey, R.M., et al.: Measuring game engagement: multiple methods and construct complexity. Simul. Gaming **45**(4–5), 528–547 (2014). https://doi.org/10.1177/1046878114553575
14. Martey, R.M., et al.: Measuring game engagement: multiple methods and construct complexity. Simul. Gaming **45**(4–5), 528–547 (2014)
15. Mayes, D., Cotton, J.: Measuring engagement in video games: a questionnaire. Proc. Hum. Factors Ergon. Soc. Annu. Conf. **45**, 692–696 (2001). https://doi.org/10.1177/154193120104500704
16. McGrath, C.H., Guerin, B., Harte, E., Frearson, M., Manville, C.: Learning gain in higher education (2015)
17. Michael, D.: Serious Games: Games that Educate. Train and Inform, Course PTR (2006)
18. Csikszentmihalyi, M.: Flow and the Foundations of Positive Psychology. Springer, Dordrecht (2014). https://doi.org/10.1007/978-94-017-9088-8

19. Niemelä, M., Kärkkäinen, T., Äyrämö, S., Ronimus, M., Richardson, U., Lyytinen, H.: Game learning analytics for understanding reading skills in transparent writing system. Br. J. Educ. Technol. **51**, 2376–2390 (2020)
20. Oktaviani, A., Fauzan, A.: Teachers perceptions about the importance of English for young learners. Linguist. Eng. Educ. Art J. **1**(1), 1–15 (2017). https://doi.org/10.31539/leea.v1i1.25
21. Palmberg, R.: Computer games and foreign-language vocabulary learning. ELT J. **42**, 247–252 (1988)
22. Pearce, J.M., Ainley, M., Howard, S.: The ebb and flow of online learning. Comput. Hum. Behav. **21**(5), 745–771 (2005). https://doi.org/10.1016/j.chb.2004.02.019
23. Sepyanda, M.: The importance of English subject in elementary school curriculum. Engl. Lang. Teach. Res. **1**(1) (2017)
24. Vlachopoulos, D., Makri, A.: The effect of games and simulations on higher education: a systematic literature review. Int. J. Educ. Technol. High. Educ. **14**(1), 1–33 (2017). https://doi.org/10.1186/s41239-017-0062-1
25. Vogel, J.J., Vogel, D.S., Cannon-Bowers, J., Bowers, C.A., Muse, K., Wright, M.: Computer gaming and interactive simulations for learning: a meta-analysis. J. Educ. Comput. Res. **34**(3), 229–243 (2006). https://doi.org/10.2190/FLHV-K4WA-WPVQ-H0YM
26. Zheng, R.Z., Gardner, M.: Handbook of Research on Serious Games for Educational Applications (2016)

Mixed Reality

Software Architecture for Location-Based Games Designed for Social Interaction in Public Space

Xavier Fonseca[1]([✉]) [iD], Stephan Lukosch[2] [iD], and Frances Brazier[3] [iD]

[1] Polytechnic Institute of Porto, Porto, Portugal
xavier.fonseca@portic.ipp.pt
[2] HIT Lab NZ, University of Canterbury, Christchurch, New Zealand
[3] Faculty of Technology, Policy and Management, TU Delft, Delft, Netherlands

Abstract. Location-based games (LBGs) are becoming increasingly more popular, especially those that focus on social interaction in public space. They have been successful to various extents at bringing players together to interact in public space; yet there is lack of knowledge and consensus on how to design these games from a technical perspective. This paper proposes a software architecture that stems from a cross-game analysis of representative games of this genre, in which 6 core architectural components are identified: **Augmentation, Navigation, Interaction, State Progression, Participation**, and **Administration**. These components support the game experience of players by enabling orientation and navigation of the players' own physical environment, their interaction with the game and other people, the traditional game-like experience, management of the entire game ecosystem, and the ability to allow players to fuel game play. An LBG prototype, *Secrets of the South*, is presented as proof of concept for this software architecture and its key components. This prototype shows that the identified components are pivotal to the gameplay of LBGs for natural interactions in public space and shows how practitioners can be guided in their preparation whilst maintaining their freedom to technically implement this architecture according to the given structure.

Keywords: Location-based games · Software architecture · Social interaction · Public space

1 Introduction

Location-based games (LBGs) are a type of games where the gameplay progresses based on the player's location. They offer unique gaming experiences when compared to traditional games, by effectively blending the real physical environment of players with a digital environment [1–3]. LBGs offer unique functionalities when compared

Supplementary Information The online version contains supplementary material available at https://doi.org/10.1007/978-3-031-15325-9_16.

H. Söbke et al. (Eds.): JCSG 2022, LNCS 13476, pp. 213–228, 2022.
https://doi.org/10.1007/978-3-031-15325-9_16

to traditional games [1, 4, 5], and they have been shown to be capable of triggering engagement from players worldwide in playful ways [6]. Yet, designers and developers of games have no guidance on how to create such games from the perspective of system design. On the one hand, in the literature different components and names are used to describe similar functionality, which in turn leaves room for interpretation on the precise functionality provided. On the other hand, completely different components are proposed by designers and developers as key, causing lack of consensus on what is needed in an LBG at large. Plus, designers and developers discuss key functionality that are not key to the game architecture itself [7, 8], but to its application. And on top of this, LBGs can be defined differently across researchers, for instance including gameplays that make use of geographical information without any physical interaction of players [9].

This paper provides guidance to designers and developers on the functionality that LBGs must implement to be able to promote real social interaction in public space. Social interaction is a social exchange that supports more complex social phenomena, thus acting as a building block of society [10]. Promoting it can address known social barriers such as the feeling of "not belonging" in a neighbourhood, lack of engagement with the local environment and its citizens, and lack of wellbeing [11]. Digital LBGs are an established method to making citizens come together and turn their own environment into a playful experience [12–16]. The requirements for such LBGs are known [5, 17–19], and these mandate a specific software architecture and architectural components to be implemented. Yet, there is a lack of guidance on how to turn such requirements into a technological artifact (the LBG). To understand which architectural components must be implemented, this paper first analyses several existing LBGs. It identifies commonalities across these games and provides 1) a list of key components for LBGs for social interaction in public space, 2) a software architecture containing such key components, and 3) a proof of concept illustrating how this software architecture is instantiated in the LBG "Secrets of the South", a game that has shown to provide opportunities for players to come together and interact in their neighbourhood [5, 18, 20]. This paper complements prior research of the authors on meaningful social interaction through location-based games [3, 5, 17–23] by specifically focusing on requirements for a systems' architecture for LBGs for social interaction.

The next section reviews the literature on software architectures for LBGs and identifies a lack of guidance that designers and developers of LBGs currently face from a system's perspective. Section 3 presents the research methodology deployed, and Sect. 4 the data analysis based on the cross-game analysis performed. Section 5 proposes a software architecture for LBGs for social interaction in public space. Section 6 illustrates the use of this architecture on a proof of concept based on the LBG Secrets of the South, and reflects on limitations. Section 7 concludes this paper. Supplementary material to this article can be found in [24], containing both an extensive cross-game analysis, and the detailed game design of the proof of concept.

2   Software Architectures for Location-Based Games

Research on software architectures for LBGs show a lack of consensus at various levels on what these should offer. A few architectural components are proposed consistently, such as the mobile device (and the application it runs), the servers supporting the game, and content management systems with authoring capabilities [6, 25–27]. Most of the components proposed, however, are either 1) unique when compared to components other designers and developers propose, 2) use distinct names for components that are nonetheless similar in functionalities, or 3) do not refer to the system's architecture. With regard to different components and names being used to describe similar functionalities, examples include: a content management system and authoring tools [25], game content generation [26], map-based authoring [6], or simply editor [27]. All four focus on management of the content provided by a game and the ability to author such content. However, these names leave room for interpretation on the exact functionality these components provide: is the content to be linked directly to a map and the surroundings of the player; is it superimposed on a map; is it some other type of information provided to players; or does it refer to game art? Examples of key components that have been proposed as such, but are not necessarily key to LBGs in general include client-server-middleware handling request management [25], and components to support multiple external service providers [6, 27].

Such lack of consensus leads to confusion on what is needed in an LBG at large. Several articles on LBGs focus on guidance but not from the system's perspective. These include 1) design frameworks, 2) design patterns, 3) game engines, and 4) functionality that is key to application design, not the system itself. Frameworks and patterns (1 and 2) guide game creators in selecting individual application related functionality [28] and knowing how to combine them to solve a particular problem [29–31]. With respect to game engines (3) the guidance provided is at the level of programming frameworks and software environments on the smartphone [26, 32–36]. With regard to functionality that is key to application design (4), several articles refer to functionality such as storytelling [7] and design and play setups [8, 37], which address the design of the application itself and not the overall software architecture.

As a result, descriptions of LBGs are not consistent on focus or terminology. With respect to the mobile device, for example, recent work either does not refer to the functionality needed/provided [25], or it refers to functionality to which other researchers do not refer (e.g. an interface, content, middleware, and positioning technology in [6], rendering, data exchange, and game input in [27], or simply GPS and internet in [38]). Descriptions of LBGs differ significantly with respect to the description of the servers involved: they can be centralized or dedicated [26], linked over a 'networking layer' [6, 27], and/or provide multiple services (e.g. management of missions, mechanics, messages, components, and players [6, 27, 38]). These different approaches to LBGs contribute to the misinformation and lack of guidance, for the multitude of approaches and different perspectives, different names used for similar functionalities, and unique functionality not stressed elsewhere, conceal what should really be offered in such games.

This creates a clear need for a software architecture that can guide game designers and developers in the creation of future LBGs. Such an architecture bears the ability to provide a high-level system's perspective of the design of LBGs and their key components. It also furthers existent knowledge on (the minimum of) what is required to be implemented by such games and why. In the following, this paper addresses this gap by enhancing the understanding of which key components are essential for a specific type of LBG: location-based games for social interaction in public space.

3 Research Methodology

This paper focuses on LBGs, i.e., games that use locative features of smartphones, and that potentially trigger social interaction (direct or indirect, offline, or digitally) in outdoor space. It starts off by selecting the games to be analysed (in the following section). The selection procedure started with an online search for lists of the best LBGs, containing reviews and public opinions of what players love(d) to play. The online search was conducted using DuckDuckGo[©] and Google[©] search engines, both with the queries "best location-based games" and "digital location-based games". Six websites with lists of games[1,2,3,4,5,6] with LBGs up to the period of 2022 were chosen. The following criteria were used to select a limited number of games from these lists: games displaying 1) strong potential for social interaction, 2) with millions of players, and 3) mentioned multiple times across these websites. The rationale for these criteria is that location-based games fostering interaction, particularly face-to-face, are the focus of this research. Games that can bring players physically together, either because they want to play together/against one another or because they need other people to explore new modes of play, bear a potential for games with more serious purposes. Games that contain millions of players, and are mentioned multiple times across the internet, show their success, and can highlight features that worked for them and might prove to be essential for the desired type of game play.

Regarding data analysis, the selected games were analysed with the focus of understanding their key functional components. The analysis focuses on 1) their goals, 2) prominent features, and, when possible, 3) choices at the software/system architecture level that are clearly needed to support the game. The next step consisted of cross checking the identified components across all analysed games, to identify commonalities in high-level functionality, as high-level features. These high-level features are then used to propose key components for a software architecture with a well-defined structure that allows developers to choose different ways of implementation. The analysis was done by one author and cross-validated by the two other researchers; contributions proposed in Sect. 6 also follow the same process. Given the size of the documentation of the game

---

[1] https://www.quertime.com/article/20-extremely-addicting-gps-location-based-mobile-games/, 20 extremely addicting LBGs, July 2018, last visited on 30-Jul-22.

[2] https://www.pockettactics.com/guides/location-based-games-ios-android/, The best location-based & GPS games on mobile, Jan. 2020, last visited on 30-Jul-22.

[3] https://www.redbytes.in/gps-mobile-game-development-ios-android-2018/, Best GPS LBGs on iOS and Android 2018, Oct. 2017, last visited on 30-Jul-22.

[4] https://www.digitaltrends.com/gaming/best-location-based-gps-games/, 5 great location-based games that aren't 'Pokémon Go', Jul. 2016, last visited on 30-Jul-22.

[5] https://beebom.com/best-location-based-gps-games/, 8 Best location based GPS games you can play, Jul. 2017, last visited on 30-Jul-22.

[6] https://www.digitaltrends.com/gaming/best-location-based-gps-games/, The 10 best location-based games, May 16. 2022, last visited on 30-Jul-22.

analysis, and page limit for this paper, such cross-game analysis is available as supplementary material to this article in [24]. This article provides a summary of the detailed analysis found in such supplementary material.

4 Analysis of Location-Based Games Triggering Social Interaction

The purpose of this section is to analyse successful and representative games on their key functionalities, and architectural components supporting such functionalities. Based on the first criterion (heavy social interaction, preferably offline), *Geocaching*, *Recoil*, *Pokémon Go*, *Ingress* and *Orna* are selected due to their strong capacity to instigate dynamics of play with multiple people offline. *Geocaching* and *Orna* bring people together to form teams; *Pokémon Go* and *Ingress* offer events worldwide where people compete in-situ; and *Recoil* is a multiplayer-based game where people must come physically together to play. Regarding the second criterion (millions of players), *Pokémon Go* and *Parallel Kingdom* are selected, as the former reported 45 million players worldwide[7], and the latter 2 million[8]. Other potential choices could be *Ingress* and *Landlord*, both with little over 400 thousand players each, but no other game comes close to these numbers of players. Lastly, *CodeRunner*, *Ingress*, *Pokémon Go*, *Geocaching*, and *Orna* are selected because they are mentioned multiple times across the selected websites (at least 3 out of 6 times).

Based on the selection of all the criteria, 7 games were selected for the analysis: *CodeRunner*, *Geocaching*, *Ingress*, *Orna*, *Parallel Kingdom*, *Pokémon GO*, and *Recoil*. Other criteria and other games could be selected for this game analysis, yet the purpose is to understand what the essential building blocks for such games are to be successful from the design and software/system's perspective. This can be done, not by analysing an exhaustive list of games, but by selecting games that are different and vary from one another, and that were/are substantially played and enjoyed by large communities of players. Other literature reviews can be done, with different LBGs and for different purposes [39], but the game selection for this article reflects the adopted criteria. The analysis done was based on playtesting and on online reviews whenever possible.

4.1 Summary of Game Analysis

Table 1 depicts the key functionalities identified during game analysis, and shows if, and how often, these functionalities are implemented in the 7 games analysed.

---

[7] https://www.businessofapps.com/data/pokemon-go-statistics/, Pokémon Go revenue and usage statistics (2019), May 2019, last visited on 30-Jul-22.
[8] https://www.pocketgamer.com/games/004719/parallel-kingdom/, Parallel Kingdom, last visited on 30-Jul-22.

4.2 Data Analysis: Key Components for Location-Based Games for Social Interaction

The cross-game analysis that is summarized in Table 1 and detailed in the supplementary material [24], led to the identification of 6 distinct structural components: **Augmentation**, **Navigation**, **Interaction**, **State Progression**, **Participation**, and **Administration**. These are defined in Table 2.

These 6 key components have shown to be included in the 7 games analysed: positioning of players in their environment (*Augmentation*), direction and orientation of players in space through informational and visual cues (*Navigation*), multimodal interaction with other players and the environment (*Interaction*), progression of a game (*State Progression*), contribution and involvement of players both at the level of content and maintenance of game play (*Participation*), and the centralized orchestration and management of the game (*Administration*). As such, these components are argued to be essential for a high-level software architecture for location-based game designed to foster social interaction in public space.

5 Software Architecture for LBGs for Social Interaction

From the data analysis performed across the games mentioned above, and the 6 key components identified, a software architecture featuring these components can be defined. Figure 1 refers to a mobile computing device (MCD), services required to support the game, and a Portal. The hardware (including communication devices, memory, sensor, and actuators) and software (including an operating system and libraries) on the MCD can run a mobile game application (note – memory is not in picture). The portal refers to an interface (e.g., local, or web-based) that players can use to submit, and potentially also author content to the game.

The 6 key components are represented in Fig. 1 as follows: the first three components *Augmentation*, *Navigation*, and *Interaction* are inside the Game Application (under the same names); the components *State Progression*, *Participation*, and *Administration*, map respectively to **State Progression Service**, **Authoring Service**, and **Administrative Service**. The key components *Augmentation* and *Navigation* are supported by the **Positioning Service**, responsible for localization and context awareness services working in tandem with the locative features of the MCD. The **Authoring Service** powers the Portal, i.e., an interface (e.g., Desktop, or web) with a storage system that can capture the contributions of players, optionally authoring as well. The **Administrative Service** enables the access to any interface to manage the game.

6 Proof of Concept: The "Secrets of the South"

To illustrate the applicability of the software architecture, this section presents a proof of concept with the LBG Secrets of the South (SotS), which instantiates the proposed architecture. SotS was created by the authors to promote social interaction and provide opportunities for such social exchange to be meaningful to those interacting [3, 5, 17–23, 37, 40]. As part of a 4 year doctoral programme, initial design choices for the game were

Table 1. Summary of the game analysis. Grey boxes are features not common or apparently not included. Green check mark for games that include the feature. Vertical blue bars for the number of games sharing the feature.

Specific Features	Commonalities (1-7)	CodeRunner	Geocaching	Ingress	Orna	Parallel Kingdom	Pokémon Go	Recoil
Map (e.g. 2D, 3D)	▁▃▄▅▆	✓	✓	✓	✓	✓	✓	✓
Game info on the map (e.g. icons)	▁▃▄▅▆	✓	✓	✓	✓	✓	✓	✓
Info aligned with surroundings (e.g. portals at POI)	▁▃▄▅	✓	✓	✓	✓	✓	✓	
Location usage to advance game play (e.g. GPS)	▁▃▄▅▆	✓	✓	✓	✓	✓	✓	✓
Augmented Reality	▁						✓	✓
Visual indications on where to go/navigate/orient (e.g. arrows)	▁▃▄	✓	✓	✓	✓			✓
Touch, swipe, or hand manipulation (e.g. zoom out of a map)	▁▃▄▅▆	✓	✓	✓	✓	✓	✓	✓
Players come together offline for interaction and joint game play	▁▃▄▅		✓	✓	✓	✓	✓	✓
Interaction with real-world objects	▁	✓	✓					
Special forms of navigation (e.g. slower the better, or tele transport)	▁					✓	✓	
Game statistics, leader boards, resources, character level	▁▃▄▅		✓	✓	✓	✓	✓	✓
Task completion, missions, puzzle solving	▁▃▄▅▆	✓	✓	✓	✓	✓	✓	✓
Unlock new features, access to unique items, different modes of play	▁▃▄		✓	✓	✓		✓	✓
Player contribution with new content, POI, challenges, or software	▁▃▄	✓		✓	✓		✓	✓
Maintenance/enforcement of game play, game community, and values	▁	✓	✓					
Peer review of players' contributions and conduct	▁▃	✓	✓	✓				
Creation, management, and review of game content or players' contribution, made by the company	▁▃▄▅	✓	✓		✓	✓	✓	✓
Centralized orchestration of game (e.g. events, community support, structure, API control, players, or target specific content)	▁▃▄		✓	✓	✓	✓	✓	
Players administer game play	▁							✓

1) to be played by children, 2) in their neighbourhood, 3) to involve everyone, and 4) to be fun [23]. Additional requirements were elicited from children during workshops designed to this purpose [17, 19]. The next stage explored the functionality that needs to be included in a design and implementation for the promotion of social interaction

Table 2. Definition of Key Components offered by the software architecture.

Key component	Description
Administration	Management of the state of the game and all its components, from statistics, players, and game content. Also included is community support, event creation, mediation of conflict between players, control of the access to the game through APIs, targeting of content to players, and the release of new features and updates. If players contribute content, that content is approved, rejected, or curated here
Augmentation	Enhancement of players' perception on their real-world surroundings and the digital game state: their positioning and representation regarding the real world, other surrounding players, and areas in the real world where they should go to advance
Interaction	Mechanisms used by players to control or interact with the digital game world. This component supports the components of augmentation and navigation, and can be based on, for e.g., human-computer interfaces, multimodal interaction, AI, tangible interfaces, and multi-player features
Navigation	Support to player navigation from its current position to another location. An effective guidance at providing players with the correct orientation and that disappears when not needed
Participation	Contribution made by players towards the game, whether it is the content (storyline, individual tasks, or physical objects), community maintenance, or game art media. Players can create/manage their contributions via a digital authoring service or tool
State progression	Game mechanics and elements that support gameplay throughout time: task completion, game statistics, character levels, acquired (rare) items, different modes of play, and the counting of resources found in the real/digital world

in public space through LBGs. This stage consisted of iterative software development and play test sessions during the process [18, 20]. The proposed software architecture (Fig. 1) comes right from early stages of the iterative process and is therefore implemented in all developed prototypes. As last stage, further workshops were done with children/teenagers (10–16 age group) to 1) jointly create content for the game that not only is appropriate but also appeals to this target group, and 2) validate the game in its capacity to provide opportunities that promote meaningful social interaction [5]. The game has shown to be successful at creating opportunities for social interaction (within a group of friends, with strangers, and with the environment) through co-located challenges of different types and difficulties, which, in turn, provides a game play experience that children enjoy and that is positive to them (i.e., bears meaning to them) [5, 18]. For this reason, this game is selected as a proof of concept for this architecture.

Figure 2 shows screenshots from the SotS[9]: a LBG that uses smartphones to mediate outdoor activities (called challenges) for social interaction. Players are presented with

[9] https://play.google.com/store/apps/details?id=com.Xav13rua.SecretsOfTheSouthv2, Secrets of the South mobile application, last visited on 30-Jul-22.

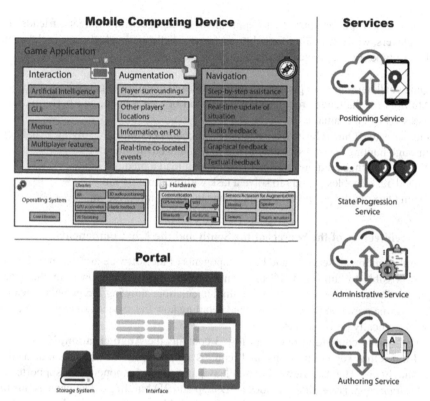

Fig. 1. Software architecture for an LBG for social interaction. Monochromatic colour scheme represents layers usually not built during game development, Polychromatic scheme otherwise.

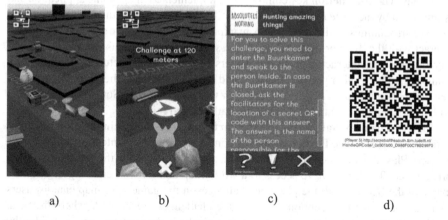

Fig. 2. Secrets of the South. a) 3D map with challenges, b) compass and text navigation towards a challenge, c) a game challenge, and d) an example of QR code for interaction.

tasks in outdoor public space that require them to engage with strangers, friends, and other players, while searching for solutions for the challenges and advance in the game. Different types of challenges are distinguished:

- Quiz challenges require players to answer a closed question to get points.
- Multiplayer challenges require players to form or join a team, and performance is assessed by an evaluator.
- Hunter is like Quiz (closed question), providing the possibility of solving a challenge through hunting for and scanning a QR code in the environment.
- Voting challenges require players to take and upload a picture.
- Timed Task enables players to solve a task within a time period.
- Open Quiz challenges pose open questions to collect information.

6.1 Architecture of the Secrets of the South and the Key Components

By implementing all services and key components of the software architecture (Fig. 1), it was possible to build an LBG that can promote social interaction in public space. Figure 3 illustrates the outcome of this implementation, showing the game application and the game portal on the upper part, and detailing how the services were implemented more specifically on the lower part.

The mobile computing device in Fig. 3 contains the **Augmentation, Navigation,** and **Interaction** key components, and requires support from the services indicated in the same figure. The **Augmentation** and **Navigation** key components are supported by the *Positioning Service*, that provides a 3D map and 3D buildings. The game sends the GPS coordinate of a smartphone to this service, which returns a stream of map tiles covering hundreds of metres in every direction of the player's location. This is used by the game to position a player and surrounding challenges and enable the location-based game play. The **Interaction** key component is implemented in the game application and is supported by the *State Progression Service*. The GUI focuses on the 3D representation of the surroundings and enables map manipulation: players can use their fingers to interact with the 3D world. The *State Progression Service* presents the challenges and supports indirect interaction between players (e.g., to attach pictures taken during a challenge, to view other players' pictures, and to vote for them). The **State Progression** key component is supported by *State Progression Service*. The SotS provides players with a personal area containing gameplay statistics and ranks.

The SotS game portal implements the **Participation** and **Administration** key components as follows. The **Participation** key component is implemented by the *Authoring Service*. Players can access the online game portal, which, after the login, provides a private area. There they have access to a world map and a list of challenges. Both the map and the list show all the playable challenges in the game. The map enables users to acquire a general perception of where the challenges are located (where they can be played). The list of challenges also indicates which challenges were created by the logged player and can be edited and deleted.

Lastly, the **Administration** key component is implemented by the *Administrative Service*. The game is managed in 3 possible ways: 1) the online system (or at the database level), 2) the PlayFab service, or 3) in the mobile game. In 1), a user with administrator

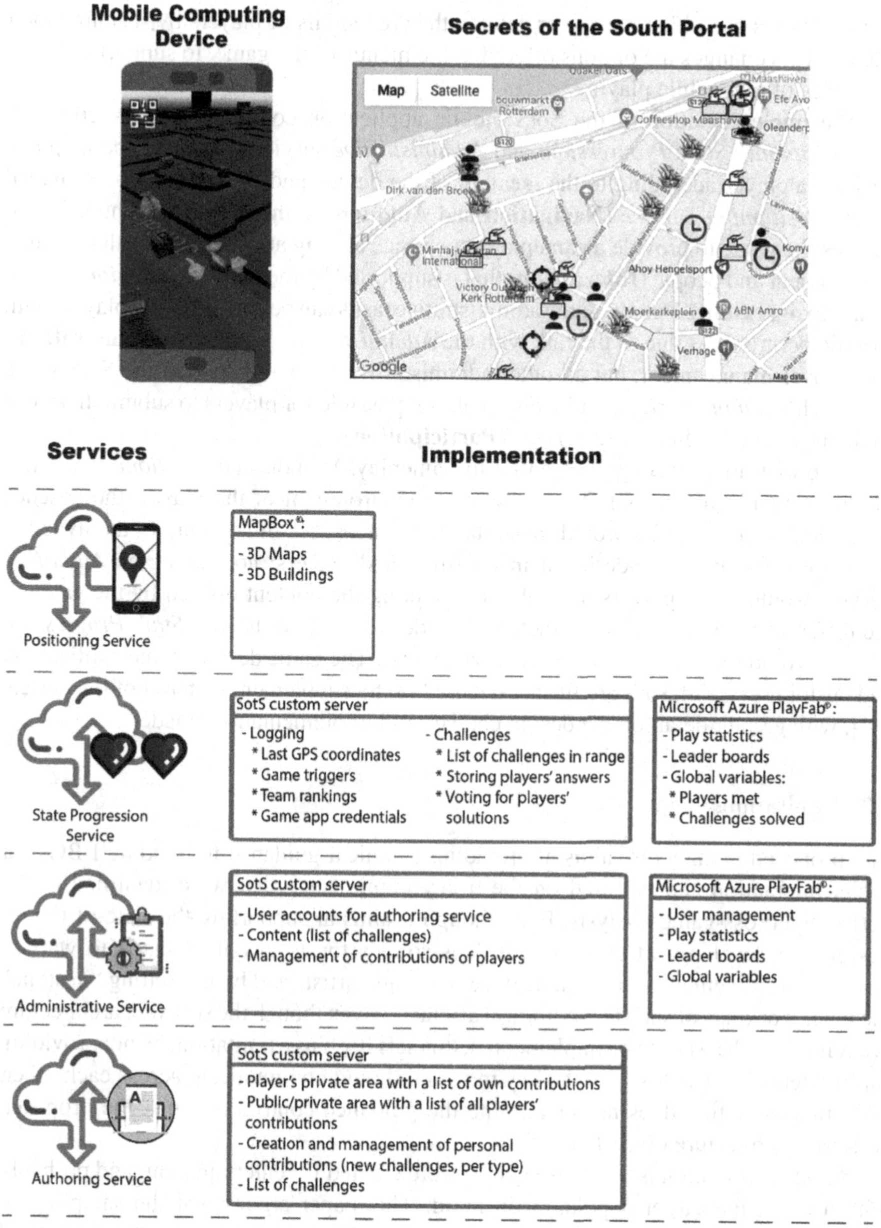

Fig. 3. Implementation of the software architecture in the game (Mapbox (https://www.mapbox.com/); Azure Playfab (https://playfab.com/); and the SotS custom server (https://github.com/xavierfonsecaphd/SecretsOfTheSouth)).

rights can not only create content but also manage other users' challenges and accounts. In 2), an administrator can operate leader boards and statistics. In 3), and during play, administrators can either elevate or demote the credentials of players by scanning their QR ID. This changes the options offered in the menus of the game, to support different dynamics of play while playing.

The implementation of the SotS mobile application communicates directly with the *Positioning, State Progression,* and *Administrative* services to render the map and position a player according to the location of the device and the information provided by the *Positioning Service* (**Navigation** and **Augmentation** key components). It also enables the game to provide a gameplay experience aiming at interaction with the game environment and people (**Interaction**) that is supported by the *State Progression Service* (**State Progression**). Finally, some administrative tasks can be performed by players with specific permissions due to the link with the *Administrative Service* (**Administration**), e.g., player management, but all other administrative tasks are done in the SotS game portal. The *Administrative Service* also makes it possible for players to submit their own challenges, via the *Authoring Service* (**Participation**).

Note that all services are essential to gameplay. Without the *Positioning Service,* the game would not be able to represent the environment of the player; the absence of *Administrative Service* would make the game incapable of adapting to the dynamic behaviour of players, rendering it inconsistent and useless; not having an *Authoring Service* would make players incapable of adapting the content offered by the game to the different types of social interaction they desire; and not having *State Progression Service* would mean not having a functional game. The game design, game application, and custom server of SotS are further detailed in the supplement material of this article [24], with greater detail on the design choices and implementations made.

6.2   Limitations

The proposed architecture aims at providing technical guidance to building LBGs for social interaction and is based on the 6 key components that were identified in the performed cross-game analysis. Even though it aims at supporting the state-of-the-art design and development processes, it does so at a top-level only. This is to warrant freedom of implementation to game developers and artists and by not setting "in stone" the inner workings of such technological artefacts. Even though the software architecture is detailed in what should be implemented, this sets itself as a limitation, by not providing further details of exactly how the key modules should communicate across each other. Still, this limitation does not undermine the guidance contribution that the proposed software architecture offers to the field.

Another limitation is that these games were created for entertainment, and probably with a particular target population in mind. This paper argues that the sampling of game titles that the followed methodology produced is appropriate to gather high-level characteristics of very successful LBGs leading to social interaction. Due to the high diversity of the game selection used, any potential bias in the conclusions based on a small sample of games is arguably not relevant. Yet, a different sample of games could produce or introduce other key components than those found with the used sample, particularly if the (unknown) premises used to build such games focus on different purposes or target groups. This poses itself as an opportunity for further research.

7 Conclusion

Addressing the lack of guidance from a system's perspective that designers and developers face when creating a LBG, this paper identified the architectural components that are key for LBGs designed to foster social interaction in public space. It enhances the understanding of software architectures for LBGs of this type at system level that is essential for game design and development. Commonalities in essential functionality provided by 7 such LBGs have been presented, i.e., functionality without which these games would not be capable of delivering the designed game play. Six key components were identified: *Augmentation, Navigation, Interaction, State Progression, Participation*, and *Administration*. These components are key because without them: an LBG would not be able to represent the environment of the player (*Augmentation*) or assist him/her in the location-based game play that is central to this genre (*Navigation*); multimodal interaction with other players and the environment would not be possible (*Interaction*); tracking of the interaction with physical/digital objects, the game play, and every game-like progression would not exist (*State Progression*); contribution and involvement of players both at the level of content and maintenance of game play would not be possible, rendering long-term game play of an LBG designed for social interaction obsolete (*Participation*); and the centralized orchestration and management of the game, required for the consistency of the game, would render the game unplayable (*Administration*). Based on these key components, a modular software architecture was proposed. This software architecture guarantees that not only designers and developers know which components to include, but also that they benefit from an approach that grants freedom of implementation. This aids designers and developers without constraining either their creativity (through a too detailed method) nor their freedom of choice (of how to implement each component). The applicability of the software architecture was shown with a proof of concept based on the LBG *Secrets of the South* (SotS). SotS incorporates the proposed architecture, which enables the game to provide opportunities for players to interact with other people [5, 18].

The proposed software architecture provides guidance on how to create a system for an LBG that fosters social interaction in public space. It supports the identified six components and can be extended to include further components for other types of functionalities as needed. This architecture provides future game designers and developers of LBGs support for less complex game design and development processes, while leaving room for creativity and implementations.

References

1. Oppermann, L., Slussareff, M.: Pervasive games. In: Dörner, R., Göbel, S., Kickmeier-Rust, M., Masuch, M., Zweig, K. (eds.) Entertainment Computing and Serious Games. LNCS, vol. 9970, pp. 475–520. Springer, Cham (2016). https://doi.org/10.1007/978-3-319-46152-6_18
2. Nijholt, A. (ed.): Playable Cities. GMSE, Springer, Singapore (2017). https://doi.org/10.1007/978-981-10-1962-3
3. Slingerland, G., Fonseca, X., Lukosch, S., Brazier, F.: Designing outdoor playgrounds for increased civic engagement. In: Presented at the CHI 2019, 4–9 May, Glasgow, UK (2019)
4. Mullen, J.D.: Location-based games and augmented reality systems. Google Patents (2013)

5. Fonseca, X., Slingerland, G., Lukosch, S., Brazier, F.: Designing for meaningful social interaction in digital serious games. Entertainment Comput. **36**(100385), 1–23 (2020). https://doi.org/10.1016/j.entcom.2020.100385

6. Paelke, V., Oppermann, L., Reimann, C.: Mobile location-based gaming. In: Meng, L., Zipf, A., Winter, S. (eds.) Map-Based Mobile Services, pp. 310–334. Springer, Heidelberg (2008). https://doi.org/10.1007/978-3-540-37110-6_15

7. Naliuka, K., Carrigy, T., Paterson, N., Haahr, M.: A narrative architecture for story-driven location-based mobile games. In: Luo, X., Cao, Y., Yang, B., Liu, J., Ye, F. (eds.) ICWL 2010. LNCS, vol. 6537, pp. 11–20. Springer, Heidelberg (2011). https://doi.org/10.1007/978-3-642-20539-2_2

8. Avouris, N.M., Yiannoutsou, N.: A review of mobile location-based games for learning across physical and virtual spaces. J. UCS **18**(15), 2120–2142 (2012)

9. Ahlqvist, O., Schlieder, C.: Geogames and geoplay. Orgs (2018). https://doi.org/10.1007/978-3-319-22774-0

10. LumenLearning: Understanding Social Interaction. Lumen Learning. https://courses.lumenlearning.com/boundless-sociology/chapter/understanding-social-interaction/. Accessed 2022

11. Government: Guidance on meaningful interaction: how encouraging positive relationships between people can help build community cohesion. NCF, National Community Forum, Communities and Local Government (2009). 978-1-4098-09616. https://rqvvs.qc.ca/documents/file/Dossiers/guidanceonmeaningfulinteraction.pdf

12. Peters, K., Elands, B., Buijs, A.: Social interactions in urban parks: stimulating social cohesion? Urban Forest. Urban Greening **9**(2), 93–100 (2010)

13. Verhaegh, J., Soute, I., Kessels, A., Markopoulos, P.: On the design of Camelot, an outdoor game for children. In: Proceeding IDC 2006, Proceedings of the 2006 Conference on Interaction Design and Children, pp. 9–16. ACM, New York (2006)

14. Görgü, L., et al.: Freegaming: mobile, collaborative, adaptive and augmented exergaming. Mob. Inf. Syst. **8**(4), 287–301 (2012). https://doi.org/10.3233/MIS-2012-00147

15. Cheok, A., et al.: Human Pacman: a mobile entertainment system with ubiquitous computing and tangible interaction over a wide outdoor area. In: Chittaro, L. (ed.) Mobile HCI 2003. LNCS, vol. 2795, pp. 209–223. Springer, Heidelberg (2003). https://doi.org/10.1007/978-3-540-45233-1_16

16. Chittaro, L., Sioni, R.: Turning the classic snake mobile game into a location–based exergame that encourages walking. In: Bang, M., Ragnemalm, E.L. (eds.) PERSUASIVE 2012. LNCS, vol. 7284, pp. 43–54. Springer, Heidelberg (2012). https://doi.org/10.1007/978-3-642-31037-9_4

17. Fonseca, X., Lukosch, S., Lukosch, H., Tiemersma, S., Brazier, F.: Requirements and game ideas for social interaction in mobile outdoor games. In: CHI PLAY 2017 Extended Abstracts, Publication of the Annual Symposium on Computer-Human Interaction in Play, pp. 331–337 (2017). https://doi.org/10.1145/3130859.3131304

18. Slingerland, G., Fonseca, X., Lukosch, S., Brazier, F.: Location-based challenges for playful neighbourhood exploration. Behav. Inf. Technol. (2020). https://doi.org/10.1080/0144929X.2020.1829707

19. Fonseca, X., Lukosch, S., Lukosch, H., Brazier, F.: Requirements for location-based games for social interaction. IEEE Trans. Games **1**(1), 1–14 (2021). https://doi.org/10.1109/TG.2021.3078834

20. Fonseca, X., Lukosch, S., Brazier, F.: Fostering social interaction in playful cities. In: Brooks, A.L., Brooks, E., Sylla, C. (eds.) ArtsIT/DLI -2018. LNICSSITE, vol. 265, pp. 286–295. Springer, Cham (2019). https://doi.org/10.1007/978-3-030-06134-0_33

21. Fonseca, X.: Location-based games for social interaction in public space. Doctoral thesis, TU Delft (2021). https://doi.org/10.4233/uuid:9db1a0c4-89ba-4f9b-b32a-47b7bca5b55e

22. Fonseca, X., Lukosch, S., Brazier, F.: Social cohesion revisited: a new definition and how to characterize it. Innov. Eur. J. Soc. Sci. Res. **32**(2), 231–253 (2018). https://doi.org/10.1080/13511610.2018.1497480

23. Fonseca, X., Lukosch, S., Brazier, F.: Secrets of the south: a location-based game for the development of 21st century social skills and promotion of social interaction. In: Proceedings of DELbA 2020 - Workshop on Designing and Facilitating Educational Location-Based Applications (DELbA 2020) Co-located with the Fifteenth European Conference on Technology Enhanced Learning (EC-TEL 2020), Heidelberg, Germany, 15 September 2020, vol. 2685 (2020)

24. Fonseca, X., Lukosch, S., Brazier, F.: Supplementary material to the article: software architecture for location-based games designed for social interaction in public space. https://www.researchgate.net/publication/358348885_Supplementary_Material_to_the_article_Software_Architecture_for_Location-based_Games_Designed_for_Social_Interaction_in_Public_Space

25. Söbke, H., Streicher, A.: Serious games architectures and engines. In: Dörner, R., Göbel, S., Kickmeier-Rust, M., Masuch, M., Zweig, K. (eds.) Entertainment Computing and Serious Games. LNCS, vol. 9970, pp. 148–173. Springer, Cham (2016). https://doi.org/10.1007/978-3-319-46152-6_7

26. Kasapakis, V., Gavalas, D.: Pervasive gaming: status, trends and design principles. J. Netw. Comput. Appl. **55**, 213–236 (2015). https://doi.org/10.1016/j.jnca.2015.05.009

27. Nolêto, C., Lima, M., Maia, L.F., Viana, W., Trinta, F.: An authoring tool for location-based mobile games with augmented reality features. In: 2015 14th Brazilian Symposium on Computer Games and Digital Entertainment (SBGames), pp. 99–108 IEEE (2015)

28. Björk, S., Holopainen, J.: Games and design patterns. In: The Game Design Reader, pp. 410–437 (2006)

29. Dormann, C., Whitson, J.R., Neuvians, M.: Once more with feeling: game design patterns for learning in the affective domain. Games Cult. **8**(4), 215–237 (2013). https://doi.org/10.1177/1555412013496892

30. Bjork, S., Holopainen, J.: Patterns in Game Design (Game Development Series). Charles River Media (2004)

31. Reuter, C., Wendel, V., Göbel, S., Steinmetz, R.: Game design patterns for collaborative player interactions. In: DiGRA (2014)

32. McShaffry, M., Graham, D.: Game Coding Complete, 4th edn. Cengage Learning PTR (2014)

33. Cowan, B., Kapralos, B.: A survey of frameworks and game engines for serious game development. In: 2014 IEEE 14th International Conference on Advanced Learning Technologies, pp. 662–664. IEEE (2014)

34. Cowan, B., Kapralos, B.: An overview of serious game engines and frameworks. In: Brooks, A.L., Brahnam, S., Kapralos, B., Jain, L.C. (eds.) Recent Advances in Technologies for Inclusive Well-Being. ISRL, vol. 119, pp. 15–38. Springer, Cham (2017). https://doi.org/10.1007/978-3-319-49879-9_2

35. Craighead, J., Burke, J., Murphy, R.: Using the unity game engine to develop SARGE: a case study. In: Proceedings of the 2008 Simulation Workshop at the International Conference on Intelligent Robots and Systems (IROS 2008) (2008)

36. Siakavaras, I., Papastergiou, M., Comoutos, N.: Mobile games in computer science education: current state and proposal of a mobile game design that incorporates physical activity. In: Mikropoulos, T.A. (ed.) Research on e-Learning and ICT in Education, pp. 243–255. Springer, Cham (2018). https://doi.org/10.1007/978-3-319-95059-4_15

37. Gião, J., Sarraipa, J., Francisco-Xavier, F., Ferreira, F., Jardim-Goncalves, R., Zdravkovic, M.: Profiling based on music and physiological state. In: Mertins, K., Jardim-Gonçalves, R., Popplewell, K., Mendonça, J.P. (eds.) Enterprise Interoperability VII. PIC, vol. 8, pp. 123–135. Springer, Cham (2016). https://doi.org/10.1007/978-3-319-30957-6_10

38. Jacob, J.T.P.N., Coelho, A.F.: Issues in the development of location-based games. Int. J. Comput. Games Technol. **2011**, 1–7 (2011)

39. Laato, S., Pietarinen, T., Rauti, S., Paloheimo, M., Inaba, N., Sutinen, E.: A review of location-based games: do they all support exercise, social interaction and cartographical training? In: CSEDU (1), pp. 616–627 (2019)

40. Fonseca, X., Lukosch, S., Brazier, F.: Design framework for social interaction with location-based games. Int. J. Serious Games **9**(1), 59–81 (2022). https://doi.org/10.17083/ijsg.v9i 1.48

Paper Beats Rock: Elaborating the Best Machine Learning Classifier for Hand Gesture Recognition

Philipp Achenbach$^{(\boxtimes)}$ (ID), Dennis Purdack (ID), Sebastian Wolf (ID),
Philipp Niklas Müller (ID), Thomas Tregel (ID), and Stefan Göbel (ID)

Serious Games Research Group, Technical University of Darmstadt, Darmstadt,
Germany
philipp.achenbach@tu-darmstadt.de

Abstract. More and more digital experiences, such as Serious Games,
rely on gesture control as a means of natural human communication.
Therefore we investigated the suitability of the *Senso Glove: DK2* data
glove and a Support Vector Machine for recognizing static hand gestures
of the popular game Rock-Paper-Scissors in a previous work. Building
on this, we now want to increase the scope of training and testing data
and evaluate different kinds of Machine-Learning classifiers in addition
to the Support Vector Machine. For this purpose, we ingested two different datasets, optimized them using grid search, and evaluated all user
data in such a way that each user dataset was used individually for testing (leave-one-out) in order to obtain the most possible representative
and user-independent result. Our results show that for a small number of
gestures, Logistic Regression has the highest accuracy (97.6%) in predicting the results quickly. For a larger dataset, Random Forest achieves the
highest accuracy (82.4%). Random Forest and Logistic Regression give
very good results on both datasets (average 89.7%, both), but Logistic
Regression is significantly faster overall. If the training and test data are
not separated by user and are thus user-dependent, the results for both
data sets improve to 99.2% and 99.5% with Support Vector Machine,
respectively, and again Random Forest performs very well, with Logistic
Regression showing small weaknesses here. In addition, we investigated
how the accuracy of the classifiers performed when we gradually reduced
the number of gestures from 25 to three in a dataset with 25 gestures
and found that up to 11 gestures, a high accuracy of more than 94%
could be achieved.

The data recorded in the course of this work are public available
in https://github.com/serious-games-darmstadt/dataglove_senso-glove-
dk2_rps-gestures (Last visited on 30 April 2022).

Keywords: Gesture recognition · Machine Learning ·
Rock-Paper-Scissors · Classification · Data glove · *Senso Glove: DK2* ·
Support Vector Machine · Decision Tree · Random Forest ·
k-Nearest-Neighbor · Logistic Regression · Gaussian Naive Bayes ·
Perceptron · Feed-forward Neural Networks

© The Author(s), under exclusive license to Springer Nature Switzerland AG 2022
H. Söbke et al. (Eds.): JCSG 2022, LNCS 13476, pp. 229–245, 2022.
https://doi.org/10.1007/978-3-031-15325-9_17

1   Introduction

Hand gestures play a vital role in the everyday life. They help us express emotions and thoughts both in verbal and in nonverbal situations. Their importance is also increasing in computer science: As technology advances, the demand for more natural ways of interacting with computers increases. Instead of the user learning to control the devices, they are supposed to apply known behavior patterns, e.g. from communication, and the machine learns to understand them. In general, a hand gestures is the combination of a handshape, the orientation of the hand, and other parameters, such as the movement of the hand [18,19].

One use case of hand gesture recognition is Virtual Reality (VR) and Augmented Reality (AR) games or educational software. In games like *Half-Life: Alyx*[1] the player uses gestures to manipulate tools and pickup items. These game-play options increase the immersion of the player. Moreover hand tracking can be used to educate about sign languages, which are an important way to communicate with hearing-impaired people. Systems which translate sign languages or teach them can lead to more social inclusion of those people. That is why gesture recognition plays a central role in the Human-Computer-Interaction (HCI).

There are two types of gestures in general: static gestures and dynamic gestures [13]. The main difference between these two types of gestures is the presence or absence of temporal structure. In a dynamic gesture, spatial information, such as the handshape, and temporal information, such as the movement of the hand, are present. The meaning of the gesture is only revealed when both aspects are considered, so there can be multiple gestures/meanings to a handshape, depending on the executed movement of the hand. In a static gesture, on the other hand, only spatial information, such as the shape of the hand is present.

The goal of this paper is to determine the classifier which is most suited for recognizing static hand gestures with a data glove. We have chosen hand gestures that also occur in nonverbal everyday communication, but also in sign language, and thus can provide information about the recognition of these. For this we conduct two experiments using two separate datasets.

In the first experiment we classify different hand gestures using several Machine-Learning (ML) approaches to identify the most promising approaches. The ML algorithms that we optimize and compare are Support Vector Machine (SVM), Decision Tree (DT), Random Forest (RF), k-Nearest Neighbor (kNN), Logistic Regression (LogReg), Gaussian Naive Bayes (GNB), Perceptron, and Feedforward Neural Network (FNN). The datasets we use were recorded independently and consist of five and 25 different hand gestures of the well-known game Rock-Paper-Scissors (RPS), respectively. *Dataset A* with five hand gestures consists of 300 recordings per gesture, or 1500 recordings in total. *Dataset B* consists of 2250 recordings of hand gestures, including 90 recordings per gesture.

---

[1] https://www.half-life.com/en/alyx/ (Last visited on 26 April 2022).

In the second experiment, we use *Dataset B* with 25 gestures and gradually reduce the number of gestures to see how the accuracy of each classifier evolves as the number of classes changes.

Table 1. Signs of different variants of RPS game [9]

No.	Shape	Name	No.	Shape	Name	No.	Shape	Name
1		Rock	11		Devil	21		Moon
2		Scissors	12		Snake	22		Bowl
3		Paper	13		Tree	23		Alien
4		Sponge	14		Dragon	24		Nuke
5		Water	15		Lightning	25		Dynamite
6		Fire	16		Sun	I		Rock
7		Air	17		Axe	II		Scissors
8		Woman	18		Monkey	III		Match
9		Gun	19		Man	IV		Paper
10		Wolf	20		Cockroach	V		Well

Table 1 shows the 27 used gestures which differ in their handshape and orientation. The gestures 1 to 25 and I to V are both part of different RPS games designed by Lovelace [9]. Because the data recording was independent, the gestures from *Dataset A* with five gestures differed from *Dataset B* with 25 gestures.

How the rules are played can be seen on the creators page[2].

---

[2] https://www.umop.com/rps.htm (Last visited on 29 April 2022).

2 Related Work

Gesture recognition is divided in vision-based and sensor-based approaches. First approach is widely used, as all the data needed for gesture classification can be captured by one or a few cameras at once [13]. Depending on the specific implementation, camera-based methods can also be comparatively inexpensive. Some approaches only require a single webcam to classify gestures [3].

In sensor-based approaches, various sensors, such as Inertial Measurement Units (IMUs) or flex sensors, are attached to the user's body, e.g. by wearing a data glove, to directly measure their movements. This has several advantages: The extracted values from these sensors typically need less pre-processing compared to the output of most camera systems. They are also more independent of the user's surroundings. When working with cameras, it can be difficult to detect important parts in the image if, for example, lighting changes often [13]. Working with cameras may also raise privacy concerns, whereas the data in most sensor-based approaches reveal very little about the users.

We focus in this paper on the sensor-based approach since it achieves a more mobile approach and is more private than a vision-based approach which uses one or more cameras.

In the following we will take a closer look at a selection of previous sensor-based works (see also Table 8): Achenbach et al. used a *Senso Glove: DK2* from *Senso Device Inc.*[3] to recognize the five static hand gestures *Rock, Paper, Scissors, Match, Well* from the popular game RPS. As this is the same glove used in this work, the technical details can be taken from Sect. 3.1. The performance was evaluated by eleven persons. Each person signed all five gestures ten times each, resulting in 550 samples in total. The data of ten persons were used to train an SVM, with the remaining data being used for hyperparameter optimization and as a first test, in which the model achieved 100% accuracy. In a second test, four different persons randomly signed 20 gestures each, resulting in an accuracy of 87.5%.

Ma et al. have developed a custom data glove to detect five simple static hand gestures: Bending each finger [10]. The data glove consists of a flex sensor on the back of each finger as well as one IMU on the wrist. Data were collected from ten people. Each one signed all five gestures ten times. The authors compared several machine learning models by dividing the recorded data into a training set and a test set. The training set is typically much larger and is used to train a classifier on a specific classification problem. The test set is then used to evaluate the approach. They tested an FNN with four layers, SVM, kNN, Long Short-Term Memory (LSTM) and Gated Recurrent Unit (GRU). The characteristic properties of the data for classification are also called features. Features have been extracted from the time domain and the frequency domain. They also tested the impact of feature extraction by applying it to three of the five models. The models with feature extraction (FNN, SVM, kNN) performed far better than

---

[3] https://senso.me (Last visited on 15 April 2022).

the remaining two, with FNN achieving the highest accuracy with 94.3% and SVM the second highest with 89.3%.

Plawiak et al. used the data glove *DG5 VHand* from *DGTech Engineering Solutions*[4] [14]. The glove consists of five flex sensors, one for each finger, accelerometers for all three axis and gyroscopes for roll and pitch of the hand. Data were recorded with ten people, each recording 22 gestures with ten repetitions per gesture. The gestures included an *OK*-sign, *Thumbs up* and *Hello*, the latter being a dynamic gesture. This is why the models need multiple sensor samples of a single gesture to detect movement. The authors used three models to classify their data: Probabilistic Neural Network (PNN), SVM and kNN. All models were first trained with a different number of sensor samples per gesture (20, 40 or 60). In a second test, the models were trained with Principal Component Analysis (PCA) (top 8, 5, 3 eigenvectors), to reduce the volume of data, and with a fixed number of samples per gesture (20). The best performance for all models was achieved with PCA and eight eigenvectors. SVM scored the highest accuracy with 98.32%, kNN is in second place with 97.36% and PNN scored 97.10%.

One disadvantage of using sensor-based approaches compared to camera-based works is the often considerably higher cost. Shukor et al. [17] have therefore developed a lower-cost alternative to many commercially used data gloves. Instead of using flex-sensors to detect the degree of bent for each finger, they use tilt-sensors, which measure whether a finger is bent at all. The returned value is binary instead of continuous, so the degree of bent is lost, however, the tilt-sensor is much less expensive than its flex-sensor counterpart. The authors use two of these sensors for each finger as well as an accelerometer to classify six static and three dynamic gestures. Each gesture was signed by four participants and repeated ten times by each of them. The data samples were compared with a distance function to prerecorded gestures stored on the micro-controller. The static gestures had an accuracy of 94.16%, while the dynamic gestures managed 78.33%. Overall the system achieved 88,88% accuracy.

Pezzuoli et al. [13] use the data glove *Talking Hands* to classify 27 dynamic gestures using kNN, linear SVM, RF (multi-layer perceptron) Neural Network (NN) and GNB. The data glove consists of ten flex-sensors to measure the bend of the fingers, one IMU to detect hand- and one to detect arm orientation. Each IMU provides one quaternion, thus describing the arm and hand rotation. Because a lot of features are captured every time a gesture is performed, the authors perform a dimensionality reduction by trying to find a function that fits through the data points provided by the sensors. Afterwards each gesture, regardless of length, can be described by a 96-dimensional vector. The authors performed two experiments to evaluate their approach. In the first experiment 27 non-sign language gestures were recorded by five users with six repetitions per gesture. The data of one user was used for testing, while the rest was used for training the models. SVM achieved the highest accuracy with 96.7% with kNN being second and RF being third with 96.6% and 96.2% respectively. In a second

---

[4] http://www.dg-tech.it/vhand3/products.html (Last visited on 15 April 2022).

experiment, a publicly available database with 95 gestures of the Australian Sign Language with 27 samples per sign was used to compare this paper to other approaches. In this test, NN scored 97.4% accuracy with kNN being second (92.9%) and RF being third (92.6%).

Saggio et al. [16] compared the performance of kNN and Convolutional Neural Network (CNN) on a dataset consisting of ten of the most common gestures of the Italian Sign Language. A data glove with ten flex-sensors on one hand as well as three IMUs on each arm was used to record the data. Seven signers were asked to repeat each gesture up to 100 times after seeing a professional signer perform them as a reference. The dataset was split 80/20 into a training and test set. The best results for kNN (96.6%) were achieved with $N = 140$ samples in the training set and $k = 1$ nearest neighbors. CNN achieved an accuracy of 98.0% with one convolutional layer with 20 filters of size 16, Rectified Linear Unit (ReLu) activation functions and batch normalization. No pooling layers were used.

3   Towards Gesture Recognition

3.1   Data Acquisition and Pre-processing

In our two experiments, hand gestures of the popular game RPS are captured with the help of a data glove.

As already mentioned, Hand gestures can be divided in static and dynamic. Dynamic gestures possess a degree of movement and therefore are more difficult to detect. We limited our experiments to static gestures. Therefore, the recorded data consider the handshape and, only in the larger *Dataset B*, the orientation of the hand. A snapshot of the data is taken at an exact point in time, since, as just mentioned, we do not need the temporal information. This point in time is announced and indicated to the player by the recording tool. The player, therefore, knows exactly when his hand must have assumed the desired configuration, consisting of handshape and possibly orientation.

Both datasets have in common that they represent hand gestures of the well-known game RPS. The data were recorded as follows: Each participant was shown a graphic of the hand gesture during data collection, which should be imitated ten times in succession. Participants could see a visualization of their own execution of the gesture and were therefore influenced by any drifts and deviations. However, the gesture executions of other subjects could not be seen. After each gesture, the data glove with its built-in IMUs was recalibrated using the included software to reduce possible measurement errors caused by displaced sensors in the glove. If any errors were detected during recording using visualization, the data was discarded and re-recorded. An example of an error is a strong drift of the thumb, which was already observed during data acquisition.

To ensure that the results of the experiments were user-independent, the data of the different users was firmly separated, so that a user's data was part of either the test data or the training data, never both!

Dataset A has been expanded from a previous work and consists of five different hand gestures (see Table 1, gesture $I - V$) [1]. The data consists of 15
features, all of which are handshape only and can be looked up in Table 2.
30 participants, between seven and 72 years old, under the conditions already
mentioned before, repeated each of the five gestures ten times, resulting in a
total of 1500 recordings.

Dataset B consists of 25 different hand gestures (see Table 1, gesture $1 - 25$)
[1]. Compared to *Dataset A*, the orientation of the hand was recorded here in
addition to the handshape. For example, the gestures *axe*, *paper* and *water*
have all the same handshape but a different hand orientation. Therefore the
quaternion of the palm rotation was added as new features to accomplish the
addition of hand gestures which differ only in the hand orientation, so 19
instead of 15 features were used here (see Table 2). The data were recorded
by nine participants (two female, seven male) between 23 and 57 years old,
resulting in a total of 2250 recordings.

Fig. 1. *Senso Glove: DK2* data glove [1]

The data glove we used to record data for our datasets was also used by us
in a previous work [1]. It is a *Senso Glove: DK2* from *Senso Device Inc*[5] with
eight IMUs and two magnetometers. Internal data processing enables precise and
cameraless capture of fingers and hand movements. Figure 1 shows the *Senso
Glove: DK2* with one IMU on the middle phalanx of each finger. An additional
second IMU is attached to the thumb. The human thumb has one more range

---

[5] https://senso.me (Last visited on 28 April 2022).

of motion than the other fingers, so two sensors are required to provide accurate information. There is also a sensor on the back of the hand and the wrist. All eight IMUs represent a combination of accelerometers and gyroscopes. These precisely measure the current orientation of the respective part of the hand. The sensors on the wrist and palm additionally contain a magnetometer whose values can also be accessed.

The SDK provided by the data glove can be used to access the values shown in Table 2. The values are supplied at a rate 10 Hz and sent via Bluetooth to a PC.

Table 2. Sensor values provided by *Senso Glove SDK* used in dataset A/B [1]

Part of hand	Value	Datatype	Floats	Dataset A	Dataset B
Thumb	Rotation	Quaternion	4	✓	✓
Thumb	Bend	Float	1	✓	✓
Thumb	Angles	Vector2	2	✓	✓
Index Finger	Angles	Vector2	2	✓	✓
Middle Finger	Angles	Vector2	2	✓	✓
Ring Finger	Angles	Vector2	2	✓	✓
Pinky Finger	Angles	Vector2	2	✓	✓
Palm	Rotation	Quaternion	4	✗	✓
Palm	Position	Vector3	3	✗	✗
Palm	Magnetometer	Vector3	3	✗	✗
Wrist	Rotation	Quaternion	4	✗	✗
Wrist	Magnetometer	Vector3	3	✗	✗
				$\Sigma 15$	$\Sigma 19$

Using only static gestures has the advantage that we do not need to extract features from the time-domain. Recording the data at a fixed time ensures that segmentation of the gestures is not necessary. Therefore, the recorded data can be used for classification without any preprocessing. The recordings are simply scaled linearly to the range of values $[0, 1]$ using min-max normalization. Converting the given quaternions to Euler angles did not give better results.

3.2 Data Processing

As seen in Sect. 2, there is a wide range of different models used to classify gestures. In the following, we will briefly look at some of the more commonly used ones, which will be examined in this paper.

Support Vector Machines (SVMs) are used to separate data [21] by mapping the data into a vector space and creating a linear hyperplane that splits the data into two classes. Using the *kernel trick*, a non-linear hyperplane can be created. SVMs are max-margin classifiers, meaning the calculated hyperplane splits the data such that the margin between the closest data point of each class and the hyperplane is maximized. This way the model is more robust when classifying unseen data.

When classifying more than one class, multiple SVMs are used. Each of them either classifies one class against all other classes (*One-against-All*) or one class against a single one of the others (*One-against-One*). Often a majority vote of all SVMs is used to calculate the final output of the model.

Decision Trees (DTs) can be seen as a collection of *if ... then ... else ...* rules [20]. In each iteration, the input data is split into different groups based on the value of one of its features. The order in which these features are used to split the data can have a big impact on the classification performance. It is therefore advised to test different orders. Ordering all features based on their information gain and starting with the one with the highest information often produces good results.

Random Forests (RFs) are a combination of multiple DT, a so-called ensemble approach [5]. Each of the trees only gets a random subset of the input data and the corresponding features. The decision of the whole classifier is calculated by a majority vote of all trees. A single tree within an RF can overfit the data easily and is therefore often weaker compared to a full DT. However, by combining multiple of these weaker trees, the classification performance typically increases, while overfitting less overall compared to regular DT.

k-Nearest Neighbor (kNN) classifies input data based on neighbouring data points seen during training [6]. k denotes the number of neighbours to be considered when classifying new data. The distance to these neighbouring points can also be considered, i.e., data points with a shorter distance to the input data can be weighted more, as they are more likely to be similar to the input data. A decision is formed by a (weighted) majority vote of all k neighbours.

Logistic Regression (LogReg) creates a logistic function, which models the probability of an input sample belonging to one of two classes based on one feature by taking the natural algorithm of the odds ratio of the feature [8].

Gaussian Naive Bayes (GNB) is based on Bayes Theorem [2]. It tries to predict an event A based on the priori and posteriori probabilities of the event as well as another event B that is supposed to have already taken place. For classification, event B could be a feature of the input data and event A could be one of the classes we try to predict. The classifier can produce good results, even though the *naive* assumption that all features are independent is usually not true.

Perceptron is the simplest form of an Artificial Neural Network [15]. In its basic form, the model consists of a single neuron. All input features are weighted and added together with a bias value: $\sum_{i=1}^{N} w_i x_i + b$, where x_i are the input values, w_i are the corresponding weights, b is the bias and N is the number of inputs. If the result is greater than zero, the perceptron's output will be one and zero otherwise. With this, the model is able to solve linearly separable problems. For more complex problems multi-layer perceptrons were developed.

Feed-forward Neural Networks (FNNs) consist of multiple neurons. Each of them function similar to perceptrons. The neurons are organized in different layers. Each layer often consists of multiple neurons. The neurons in one layer get their inputs from the neurons in the previous layer and propagate their outputs into the neurons in the next layer. The final layer then computes the output for the entire network. Information only ever flows in one direction. There are no cycles in FNNs.

An *Apple MacBook Pro*[6] (14", 2021) with *Apple M1 Pro* processor (10-core CPU with 8 performance cores and 2 efficiency cores, 16-core GPU, 16-core Neural Engine and 200 GB/s memory bandwidth) and 16 GB Ram was used to optimize, train and classify the various ML algorithms. All classifiers were implemented using *Python* (version 3.9.10) and *scikit-learn* (version 1.0.2). All used classes and hyperparameters can be found in the official documentation[7].

4   Experiments

In this work, two experiments were performed to investigate the performance and accuracy of the ML classifier.

4.1   Experiment 1

In the first experiment, we perform hyperparameter optimization on the training data using grid search with k-fold cross-validation ($k = 10$). The leave-one-out principle was applied, so training and test data were separated in such a way that data from one participant was used as test data and all other data was used as training data. In this way, all possible combinations were iterated. In order to compare the performance of the classifiers, the *F1-score*, the *time for training*, and the *time to for prediction/classification* were stored and evaluated. A mean was then taken from the data thus obtained to investigate the performance of the the eight mentioned ML classifier.

The hyperparameters used and the ranges in which the optimum was sought can be seen in Table 3.

4.2   Experiment 2

In the second experiment, we gradually reduce the number of classes/gestures on *Dataset B* from 25 to three to see, how accuracy will change. The procedure is otherwise identical to *Experiment 1*.

---

[6] https://www.apple.com/macbook-pro-14-and-16/specs/ (Last visited on 30 April 2022).

[7] https://scikit-learn.org/stable/ (Last visited on 30 April 2022).

5   Results and Discussion

5.1   Classifier Accuracy

Table 4 shows the results of *Experiment 1*, whereas Table 5 shows the results of *Experiment 2*.

As can be seen, the F1-scores for *Dataset A* are all very high. Even the least accurate approach (Perceptron) achieves an accuracy of 94.0%. All eight classifiers manage to achieve 100% accuracy with at least one combination of training and test data. LogReg can achieve the highest F1-score which is 97.6%.

Table 3. Grid seach hyperparameter range

Classifier	Parameter	Used range
Support Vector Machine	Kernel	$\{rbf\}$
	C	$\{2^{-5}, 2^{-3}, \ldots, 2^{15}\}$
	gamma	$\{2^{-15}, 2^{-14}, \ldots, 2^{5}\}$
Decision Tree	Criterion	$\{gini, entropy\}$
Random Forest	Criterion	$\{gini, entropy\}$
	n_estimators	$\{2^{0}, 2^{1}, \ldots, 2^{10}\}$
	max_features	$\{1, 2, \ldots, 10\}$
k-Nearest Neighbor	N_neighbors	$\{1, 3, \ldots, 21\}$
	weights	$\{uniform, distance\}$
	metric	$\{euclidean, manhattan, minkowski\}$
Logistic Regression	Solver	$\{newton\text{-}cg, lbfgs, sag, saga\}$
	penalty	$\{none, l_2, l_1, elasticnet\}$
	C	$\{2^{-5}, 2^{-3}, \ldots, 2^{15}\}$
	l_1_ratio	$\{0.1, 0.2, \ldots, 1\}$
Gaussian Naive Bayes	Var_smoothing	$\{1e^{-11}, 1e^{-8}, \ldots, 1e^{3}\}$
Perceptron	Penalty	$\{none, l_2, l_1, elasticnet\}$
	max_iter	$\{10, 100, \ldots, 100000\}$
	l_1_ratio	$\{0.1, 0.2, \ldots, 1\}$
Feed-forward Neural Network	Solver	$\{lbfgs\}$
	hidden_layer_sizes	$\{(2^{2}, 2^{2}), (2^{3}, 2^{3}), \ldots, (2^{10}, 2^{10})\}$
	alpha	$\{1e^{-4}, e^{-3}, e^{-2}, e^{-1}\}$

Table 4. Comparison of different classifiers after hyperparameter optimization

| Dataset | Classifier | F1-score | | | | t_{train} (ms) | $t_{predict}$ (ms) |
		Mean	Std.Dev.	Min	Max	Mean	Mean
A	SVM	96.7 %	0.67 %	56.3 %	100.0 %	19.029	5.900
	DT	95.7 %	0.72 %	53.6 %	100.0 %	9.013	**0.055**
	RF	97.0 %	0.59 %	57.7 %	100.0 %	352.535	7.192
	kNN	95.2 %	0.72 %	56.3 %	100.0 %	0.611	1.468
	LogReg	**97.6 %**	0.38 %	65.8 %	100.0 %	58.782	0.085
	GNB	96.9 %	0.56 %	58.8 %	100.0 %	**0.424**	0.125
	Perceptron	94.0 %	0.82 %	69.2 %	100.0 %	5.134	0.067
	FNN	96.6 %	0.42 %	65.8 %	100.0 %	11934.484	1.697
B	SVM	81.0 %	0.39 %	74.8 %	94.3 %	112.207	270.300
	DT	70.6 %	0.35 %	62.9 %	79.9 %	33.085	0.120
	RF	**82.4 %**	0.32 %	72.4 %	93.2 %	1127.212	20.548
	kNN	74.3 %	0.38 %	66.3 %	83.9 %	**0.166**	7.931
	LogReg	81.9 %	0.29 %	76.0 %	90.2 %	559.639	0.119
	GNB	77.8 %	0.32 %	68.4 %	85.2 %	0.961	0.519
	Perceptron	70.4 %	0.91 %	54.4 %	83.5 %	20.330	**0.118**
	FNN	80.5 %	0.51 %	71.6 %	95.8 %	29208.535	6.771

Dataset B shows the influence of the increased number of classes/gestures from five to 25 compared to *Dataset A*. The most accurate classifier RF achieves just 82.4% accuracy, which is about 15% less than in *Dataset A*. Again, the least accurate classifier is Perceptron with 70.4%, closely followed by DT with 70.6% accuracy.

Looking at the F1-scores for both datasets, we see that RF and LogReg give very good results for both datasets (both average 89.7%). Second and third place go to SVM and FNN with average 88.9% and 88.6% accuracy, respectively.

Table 5. F1-scores of different classifiers by varying number of gestures

Classifier	3	5	7	9	11	15	25
SVM	**100.00 %**	**100.00 %**	97.88 %	**98.20 %**	97.29 %	**92.28 %**	81.05 %
DT	96.01 %	94.31 %	90.98 %	86.73 %	86.47 %	77.45 %	70.62 %
RF	**100.00 %**	97.74 %	96.19 %	91.76 %	93.35 %	90.39 %	**82.42 %**
kNN	**100.00 %**	99.10 %	**98.90 %**	97.86 %	95.75 %	89.99 %	74.31 %
LogReg	**100.00 %**	99.55 %	97.21 %	98.06 %	**97.95 %**	91.83 %	81.89 %
GNB	**100.00 %**	**100.00 %**	97.35 %	96.62 %	96.32 %	90.24 %	77.84 %
Perceptron	**100.00 %**	94.24 %	90.70 %	87.55 %	89.77 %	82.17 %	70.38 %
FNN	**100.00 %**	98.63 %	96.99 %	95.70 %	97.36 %	91.27 %	80.53 %
Average	99.50 %	97.94 %	95.78 %	94.06 %	94.28 %	88.20 %	77.38 %

If we now focus on Table 5, we see that all classifiers provide a consistently very good result in terms of accuracy up to eleven gestures. Exceptions are DT, which is also the only one that does not reach 100% accuracy when classifying three gestures, and Perceptron where the accuracy already decreases strongly from three to five gestures.

5.2   Classifier Performance

To examine the performance of each classifier, we must also consider the time to train and the time to predict/classify. If we take a closer look at Table 4, we see that there are extreme differences in the training time as well as in the prediction time.

FNN, for example, takes by far the most time in training, but can classify relatively quickly. DT, LogReg, and Perceptron are the fastest algorithms, regardless of the number of gestures. kNN and GNB are trained the fastest, with kNN performing better with an increasing number of gestures and being the only classifier that becomes faster as the number of classes increases. However, since the time is very small at less than one millisecond, this may be due to the workload of the measuring computer and may be coincidence.

A fivefold increase in the number of gestures doubles to quadruples the time required for training for most classifiers. Exceptions are SVM with a close six-fold increase in time, LogReg with an almost tenfold increase, and the already mentioned kNN, which is the only classifier that can improve its time to a close quarter. In terms of time to classify, the classifiers are all in the range of a factor of 1.4 to 5.4, only SVM increases its time by a factor of forty-five, which shows us that this classifiers performs poorly when it comes to scaling classes.

In general, it can be said that four out of eight classifiers needed less than 1 ms for prediction, regardless of the number of gestures. With the exception of SVM and RF all classifiers need less than 10 ms, RF up to 20 ms depending on the number of gestures and SVM as already mentioned with up to 270 ms much more.

Overall, we can say that while RF and LogReg provide accurate results regardless of the number of classes, LogReg takes a factor of 85 to 170 less time to predict than RF and is also up to five times faster in training. Nevertheless, RF offers itself as an alternative, since it is still in an acceptable range with about 1s for training and 20 ms for prediction, especially since the training time is not necessarily time-critical. SVM and FNN on the other hand also provide accurate results, but are much slower in comparison than the mentioned ones.

5.3   User Independence

The experiments just mentioned were all evaluated with a fixed training and test data set separated by user and are therefore user independent. In order to obtain a better comparability with other work, we have now examined *Experiment 1* again with randomly composed training and test data in a ratio of 80 to 20. For this, we used fixed hyperparameters that are in the ranges given in Table 3 and gave good results in *Experiment 1*. Subsequently, the optimized classifiers were trained and tested 100 times. The training and test data were randomized again before each run. The average accuracy, as well as the standard deviation of the maximum and minimum, can be found in Table 6.

Table 6. Accuracies of different classifiers with 80 to 20 train/test data split

Classifier	5 gestures accuracy				25 gestures accuracy			
	Mean	St.Dev.	Min	Max	Mean	St.Dev.	Min	Max
SVM	**99.2%**	0.56%	97.3%	100.0%	**99.5%**	0.31%	98.4%	100.0%
DT	97.7%	0.89%	95.3%	99.3%	92.6%	1.30%	89.3%	94.9%
RF	98.7%	0.59%	97.3%	100.0%	99.3%	0.38%	98.0%	100.0%
kNN	99.0%	0.45%	97.7%	99.7%	99.4%	0.33%	98.4%	100.0%
LogReg	98.4%	0.67%	96.3%	99.7%	96.5%	0.88%	94.2%	98.9%
GNB	97.5%	0.81%	95.3%	99.3%	89.9%	1.38%	86.9%	93.1%
Perceptron	96.5%	2.01%	85.0%	99.7%	85.7%	3.28%	76.4%	92.7%
FNN	99.1%	0.59%	97.7%	100.0%	98.8%	0.56%	96.9%	100.0%

As can be seen, the results for both datasets are much better than for user-independent data in Table 4. *Dataset B* can achieve better results with significantly more gestures in some cases than *Dataset A*, so it can be argued that both datasets can achieve similar results if data are user-dependent.

It is worth noting that Perceptron is again the least accurate classifier, indicating that this classifier is not suitable for this type of classification. LogReg now performs rather mediocre in comparison, showing that the approach has advantages with user-independent data.

The fact that the accuracy of dataset B is higher than for dataset A, despite the higher number of classes, may be due to the data quality on the one hand, but also to the selected hyperparameters, which are fixed here and have not been optimized.

5.4   Outlier

During our investigations in *Experiment 1*, we found that large variations in F1-scores were visible in one run. For example, in SVM, 29 of the 30 runs could show F1-scores ranging from 86.81% to 100% (mean 98.07%), except for the run with participant 13 as test data. Here, only an F1 score of 56.28% could be determined. The other classifiers showed similar behavior and across all classifiers the best F1 score of only 69.21% was obtained with Perceptron. We therefore assume that the quality of this data set is very low and ran *Experiment 1* again excluding the data from participant 13. The results can be seen in Table 7. The accuracy could be increased by 1.4% on average and every classifier could improve his F1-score. As a positive side effect, the times could also be improved, which can

Table 7. Dataset A results without data from participant #13

| Classifier | F1-score | | | | t_{train} (ms) | $t_{predict}$ (ms) |
	Mean	Std.Dev.	Min	Max	Mean	Mean
SVM	98.0 %	0.07 %	90.0 %	100.0 %	7.316	2.223
DT	97.1 %	0.14 %	83.3 %	100.0 %	6.077	0.051
RF	98.5 %	0.06 %	89.7 %	100.0 %	397.406	8.482
KNN	96.8 %	0.17 %	85.6 %	100.0 %	0.413	1.047
LogReg	**99.0 %**	0.03 %	92.1 %	100.0 %	53.031	0.076
GNB	98.0 %	0.08 %	90.0 %	100.0 %	**0.379**	0.111
Perceptron	94.8 %	0.57 %	68.7 %	100.0 %	3.439	**0.049**
FNN	98.4 %	0.07 %	90.0 %	100.0 %	8185.472	0.951

certainly be explained by a more problem-free classification, but could also be due to fluctuations in the computer's workload.

Comparing to Table 5 we can now also see that the classification of five gestures from *Dataset B* gives about the same results as in *Dataset A*. That shows that the classifiers give similar results for the same number (but not type) of gestures.

5.5 Comparison with Related Work

Table 8 lists comparable works, sorted by the number of gestures to be recognized. For better comparability, we use the user-dependent results from Table 6

Table 8. Comparison of recognition accuracy with related work

Author(s)	Sensor	Classifier(s)	HS	Mo	Or	#G	#P	Accuracy
Achenbach et al. [1]	Data glove	SVM	✓	-	-	5	11	87.50%
Ma et al. [10]	Data glove	FNN	✓	-	-	5	10	94.30%
This work	**Data glove**	**SVM**	✓	-	-	**5**	**30**	**99.2%**
Melo [11]	Leap Motion	HMM	✓	✓	✓	6	-	57.29%
Melo [11]	Data glove	HMM	✓	✓	✓	6	-	76.00%
Billiet et al. [4]	Microsoft Kinect	kNN	✓	-	-	8	8	95.50%
Shukor et al. [17]	Data glove	Distance Function	✓	✓	-	9	4	88.88%
Saggio et al. [16]	Data glove	CNN	✓	✓	-	10	7	98.00%
Plawiak et al. [14]	Data glove	SVM	✓	✓	✓	22	10	98.32%
This work	**Data glove**	**SVM**	✓	-	✓	**25**	**9**	**99.5%**
Pezzuoli et al. [13]	Data glove	SVM	✓	✓	✓	27	5	96.70%
Kumar et al. [7]	Microsoft Kinect	HMM	✓	✓	✓	30	8	83.77%
Mittal et al. [12]	Leap Motion	CNN, LSTM	✓	✓	✓	35	6	89.50%

In table header the following abbreviations were used: Handshape (HS), Movement (Mo), Orientation (Or), Gestures (G), Participants (P)

for the comparison, as done, for example, by Pezzuoli et al. [13]. Here our SVM can obtain the best results in the comparison with 99.2% and 99.5%, respectively.

The user-independent results still represent the highest accuracy in a direct comparison with *Dataset A* and our LogReg at 97.6%, while *Dataset B* slightly underperforms with our RF and 82.4%.

6   Conclusion and Future Work

In this paper, we investigated different classifiers to find the most suitable one to detect static hand gestures. Regardless of the number of classes, RF and LogReg perform best, with preference given to the former for user-independent data, though LogReg is faster for this in any case. For *Dataset A* with five gestures a F1-score of 97.6% can be achieved, for *Dataset B* with 25 gestures it is 82.4%. If user-dependent data is also allowed, i.e., data from users who have already participated in the training data, the accuracies increase significantly to over 99% for both data sets when using a SVM. The use of outlier detection can also increase the accuracy of our approach. On a trial basis, an erroneous user record was analyzed and removed from *Dataset A*. This increased the F1-score by an average of 1.4% across all classifiers in *Experiment 1*.

Experiment 2 showed us that most classifiers (exceptions were DT and Perceptron) had no trouble classifying up to eleven gestures and had accuracies between 93.35% and 97.95%. From eleven gestures on, the accuracy of the classifiers dropped sharply, which is due to the high number of classes.

For a future work we would like to use a more precise glove to be able to recognize and distinguish even more gestures and handshapes. In particular, the aforementioned strong drift of the thumb must be prevented. These could be taken from sign language, for example. There, the handshapes are similar and partly identical to the gestures studied in this work. However, there are significantly more - it is estimated that a classification of 60 to 120 gestures consisting of handshape only (no orientation) would be useful for this future work. To complement this, we want to investigate feature selection and see if we can achieve better results by selecting features more precisely. The already mentioned outlier detection will also be extended.

References

1. Achenbach, P., Müller, P., Wach, T., Tregel, T., Göbel, S.: Rock beats Scissor: SVM based gesture recognition with data gloves. In: 2021 IEEE International Conference on Pervasive Computing and Communications Workshops and other Affiliated Events (PerCom Workshops), pp. 617–622 (2021)
2. Berrar, D.: Bayes' theorem and naive Bayes classifier. Encyclopedia of Bioinformatics and Computational Biology: ABC of Bioinformatics **403** (2018)
3. Bhuiyan, R.A., Tushar, A.K., Ashiquzzaman, A., Shin, J., Islam, M.R.: Reduction of gesture feature dimension for improving the hand gesture recognition performance of numerical sign language. In: 2017 20th International Conference of Computer and Information Technology (ICCIT), pp. 1–6. IEEE (2017)

4. Billiet, L., Oramas Mogrovejo, J.A., Hoffmann, M., Meert, W., Antanas, L.: Rule-based hand posture recognition using qualitative finger configurations acquired with the kinect. In: Proceedings of the 2nd International Conference on Pattern Recognition Applications and Methods, pp. 1–4 (2013)
5. Breiman, L.: Random forests. Mach. Learn. **45**(1), 5–32 (2001)
6. Fix, E., Hodges, J.L.: Nonparametric discrimination: consistency properties. Randolph Field, Texas, Project, pp. 21–49 (1951)
7. Kumar, P., Saini, R., Roy, P.P., Dogra, D.P.: A position and rotation invariant framework for sign language recognition (SLR) using Kinect. Multimed. Tools Appl. **77**(7), 8823–8846 (2017). https://doi.org/10.1007/s11042-017-4776-9
8. LaValley, M.P.: Logistic regression. Circulation **117**(18), 2395–2399 (2008)
9. Lovelace, D.C.: Rock-Paper-Scissors Variants (2003). https://www.umop.com/rps.htm
10. Ma, W., Hu, J., Liao, J., Fan, Z., Wu, J., Liu, L.: Finger gesture recognition based on 3D-accelerometer and 3D-gyroscope. In: Douligeris, C., Karagiannis, D., Apostolou, D. (eds.) KSEM 2019. LNCS (LNAI), vol. 11775, pp. 406–413. Springer, Cham (2019). https://doi.org/10.1007/978-3-030-29551-6_36
11. de Melo, P.M.P.: Gesture recognition for human-robot collaborative assembly (2018)
12. Mittal, A., Kumar, P., Roy, P.P., Balasubramanian, R., Chaudhuri, B.B.: A modified LSTM model for continuous sign language recognition using leap motion. IEEE Sens. J. **19**(16), 7056–7063 (2019)
13. Pezzuoli, F., Corona, D., Corradini, M.L.: Recognition and classification of dynamic hand gestures by a wearable data-glove. SN Comput. Sci. **2**(1), 1–9 (2020). https://doi.org/10.1007/s42979-020-00396-5
14. Plawiak, P., Sośnicki, T., Niedźwiecki, M., Tabor, Z., Rzecki, K.: Hand body language gesture recognition based on signals from specialized glove and machine learning algorithms. IEEE Trans. Industr. Inform. **12**(3), 1104–1113 (2016)
15. Rosenblatt, F.: The perceptron: a probabilistic model for information storage and organization in the brain. Psychol. Rev. **65**(6), 386 (1958)
16. Saggio, G., Cavallo, P., Ricci, M., Errico, V., Zea, J., Benalcázar, M.E.: Sign language recognition using wearable electronics: implementing k-nearest neighbors with dynamic time warping and convolutional neural network algorithms. Sensors **20**(14), 3879 (2020)
17. Shukor, A.Z., et al.: A new data glove approach for Malaysian sign language detection. Procedia Comput. Sci. **76**, 60–67 (2015)
18. Stokoe, W.: Sign Language Structure. Linstok Press, Silver Spring, MD (1960)
19. Stokoe, W.C., Casterline, D.C., Croneberg, C.G.: A dictionary of American Sign Language on linguistic principles. Linstok Press (1976)
20. Swain, P.H., Hauska, H.: The decision tree classifier: design and potential. IEEE Trans. Geosci. Electron. **15**(3), 142–147 (1977)
21. Vapnik, V., Chervonenkis, A.: On a class of algorithms of learning pattern recognition. Autom. Remote. Control. **25**, 937–945 (1964)

Learning with Augmented Reality Headsets? Experiences of a Use Case in Vocational Education

Pia Spangenberger[1]([⊠]) [iD], Felix Kapp[2] [iD], Nadine Matthes[1], and Linda Kruse[3]

[1] Institute of Vocational Education and Work Studies, Technische Universität Berlin, Berlin, Germany
{pia.spangenberger,nadine.matthes}@tu-berlin.de
[2] Chair of Human-Machine-Systems, Technische Universität Berlin, Berlin, Germany
Felix.kapp@tu-berlin.de
[3] School of Design, Department of Media Design, University of Applied Sciences Mainz, Mainz, Germany
Linda.kruse@hs-mainz.de

Abstract. For over a decade augmented reality (AR) technology has been discussed as educational tool. Latest technical advancements such as voice control, hand-tracking and moving virtual objects in augmented interaction using AR head-mounted-displays (HMDs) widen the opportunities for educational use even further. Still, the question remains how AR headsets can contribute to learning. As an example, we will present a use case in vocational education in which students shall practice the reading of hydraulic diagrams using advanced AR headsets. We developed a first prototype and examine its feasibility for a learning concept. In particular, we tested a) use of hand-tracking to select and move technical components, and b) use of voice commands and the gaze cursor to highlight the technical components by their names. Based on the experiences, we will analyse the strengths, weaknesses, opportunities and threats of our learning concept in a SWOT analysis. Finally, advantages and disadvantages of implementing advanced AR headsets in vocational education practice will be discussed.

Keywords: AR · HMDs · HoloLens2 · Technical subjects · Vocational education · Metal engineering · Electrical engineering

1 Introduction

Augmented reality (AR) can be described as a condition in which the real-world environment is enhanced by computer-generated perceptual information, such as 3D virtual objects [1]. Users experience virtual objects while still seeing or interacting with the real environment. Using either smartglasses, tablets or a smartphone, they can perceive or interact with virtual information in real time. Recent technological innovation even allows a deeper experience by wearing AR devices on the own physical body, increasing the perceived local presence of virtual objects through headsets with see-through holographic lenses or smart contact lenses [2]. Based on prior definitions and concepts of

---

The original version of this chapter was revised: multiple orthographic errors in the paper were corrected. The correction to this chapter is available at
https://doi.org/10.1007/978-3-031-15325-9_20

H. Söbke et al. (Eds.): JCSG 2022, LNCS 13476, pp. 246–258, 2022.
https://doi.org/10.1007/978-3-031-15325-9_18

AR, VR and Mixed Reality, such as Milgram and Kishino's [3] virtual environment continuum or prior work by Azuma [1], Rauschnabel et al. [2] propose an AR continuum that 'ranges from assisted reality (with low levels of local presence) to mixed reality (with high levels of local presence)' (see Fig. 1).

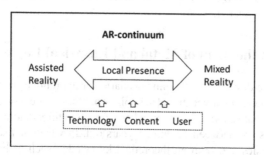

Fig. 1. AR-continuum according to Rauschnabel et al. [2]. Own illustration.

Via common mobile phones, Google Glasses or AR headsets augmented reality (AR) technology has find its way into assisting working processes in the industry and into the gaming market [2, 4–6]. For instance, Zhang et al. [4] demonstrated the use of advanced AR technology for city modelling. Collecting use cases in the industrial service, Aleksy et al. [5], observed that AR technology can be beneficial for service workers regarding remote support or repair support. Location-based AR games such as Pokémon GO have reached consumers worldwide using their own smartphones to find virtual objects called Pokémon within their own neighbourhood [6].

Against this background, AR technology has also gained interest in the context of education [7–13] and vocational education [14–17]. For instance, in technical subjects in the field of vocational education Guth et al. [14] used AR technology in a learning scenario to provide learners with additional information on a technical facility for water supply and wastewater disposal. The authors state that AR was beneficial because apprentices could gain experience with technical facilities that were not possible in reality. Furthermore, Sirakaya and Cakmak [15] argue that AR can especially be beneficial for complex assembly and maintenance processes in technical subjects because it provides 'simultaneous interaction between virtual objects and the real world' compared to diagrams or videos which are generally used ([15], p. 3). Instead of learning from a 2D illustration, apprentices could benefit from interacting with visual 3D technical components. AR learning scenarios can provide practical experiences with virtual technical components which are essential for the learning process in the field of technical vocational education, e.g., electrical engineering [16]. Furthermore, AR learning environments can allow autonomous learning to foster self-management of one's learning process, which is also relevant for apprentices in the field of vocational education [17].

The latest generation of AR HMD (head-mounted-displays) introduced new technological features such as voice control and gesture control that have the potential to enhance the benefits of AR technology as educational tool in the field of vocational education even further. However, research findings on effective advanced AR learning applications using standalone HMDs in vocational education practice are still rare [11, 16].

The present article presents a first concept on how to use latest AR technology in an educational context. We therefore developed a specific use case for vocational education (learning goal: learn how to read and understand a hydraulic diagram) and developed a first prototype. Our experience with the development of the concept and the prototype are summarized in a SWOT analysis of advanced AR headsets for educational settings, which we present in Sect. 4.

2   Use Case in the Field of Metal and Electrical Engineering

In our use case, we developed a learning scenario for apprentices in the field of metal and electrical engineering at vocational schools. Apprentices are working at a company and go to a vocational school on a rotation basis for up to three-and-a-half years. Commonly, apprentices are between 17 and 25 years old. In vocational schools they learn about technical basics and relevant theoretical knowledge such as basis principals of technical systems, machines or specific technical components. In the classroom practical application of competencies on actual sights are limited due to safety restrictions and limited space or time in a vocational school setting. Instead, vocational teachers often use videos, or computer-based simulations, if available, to provide experiences for apprentices in practice.

2.1   Learning Objectives and Learning Content

The learning objective of our learning scenario is to foster reading and understanding hydraulic diagrams. Reading hydraulic diagrams is an essential competency in technical education especially in the field of metal and electrical engineering. The reading of hydraulic diagrams is difficult for apprentices to learn because of their complexity [18]. Apprentices have to understand relationships between technical components and their functions for complete machines or plants. Apprentices should be able to read diagrams by means of recognizing symbols of a diagram, knowing their function and combine these symbols with a technical component. In our concept we use hydraulic diagrams because it is one technical component of the hydraulic brake pressure system of a wind energy plant. The hydraulic brake pressure system is a complex technical system that is an essential part of a complete wind energy plant. It is located in the gondola to control the rotation speed of the rotor blades in case of repair or maintenance work. Without a basic knowledge of the hydraulic diagram, its technical components and functions, the maintenance or repair of a wind energy plant is hardly possible. Hence, in our learning scenario we will combine the learning objective, reading hydraulic diagram, with its functions for maintaining a wind energy plant. The hydraulic diagram contains three main components which are supported by further monitoring and control components as such as sensors or magnetic valves (see Fig. 2):

1. Three motors and hydraulic pumps (1–9)
2. Accumulator of hydraulic disc brakes (220)
3. Hydraulic disc brakes (239–244)

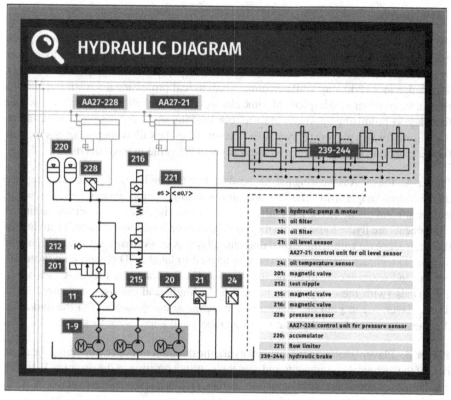

Fig. 2. Hydraulic Diagram as a simplified illustration. Own illustration.

2.2 Quest Design

We developed a learning setting that allows learners to share their thoughts, exchange opinions and discuss learning content to achieve a deeper understanding of complex hydraulic diagrams [19, 20]. We considered central components of the four-component instructional design (4C/ID) model [21]: We developed (1) an authentic learning task in which apprentices have to arrange virtual 3D technical components of a hydraulic diagram displayed in the real environment via advanced AR technology. While rearranging technical components, apprentices have to connect new learning content on technical components of a hydraulic diagram to their basic knowledge on general function of diagrams. Apprentices also receive (2) additional information through a classmate or the AR system itself. (3) The system is providing direct feedback when needed in time. (4) Apprentices will acquire new abilities by using their skills in real-time to arrange the virtual hydraulic diagram, fulfil the quest under time stress and exchanging information with their classmate. At the end, apprentices can repeat practice by changing their roles.

2.3 Gameplay

We understood our learning concept as a first step towards developing a serious game using advanced AR headsets. Serious games provide opportunities for learners to interact in learning tasks, receive feedback on own mastery experiences and foster complex knowledge in a vivid way while creating a link to real professional situations [22–24]. Hence, we considered to implement game elements such as challenges, collaboration and feedback as promising approach to foster our learning objective. The learning concept is designed for two players (Player A and Player B). In the following paragraphs we will further elaborate each player's role and actions in the game in more detail:

Player A. Player A is wearing the AR headset. Player A will be able to see the structure of the virtual diagram in AR. The diagram is holding empty spaces for each single technical component of the hydraulic diagram. In the beginning, the virtual technical components are flying loose within the room, have to be found, selected and brought into their correct place within the virtual diagram. Player A can verbally select and highlight virtual 3D technical components, verbally request to label a 3D object, grab those 3D objects and rearrange them inside their real-world environment. Player A uses voice commands (with the components names) to highlight and discover the correct part. Then, player A can grab and rearrange the technical components to fit the hydraulic diagram. For ease of use, the rotation around the x and z-axis were locked.

Player B. Player B looks at the original hydraulic diagram on paper containing the symbols of the technical components and sees their correct position in the diagram. Player B communicates the technical components' names, symbols and position to player A.

Game Goal. Arranging the technical components presented in AR into its correct position in the virtual hydraulic diagram.

Game Challenge. Both players have different information in the beginning. Player A sees 3D objects of technical components displayed in the classroom through the AR headset. Player B has a paper (or tablet) with the hydraulic diagram (see Fig. 2) but does not have a visual representation of the technical components. Under time pressure players have to rearrange the technical components in AR into its correct position in the hydraulic diagram.

Collaboration. Since both players have different information on the beginning, they have to communicate with each other to master the quest. While player B has the task of explaining symbols in the diagram, Player A has the task of explaining the functions and arranging the technical components in AR according to the explanations by player B. Only if they elaborate a common understanding of the correct arrangement of a hydraulic diagram, they will be able to master the task. Afterwards players can change their role and repeat the procedure, prospectively with another diagram (virtually and as paper version) to transfer their knowledge of the first round.

Feedback. Feedback is given twofold by a) players to each other, and b) the system. Player A will be able to point at or announce technical components and gains feedback through highlighting if their selection of technical components is correct or not. Player A has to explain the properties of each technical component to Player B to match it to a symbol at the paper plan. If they master a correct selection and arrangement in the virtual diagram the correct symbol of the technical component will appear, and the technical component itself will vanish. The game is over when all virtual technical components have vanished, and only symbols are visible to player A. Furthermore, player A will see that the rotor blades of a 3D miniature wind energy plant will start running symbolizing that players successfully mastered to activate the brake pressure system.

2.4 Hardware – Advanced AR Headset

In our use case, we used an advanced AR headset that provides an extension of "reality" (real space) by projected 3D objects. The "reality" can be completely or partially hidden and overlaid. Advanced AR technology can recognize a room's geometry and uses its measurements for further calculation: Objects can be bound to existing geometry of the room, e.g., to the wall (as a picture). As example we used the HoloLens2 by Microsoft. The technology contains gesture control (hand-tracking), real-time eye tracking, voice command and control, world-scale positioning tracking, spatial mapping as well as collaboration possibilities using Microsoft Mesh [25]. Gesture control makes use of specific gestures of one's own hands, that are recognized and interpreted by the system as input, e.g., tapping with the index finger on a virtual button ('air tap') will be interpreted as confirmation to 'select' it (similar to a mouse click). For instance, to call up the main menu one's fist has to be clenched and recognized by the camera, then tap the wrist of the fist with the other hand. Gestures like 'pinching' by placing the index finger onto the thumb allow to manipulate virtual objects by moving them around. Using 'pinching' with both hands allows to scale virtual objects or take a photo. The voice control responds to defined keywords and executes them. Voice control means, that the system recognizes certain voice commands and interprets those as input. I.e., the before mentioned 'air tap' can as well be achieved by looking at the virtual button and using the respective voice command 'select'. Keywords can be combined. The processing of the words is prolonged the longer the voice input is. A word as such as 'start' is processed faster than a sentence 'start my favourite application now.' However, both would lead to the same result. Whereby the spoken part must first be completely finished, this sentence is then analysed by the software and tries to find a matching to stored keywords. In HoloLens2 not all languages are supported. Speech recognition is based on the defined device language. In order for the system to interpret which virtual button should be selected on command, the position of the 'gaze cursors' is used. The gaze cursor uses eye-tracking to follow the user's eye focal point.

3 Prototype

The prototype was developed in Unity using the Microsoft Mixed Reality Toolkit (MRTK). Modelling started with single technical components (e.g., accumulators, sensors, valves) of the hydraulic subsystem diagram in their original size as 3D objects in

Blender (see Fig. 3). In our scenario, two main functions of the advanced AR technology were essential for player A, a) use of hand-tracking gestures to select and move technical components, and b) use of voice commands and the gaze cursor to highlight the technical components by their names. Hence, we used the modelled single technical components (e.g., accumulators, sensors, valves) of the hydraulic subsystem diagram to test grabbing and rearranging the technical components and to test voice commands necessary for player A (highlighting and discovering the correct component).

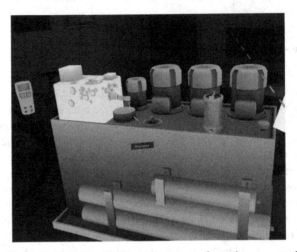

Fig. 3. Highlighting technical component after voice command

In the next step, a virtual 3D miniature model of a wind energy park (height about 1 m) was developed. It can be rotated around the y-axis and rearranged inside the room. The model was locked in size and distance to the real-world ground floor for ease of use (see Fig. 4). The wind energy park was implemented into the augmented learning scenario to visualize the consequences of mastering the rearranging technical components for the complete machine, which is in our scenario an offshore wind energy plant. If players rearrange the hydraulic diagram successfully, the rotor blades of the wind energy plant will start. We used the visualization to further evaluate gestures (hand-tracking) and additional voice commands (speech recognition) separately. Player A could determine speed of rotation blades by giving voice commands, e.g., by saying 'faster' out loud, the rotor blades start rotating faster and slower, by saying 'slower'. However, this specific command was not part of the final learning scenario but has been developed to test basic functions of the AR technology as part of testing visualization and voice commands.

Fig. 4. Miniature model of offshore wind energy plant

4   Testing and SWOT Analysis

The above-described technical features were tested by six experts (two game designers and a programmer of a game studio and three academic researchers in the field of learning psychology, instructional technology design and technical didactics). The experts tested commands and the gaze cursor to highlight the technical components by their names. They tested dragging, resizing and rotation of technical components using the hand-tracking features of the advanced AR technology. Experts also interacted with the 3D objects at the same time in the same room to test applicability for learning in a group setting. Within an online focus group their experiences were shared, written down in a protocol and documented.

Gesture Control. In most cases, the gestures worked well and were executed with 'per-ceived' low latency (e.g., tapping buttons). However, experts observed that the control of the menus only works via gestures and voice control, and the usage is not designed to use other input devices, such as keyboard, controller or mouse that allow direct error-free input. For gesture control, experts reported that it was necessary to keep the hands in the field of the camera-view directly in front of the glasses. Their gestures must be performed precisely to manipulate technical components of the diagram. Hands should not overlap if possible. If these directions were not applied by experts, hand-tracking functions did not operate.

Voice Commands. For voice control of technical components, the AR technology oper-ates using keywords. Visual feedback helped to recognize speech whether keywords are correct, and commands can be cancelled using the Windows menu. However, experts reported that the longer the keyword (e.g., 'sensor' vs. 'accumulator of hydraulic disc brakes'), the longer the speech recognition processing. Experts stated that this type of input feels more 'sluggish' than, for example, gestures. The sequence is usually that a technical component is spoken, and players have to wait if the command was recognized correctly. After recognizing the command, players have to wait to correct the command if necessary or they have to wait for the command to be executed. Experts stated that this latency caused by waiting for a respond of the system requires more attention than when a command is executed via a mouse or keyboard whereas it is interpreted correctly in any case. The needed extra attention of the player might lead to quicker fatigue and a level of frustration when commands are not recognized, incorrectly recognized or take longer to be executed compared to 'classic' input methods. Experts also observed that voice control is precise in operating only for the person wearing the glasses. Other voices of experts in the same room were not recognized by the AR technology.

Visualization. The HoloLens2 uses laser projection to display the images on parts or the full glasses. This allows, to only cover parts of glasses and be able to still see the rest of the environment besides the projections. But experts observed that the projection on the various layers of the glasses is less sharp, as the image is created through overlapping layers of light waves. Experts outlined that this is as well true to other Augmented Reality headsets like the Magic Leap. The main issue with this technology would be that text is harder to read. In Virtual Reality HMDs (e.g., Meta Quest, HTC Vive) the images are displayed through a monitor (i.e., QLED or RGB-LCD). Thus, each individual pixel can show the colour needed for the image.

Furthermore, according to the experts, the displayed names of the technical components were difficult to read depending on its size. If there was light in the room (depending on the type of lighting), it was also difficult to see the technical components or virtual model of the wind energy plant. Experts stated that in a classroom setting this has to be considered. The colour rendition can be strongly influenced by the scattered light and is formed on the glass. The surfaces do not have saturated colours. Instead, the colour prism of the glass can be seen clearly in the colour areas or depending on the presentation and animation. Experts referred to the hummingbird from the HoloLens 2 demo. In the hummingbird, the colour mantle of the glasses was positively represented in the bird and gives it a lively look. The prisms or similar fragments were received to look 'good'. However, experts mentioned that the representation or colour fastness has limits. They reported that there was always at least a weak 'hologram' effect visible.

We evaluated experts' experiences using a SWOT analysis. In the past decade, SWOT analysis has been used in the field of education to evaluate strengths, weaknesses, opportunities and threats before implementing learning technology [26–28]. Thus, in the following (Fig. 5) our observations are summarized in a SWOT matrix:

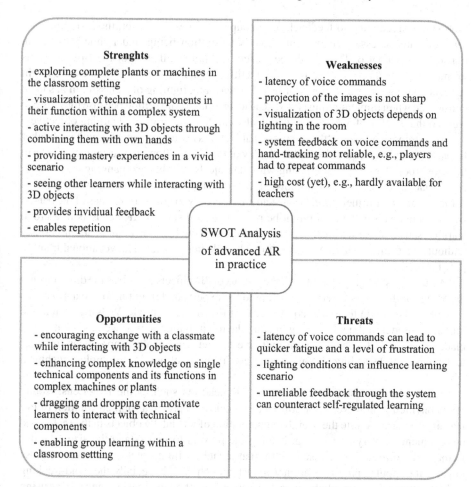

Strenghts

- exploring complete plants or machines in the classroom setting

- visualization of technical components in their function within a complex system

- active interacting with 3D objects through combining them with own hands

- providing mastery experiences in a vivid scenario

- seeing other learners while interacting with 3D objects

- provides invidiual feedback

- enables repetition

Weaknesses

- latency of voice commands

- projection of the images is not sharp

- visualization of 3D objects depends on lighting in the room

- system feedback on voice commands and hand-tracking not reliable, e.g., players had to repeat commands

- high cost (yet), e.g., hardly available for teachers

SWOT Analysis of advanced AR in practice

Opportunities

- encouraging exchange with a classmate while interacting with 3D objects

- enhancing complex knowledge on single technical components and its functions in complex machines or plants

- dragging and dropping can motivate learners to interact with technical components

- enabling group learning within a classroom settting

Threats

- latency of voice commands can lead to quicker fatigue and a level of frustration

- lighting conditions can influence learning scenario

- unreliable feedback through the system can counteract self-regulated learning

Fig. 5. SWOT analysis of the experience with advanced AR in practice. Own illustration.

5 Discussion and Conclusion

As part of a SWOT analysis, we evaluated strengths, weaknesses, opportunities and threats of using advanced AR headsets for a classroom setting in the field of metal and electrical engineering. Six experts tested hand-tracking and voice control of technical components as well as interacting with AR headsets at the same time in the same room as essential features for our learning scenario before further game development. As weaknesses we observed that a time delay in the system's respond to speech commands as well as necessary precise hand movements to activate selection processes of technical components to receive feedback might counterpart our learning objectives. While waiting for feedback of spoken words and hand-movements, players might get frustrated. The time delay might trigger an uncertainty in players because for a short moment of time it is not clear if the system doesn't respond due to an error or because of players' own wrongdoing. Within our testing, experts repeated names of technical components in slow motion after receiving no feedback for a couple of times. However, those rudimentary functions are necessary to prevent player's frustration being under time pressure in our learning scenario. Thus, with the current technological state of the HoloLens2 as example for advanced AR headsets, competitive elements such as time pressure might set a motivating game experience at risk. Furthermore, lighting of a classroom has to be considered when implementing an AR headset in a classroom setting because lighting can weaken the display of 3D objects, which also might counteract the learning objectives.

As a strength, we state 'the obvious' that learners are able to interact with each other because the see-through holographic display of the HMD allows to see another person in the same room while still interacting with 3D objects. By that, exchanging information can initiate a reflection of own knowledge to develop a common understanding of the learning content. Furthermore, the system answers only to voice commands of the person wearing the headset. Thus, it might be possible to use several AR headsets in a group learning setting. Learners will be enabled to explore the learning content autonomously without interfering each other, which is one key element of technical vocational training [14–17].

As another strength, we point out the visuals of 3D objects as well as the dragging and dropping. Both has been very convincing to the experts and might motivate apprentices to explore the single technical components of the diagram in AR. Walking around the miniature model of the wind energy plant, placing it in the room as well as seeing rotor blades starting as feedback, might motivate learners and enable apprentices to better understand single technical components and their functions in a complete technical system.

In summary, we state that advanced AR headsets such as the HoloLens2 sound very convincing, however, they still face obstacles for practical implementation of our learning scenario. While the overall augmentation of virtual 3D objects in the real-world environments is very convincing, helping the players to understand the size relations to the real world and the possibility to manipulate position, rotation and size of those objects, the input capabilities are not robust enough, yet. Especially the hand-tracking and voice control lacked reliability to be practically applied in a real learning setting using time pressure and on-time feedback, which are essential component to foster complex skills [22]. The immense lag and uncertainty of the voice command interpretation was reported by experts as frustrating and discouraging, which could have a negative impact on autonomous and self-regulated learning especially for unexperienced users (see also Akçayır and Akçayır [9]).

Concluding, we observed that some weaknesses of the AR headset might counteract our learning objectives. As already pointed out by Krüger and Bodemer [11], AR features of advanced AR such as the HoloLens2 might not be at a level yet where they are reliable enough for actual and real learning settings in practice. For instance, voice control and hand-tracking lack speed by delaying visible feedback which can lead to players' frustration. Experts have been waiting for feedback if they have performed hand-tracking gestures or voice commands correctly. On the contrary, the visualizing of 3D technical components in the real-world setting in our example were very convincing and might enhance leaners motivation to better understand complex technical systems. Furthermore, learners can exchange thoughts and ideas with each other because the

AR headset allows seeing a learning partner while interacting with 3D objects. Based on our experiences, we conclude that advanced AR headsets bring new and promising features for practical experiences of apprentices within a classroom setting. However, some technical features are (yet) not reliable enough to secure self-regulated learning environments due to the unreliability of the native input options and their latency.

References

1. Azuma, R.T.: A survey of augmented reality. Presence Teleoperators Virtual Environ. **6**, 355–385 (1997). https://doi.org/10.1162/pres.1997.6.4.355
2. Rauschnabel, P.A., Felix, R., Hinsch, C., Shahab, H., Alt, F.: What is XR? Towards a framework for augmented and virtual reality. Comput. Hum. Behav. **133**, 107289 (2022). https://doi.org/10.1016/j.chb.2022.107289
3. Milgram, P., Kishino, F.: A taxonomy of mixed reality visual displays. IEICE Trans. Inf. Syst. **77**, 1321–1329 (1994)
4. Zhang, L., Chen, S., Dong, H., El Saddik, A.: Visualizing toronto city data with hololens: using augmented reality for a city model. IEEE Consum. Electron. Mag. **7**, 73–80 (2018). https://doi.org/10.1109/MCE.2018.2797658
5. Aleksy, M., Troost, M., Scheinhardt, F., Zank, G.T.: Utilizing HoloLens to support industrial service processes. In: Barolli, L., Aina, I. (eds.) 32nd IEEE International Conference on Advanced Information Networking and Applications. IEEE AINA 2018, 16–18 May 2018, Krakow, Poland, Proceedings, pp. 143–148. IEEE, Piscataway (2018). https://doi.org/10.1109/AINA.2018.00033
6. Rasche, P., Schlomann, A., Mertens, A.: Who is still playing pokémon go? A web-based survey. JMIR Serious Games **5**, e7 (2017). https://doi.org/10.2196/games.7197
7. Söbke, H., Baalsrud Hauge, J., Stefan, I.A., Stefan, A.: Using a location-based AR game in environmental engineering. In: van der Spek, E., Göbel, S., Do, E.-L., Clua, E., Baalsrud Hauge, J. (eds.) ICEC-JCSG 2019. LNCS, vol. 11863, pp. 466–469. Springer, Cham (2019). https://doi.org/10.1007/978-3-030-34644-7_47
8. Kesim, M., Ozarslan, Y.: Augmented reality in education: current technologies and the potential for education. Procedia Soc. Behav. Sci. **47**, 297–302 (2012). https://doi.org/10.1016/j.sbspro.2012.06.654
9. Akçayır, M., Akçayır, G.: Advantages and challenges associated with augmented reality for education: a systematic review of the literature. Educ. Res. Rev. **20**, 1–11 (2017). https://doi.org/10.1016/j.edurev.2016.11.002
10. Sommerauer, P., Müller, O.: Agumented reality for teaching and learning – a literature review on theoretical and empirical foundations. Research papers, 31 (2018)
11. Krüger, J.M., Bodemer, D.: Application and investigation of multimedia design principles in augmented reality learning environments. Information **13**, 74 (2022). https://doi.org/10.3390/info13020074
12. Bacca, J., Baldiris, S., Fabregat, R., Graf, S.: Kinshuk: augmented reality trends in education: a systematic review of research and applications. Educ. Technol. Soc. **17**, 133–149 (2014)
13. Radu, I.: Augmented reality in education: a meta-review and cross-media analysis. Pers. Ubiquit. Comput. **18**(6), 1533–1543 (2014). https://doi.org/10.1007/s00779-013-0747-y
14. Guth, L., Söbke, H., Hornecker, E., Londong, J.: An augmented reality-supported facility model in vocational training. In: Lingnau, A. (ed.) Proceedings of DELFI Workshops 2021, pp. 15–27 (2021)
15. Sirakaya, M., Kilic Cakmak, E.: Effects of augmented reality on student achievement and self-efficacy in vocational education and training. Int. J. Res. Vocat. Educ. Training **5**, 1–18 (2018). https://doi.org/10.13152/IJRVET.5.1.1

16. Stender, B., Paehr, J., Jambor, T.N.: Using AR/VR for technical subjects in vocational training – of substancial benefit or just another technical gimmick? In: Proceedings of the 2021 IEEE Global Engineering Education Conference (EDUCON), Vienna, Austria, 21 April 2021–23 April 2021, pp. 557–561. IEEE, Piscataway (2021). https://doi.org/10.1109/EDUCON46332.2021.9453928
17. Barabasch, A., Keller, A.: Innovative learning cultures in VET – 'I generate my own projects'. J. Vocat. Educ. Training **72**, 536–554 (2020). https://doi.org/10.1080/13636820.2019.1698642
18. Matthes, N., Schmidt, K., Kybart, M., Spangenberger, P.: Trainieren der Fehlerdiagnosekompetenz in der Ausbildung. Qualitative Studie mit Lehrenden im Bereich Metall- und Elektrotechnik. JOTED **9**, 31–53 (2021). https://doi.org/10.48513/joted.v9i1.222
19. Greeno, J.G., Collins, A.M., Resnick, L.B.: Cognition and learning. In: Calfee, R.C., Berliner, D.C. (eds.) Handbook of Educational Psychology, pp. 15–46. Prentice Hall International (1996)
20. Anderson, R.C., et al.: The Snowball phenomenon: spread of ways of talking and ways of thinking across groups of children. Cogn. Instr. **19**, 1–46 (2001)
21. van Merriënboer, J.J.G., Clark, R.E., de Croock, M.B.M.: Blueprints for complex learning: the 4C/ID-model. ETR&D **50**, 39–61 (2002). https://doi.org/10.1007/BF02504993
22. Plass, J.L., Homer, B.D., Kinzer, C.K.: Foundations of game-based learning. Educ. Psychol. **50**, 258–283 (2015). https://doi.org/10.1080/00461520.2015.1122533
23. Wouters, P., van Nimwegen, C., van Oostendorp, H., van der Spek, E.D.: A meta-analysis of the cognitive and motivational effects of serious games. J. Educ. Psychol. (2013). https://doi.org/10.1037/a0031311
24. Spangenberger, P., Matthes, N., Kruse, L., Draeger, I., Narciss, S., Kapp, F.: Experiences with a serious game introducing basic knowledge about renewable energy technologies: a practical implementation in a German secondary school. J. Educ. Sustain. Dev. (2021). https://doi.org/10.1177/0973408220981445
25. Microsoft: HoloLens2 capabilities and solutions. Greeno. https://docs.microsoft.com/en-us/hololens/hololens-commercial-features
26. Rizzo, A., Kim, G.J.: A SWOT analysis of the field of virtual reality rehabilitation and therapy. Presence Teleoperators Virtual Environ. (2005). https://doi.org/10.1162/1054746053967094
27. Azhar, S., Kim, J., Salman, A.: Implementing virtual reality and mixed reality technologies in construction education: students' perceptions and lessons learned. In: ICERI2018 Proceedings. 11th Annual International Conference of Education, Research and Innovation, Seville, Spain, November 2018, pp. 3720–3730 (2018). https://doi.org/10.21125/iceri.2018.0183
28. Benzaghta, M.A., Elwalda, A., Mousa, M., Erkan, I., Rahman, M.: SWOT analysis applications: an integrative literature review. J. Global Bus. Insights (2021). https://doi.org/10.5038/2640-6489.6.1.1148

A Lens to the Past: Using Site-Specific Augmented Reality for Historical Interpretation

Mads Haahr[1,2]([✉]) [ID] and Pernille Henriette Wiil[3] [ID]

[1] School of Computer Science and Statistics, Trinity College Dublin, Dublin, Ireland
haahrm@tcd.ie
[2] Haunted Planet Studios, Dublin, Ireland
[3] Museet Mosede Fort Danmark, 1914-18 Greve Strand, Denmark

Abstract. This demo paper presents a locative, site-specific, augmented-reality game for a WW1 historical site. The work constitutes the preliminary results of a research collaboration between two universities, one museum and a developer of serious games. The challenge was to produce an interactive, playful and educational digital experience based on the results of research into national policy and other cultural forces in relation to food and nutrition in Denmark during WW1. The resulting game needed to have a high technology readiness level and be deployed in the historical site for use by visitors. The research collaboration produced several innovations in location-based augmented-reality games for cultural heritage that are likely to be of interest to researchers and developers working in this space: (a) a way to present complex content that requires multiple perspectives in a geolocatable double structure; (b) the use of a visual aesthetic that resonates highly with the historical period in question in order to encourage reflection that relates the past to the present; (c) an approach to adding supplementary historical information in a fashion that aims not to overload the player with information during the play experience. While we have yet to evaluate the work through a user trial, this demo paper presents our design motivations and solutions that arose from the collaboration and the complex historical material.

Keywords: Locative gaming · Augmented Reality · Cultural heritage · Historical Interpretation

1 Introduction

In this demo paper, we present a sophisticated site-specific, location-based Augmented Reality (AR) game situated in a historical WW1 fort. The game was developed as part of a research project funded by the Velux Foundations. The research project was a collaboration between Aarhus University, Trinity College Dublin, the museum Museet Mosede Fort Danmark 1914–18 and the game developer Haunted Planet Studios. A primary high-level objective of the project was to explore ways of actively integrating the process of research with the educational activities of the museum, and the game documented in this paper was one of the outputs from the research project.

H. Söbke et al. (Eds.): JCSG 2022, LNCS 13476, pp. 259–265, 2022.
https://doi.org/10.1007/978-3-031-15325-9_19

Entitled *Kampen om maden 1914–1918* (loosely translated, "the struggle for food 1914–1918"), the game had multiple objectives: It needed to engage the general public with an attractive and thought-provoking experience; it needed to encourage reflection around how ideas regarding food and nutrition that were developed during WW1 are still relevant today; and it needed to be based on the latest research into national policy and other cultural forces during WW1 in Denmark. Furthermore, it had to be based on Haunted Planet's "Longship" game engine, which had been used in previous cultural heritage experiences, such as *Bram Stoker's Vampires*, which was shortlisted for the 2016 Heritage in Motion Award.

Museet Mosede Fort Danmark 1914–18 is a World War 1 museum based in Greve, Denmark, situated on the coast south of Copenhagen and centred around a historical WW1 fort. Rather than a typical war museum, the museum tells a complex story about how national policy decisions, especially around the scarcity of food, during the First World War led to the development of ideas and thinking that became the foundation of the Danish welfare society and are still relevant today – perhaps more than ever.

2   Related Work

Location-based games date back to the early 2000s, and with the success of *Ingress* (2012) and *Pokémon GO* (2016), locative games entered the mainstream in a very serious way. The genre holds considerable potential for cultural heritage sites as a way to present historical and other types of content, and a number of experiences exist, ranging from early experiments such as Geist [1], REXplorer [2] and Viking Ghost Hunt [3] to more mature approaches, such as Jumièges 3D [4]. A study has shown that mobile augmented reality applications with historical pictures and information are of interest to end users and that the level of interest is related to the perceived usefulness and perceived enjoyment of the applications [5]. History-focused projects, such as Media Portrait of the Liberties [6] and Riot! 1831 [7] have explored how media fragments (audio, video and static images) can be situated in locations that were of historical relevance to the story material, and projects such as Geist [1], Oakland Cemetery [8] and Carletto the Spider [9] placed more complex entities across cultural sites in the form of virtual storytellers, which allow more interaction than static media fragments. Sophisticated authoring tools, such as StoryPlaces [10], have reduced the cost of developing locative cultural heritage experiences.

3   Core Game Concept

The pretext for the game experience is that mysterious apparitions from the past have appeared across the historical fort. The player must find these revenant apparitions and investigate why they have appeared right here and right now. The player's smartphone is transformed into a "detection device" to help locate and get close to the revenant apparitions. Each encounter starts with the build-up of a soundscape related to the apparition in question and ends with the player taking a photograph of the apparition.

The game contains four game modes (see Fig. 2) through which the player interacts with the game mechanics: The Map (an overlay on Google Maps) enables coarse-grained navigation, the Radar (a representation of a naval radar) enables fine-grained navigation and search mechanic, the Ghostviewer (a monochrome Augmented Reality camera) lets players take photos of the revenant apparitions. The Map Mode shows the general play area outlined in purple, but it does not show the specific points of interest, because this would make the navigation and search mechanic too easy to offer an interesting play experience. The Casebook (a list of player photos and descriptions of encounters), shown in Fig. 2 (bottom), lets players review their photos and game text to consider why exactly these apparitions have emerged right here and now. As an interactive experience, the game mechanics are concerned with navigation, capture and collection of the revenants, but the design leaves out many other mechanics known from locative games, such as explicit scoring mechanics, levelling up and territorial conquest. From a game experience point of view, *Kampen om maden 1914–1918* probably has more in common with lighter, more flow-based explorative games [12], such as *Flower* (2009), than it has with *Ingress* and *Pokémon GO*.

During the collaborative design process, our team discussed if we should call this more flow-based explorative outcome a 'game.' We considered different other more open-ended descriptions such as an 'experience,' an 'exploration' or even the more elusive 'encounter with the past.' However, in the promotion of this new type of offering, the museum needed to present an unambiguous and easily recognisable description of the activity to potential users, and therefore we retained the designation of *Kampen om maden* as a game.

A typical play experience begins with the player using the Map (Fig. 1 top left) to orient themselves and ensure they are within the play area. The player then switches to the Radar (Fig. 1 top right) and decides which of the encounters they would like to approach (e.g., the nearest) and then starts walking towards it. The player tracks the encounter on the Radar as they are moving and navigating the fort's irregular terrain. As the player approaches the encounter, its associated soundscape begins to play, evoking the encounter's theme through its sound design. When the player gets very close to the encounter, they must switch to the Ghostviewer (Fig. 1 bottom left) which shows a monochrome camera feed of the surroundings. Guided by a directional arrow on top of the camera feed, the player now scans the scene until they see the revenant apparition, which is anchored to a fixed compass direction in the location. The player then taps the camera button to capture a monochrome photo of the revenant, which is floating against the backdrop of the historical fort. After reviewing their photo in the Casebook (Fig. 2 bottom left), the player switches back to the Radar and uses it to find the revenant's companion encounter, which is now the sole encounter shown on the Radar (Fig. 1 bottom right). This companion encounter forms the second part of the geolocatable double structure mentioned earlier. After the player has used the Radar and the Ghostviewer to capture the companion encounter, the Radar now shows all remaining encounters (Fig. 1 bottom right) and the player can proceed to find the next one. Throughout the experience, shows the current game mode with a light blue glow around the relevant button, and gives cues to the player about which game mode to use next by showing a yellow pulsating glow around the relevant button. (See Fig. 1.)

To enhance the players' possibility to reflect on the messages carried by the revenant apparitions from the past to the present, the players are given the opportunity to get their personal Casebook sent to their email. This online Casebook contains additional information about the encounters, including the original historical photographs as well as links to relevant articles which the players can explore at any given time.

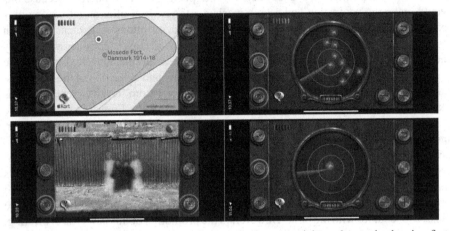

Fig. 1. Left: map mode (top) and Ghostview mode (bottom); right: radar mode showing first encounter (top) and companion encounter (bottom).

When the game is played in the historical fort, the exact location of each revenant apparition is curated to offer a good experience, for example by ensuring historically relevant and aesthetically pleasing visual backdrops to the revenants. In addition, the game has a "random mode" that allows it to be played in other locations than the fort. In random mode, the game stages itself in the player's location by placing the revenants in a randomized configuration around the player. The random mode is considered an experimental feature, and at the time of writing it does not guarantee that the revenants are placed in accessible locations, but it does allow the game to be played in a park or other open area anywhere in the world.

4 Shadow and Light

The game uses and reflects upon the fundamental dialectic figure of the poppy. The poppy, which grew on the battered grounds of battlefields, holds the dialectic relation between life and death – food and war. This dialectic is present in every part of the overall game concept, structure and mechanics and has been the driver for both the visual and the textual content.

The game experience is structured around nine double encounters. Of each double encounter, the first brings to the fore a particular problem related to food shortage and malnutrition that manifested themselves in Denmark (neutral during the war) through the dark shadows of WW1. The second part of the double encounter is a "companion encounter" that relates to the same theme as the first but shows how new solutions to the food-related problems grew out of the war shadows and formed new ways of organising Danish society. The player can choose freely between the different first encounters (see

Fig. 1 top right), but once they have engaged with a first encounter, they cannot proceed in the game until they have found the matching second encounter (see Fig. 1 bottom right). To help make this possible, the remaining first encounters will temporarily disappear from the Radar and only the matching second encounter is shown. First encounters are marked in blue and second encounters in red in order to mark the distinction visually.

The encounter visuals – the apparitions – are taken from historical photos from the time of the war and hence appear in black and white. To enhance the experience of engaging with apparitions from the past, the Ghostviewer (AR camera mode) is also in black and white (see Fig. 1 bottom left; as well as Fig. 2 top left and right). In this way the game encourages the player to see the present in the light of the past and vice versa.

The encounters with the revenant apparitions are intentionally placed on locations where the historical site in different ways create an aesthetic background, which enhances the atmospheric and symbolical experience of the apparitions and their messages from the past. In this way the site-specific nature of the game is based on the historical fort's unique atmosphere. The atmospheric experience of the apparitions are further aided by the game's elaborate soundscape.

Fig. 2. Ghostviewer (top) and casebook (bottom) for one double encounters: battlefield (left) is the first encounter and cornfield (right) is the companion encounter. The Casebook screenshots are from the online version of casebook, which contains additional information and links to historical sources.

Every apparition is accompanied by an intentionally surprising heading and a short text, which evokes the theme that the apparition symbolises. To show the dialectic relation between the apparitions that emanate from the war shadows and the ones that represent new growth, the pictures taken with the Ghostviewer are framed by either withered black branches or a blooming poppy flower décor, as shown in Fig. 2 (bottom left and right). The dialectic relation is also reflected in the text that accompanies each revenant apparition in the Casebook. For the Battlefield/Cornfield double encounter, the text for the first (Battlefield) encounter is: "The battlefields were soaked in the blood of soldiers. The slaughterhouses were soaked in the blood of animals. The war time vegetarians saw a connection." (Fig. 2 bottom left.) For the companion (Cornfield) encounter, the text is: "The cornfield produced food from the farmers' labour. It was hard work, but peaceful." (Fig. 2 bottom right.)

5   Conclusions

The game launched in 2020 and is available as a free (and free of advertising) download for both Android[1] and iOS[2] platforms. While it is intended to be experienced in the museum's historical fort, its random mode allows it to be played in an open area anywhere in the world, such as a park. User trials were scheduled for summer 2020, but were postponed due to the Covid-19 pandemic. While lockdowns in Denmark were lifted towards the end of 2021, winter weather conditions in Denmark combined with the exposed location of the historical fort has prevented user trials from taking place until the early summer of 2022.

The development of the game was an ongoing dialectical process between the characteristics of the Haunted Planet Studios' "Longship" game engine and an analytical investigation of the historical content presented in the game. The existing game engine had an inherent ghostly aesthetic character [11], which came to determine the overall idea of the game from the beginning. However, the outcome of the historical research and insight that the game should convey spurred a new development of the game mechanics so it could reflect and enhance the rather complicated results of the museum's historical research. In this way both the development of the game and the historical research went in new and unforeseen directions. Specifically, the following features were added to the game engine as a direct result of historical research:

1. The double-encounter structure was added to support the poppy dialectic. We consider the double encounters are feature that could be generally useful for locative cultural experiences that deal with complex historical material, specifically material that require two complementary perspectives to be presented as part of the same experience.
2. The ability to show the AR camera in monochrome was added to the game engine's Ghostviewer in order to give an aesthetic that resonates more with the time of WW1 than conventional colour AR views used in nearly all smartphone-based AR, including the earlier version of the Longship engine [11]. The resulting player photos are aesthetically pleasing, and highly representational to the extent that they frequently resemble real historical photos from the time of WW1. The intention is that this will encourage reflection that relates the past to the present.

---

[1] https://play.google.com/store/apps/details?id=com.hauntedplanet.branded.mosedefort.

[2] https://apps.apple.com/ie/app/kampen-om-maden/id1533193718.

3. The ability to upload the player photos to an online version of Casebook with additional information about the historical aspects was added to support player reflection.

The user trial will be an important next step to examine whether the complex structure and content of the game achieves its intended purpose. In the trial we will measure the level of engagement and reflection that players experience while playing the game and attempt to establish the extent to which the complex historical material that we have tried to capture in the game format is understood by and reflected upon by the players.

References

1. Kretschmer, U., et al.: Meeting the spirit of history. In: Proceedings of the 2001 Conference on Virtual Reality, Archeology, and Cultural Heritage, pp. 141–152 (2001)
2. Ballagas, R., Kuntze, A., Walz, S.P.: Gaming tourism: lessons from evaluating rexplorer, a pervasive game for tourists. In: Indulska, J., Patterson, D.J., Rodden, T., Ott, M. (eds.) Pervasive 2008. LNCS, vol. 5013, pp. 244–261. Springer, Heidelberg (2008). https://doi.org/10.1007/978-3-540-79576-6_15
3. Carrigy, T., Naliuka, K., Paterson, N., Haahr, M.: Design and evaluation of player experience of a location-based mobile game. In: Proceedings of the 6th Nordic Conference on Human-Computer Interaction: Extending Boundaries, pp. 92–101 (2010)
4. Happe, D., Hamon, G.: Jumieges 3D. Departement de la Seine- Maritime (2013)
5. Haugstvedt, A.C., Krogstie, J.: Mobile augmented reality for cultural heritage: a technology acceptance study. In: 2012 IEEE International Symposium on Mixed and Augmented Reality (ISMAR), pp. 247–255. IEEE, November 2012
6. Nisi, V., Oakley, I., Haahr, M.: Location-aware multimedia stories: turning spaces into places. Universidade Cátolica Portuguesa, pp.72–93 (2008)
7. Reid, J.: Design for coincidence: incorporating real world artifacts in location based games. In: Proceedings of the 3rd International Conference on Digital Interactive Media in Entertainment and Arts, pp. 18–25, September 2008
8. Dow, S., Lee, J., Oezbek, C., MacIntyre, B., Bolter, J.D., Gandy, M.: Exploring spatial narratives and mixed reality experiences in Oakland cemetery. In: Proceedings of the 2005 ACM SIGCHI International Conference on Advances in Computer Entertainment Technology, pp. 51–60, June 2005
9. Lombardo, V., Damiano, R.: Storytelling on mobile devices for cultural heritage. Rev. Hypermedia Multimedia **18**(1–2), 11–35 (2012)
10. Hargood, C., Weal, M.J., Millard, D.E.: The storyplaces platform: building a web-based locative hypertext system. In: Proceedings of the 29th on Hypertext and Social Media, pp. 128–135 (2018)
11. Haahr, M.: Literary play: Locative game mechanics and narrative techniques for cultural heritage. In: Göbel, S., Ma, M., Hauge, J.B., Oliveira, M.F., Wiemeyer, J., Wendel, V. (eds.) JCSG 2015. LNCS, vol. 9090, pp. 114–119. Springer, Cham (2015). https://doi.org/10.1007/978-3-319-19126-3_10
12. Chen, J.: Flow in games (and everything else). Commun. ACM **50**(4), 31–34 (2007)

Correction to: Learning with Augmented Reality Headsets? Experiences of a Use Case in Vocational Education

Pia Spangenberger(iD), Felix Kapp(iD), Nadine Matthes, and Linda Kruse

Correction to:
Chapter "Learning with Augmented Reality Headsets?
Experiences of a Use Case in Vocational Education" in:
H. Söbke et al. (Eds.): *Serious Games*, LNCS 13476,
https://doi.org/10.1007/978-3-031-15325-9_18

In an older version of this paper, there were orthographical errors in the text. The word "threat" was misspelled as "thread" on pages 254 and 255, which affected the meaning of the text. This has been corrected.

The updated original version of this chapter can be found at
https://doi.org/10.1007/978-3-031-15325-9_18

Author Index

Printed in the United States
by Baker & Taylor Publisher Services

Printed in the United States
by Baker & Taylor Publisher Services